Acclaim for Ian Johnson's

wild grass

A Kiriyama Prize Notable Book

"A gripping tale of a very few ordinary people and their extraordinary courage in fighting for their rights against the Communist Party leviathan." —*The Washington Post Book World*

"Elegantly written. . . . Poignant. . . . Insightful, well-crafted. . . . Likely to find a broad readership." —*Boston Review*

"Cause for hope for China's future. . . . In vivid detail, [Johnson] recounts . . . cases . . . that show that individual Chinese at last have hope that the legal system can help." —*Foreign Affairs*

"Gripping . . . taut, perceptive writing. . . . Reads in parts like a John Grisham legal thriller." —*Houston Chronicle*

"Johnson is a wonderful storyteller. . . . His book is filled with evocative passages. . . . He captures the resilient spirit of many Chinese people." —*The Christian Science Monitor*

"Johnson writes well, wielding a remarkably gentle pen against the grossest injustices or when describing the most remarkable instances of personal bravery. The people written about here could wish for no better chronicler." —*The Asian Review of Books*

"This year's best general book on China." —*China Economic Quarterly*

IAN JOHNSON

wild grass

Ian Johnson is the Berlin bureau chief for
The Wall Street Journal. In 2001, when he
was the *Journal*'s Beijing correspondent,
he won the Pulitzer Prize for his reporting
on Falun Gong. He lives in Berlin.

wild grass

THREE PORTRAITS

OF CHANGE

IN MODERN CHINA

IAN JOHNSON

VINTAGE BOOKS

A DIVISION OF RANDOM HOUSE, INC.

NEW YORK

To Jean and Denis

FIRST VINTAGE BOOKS EDITION, MARCH 2005

Copyright © 2004 by Ian Johnson

All rights reserved under International and Pan-American Copyright Conventions. Published in the United States by Vintage Books, a division of Random House, Inc., New York, and simultaneously in Canada by Random House of Canada Limited, Toronto. Originally published in hardcover in the United States by Pantheon Books, a division of Random House, Inc., New York, in 2004.

Vintage and colophon are registered trademarks of Random House, Inc.

Some of the material previously appeared in slightly different form in *The Wall Street Journal.*

The Library of Congress has cataloged the Pantheon edition as follows:
Johnson, Ian, [date]
Wild grass : three stories of change in modern China / Ian Johnson.
p.   cm.
Includes bibliographical references.
1. Political activists—China.   2. Government, Resistance to—China.
3. Dissenters—China.   4. Civil rights—China.   5. China—Politics and government—1976– .   I. Title.
JQ1516.J64 2004
323'.04'0951—dc22
2003058082

Vintage ISBN: 0-375-71919-9

Author photograph © Otto Pohl
Book design by Johanna S. Roebas

www.vintagebooks.com

Printed in the United States of America
10 9 8 7 6 5 4 3 2

Wild grass strikes no deep roots,

has no beautiful flowers and leaves,

yet it imbibes dew,

water and blood and the flesh of the dead,

although all try to rob it of life.

—LU XUN, *Wild Grass*, 1926

Contents

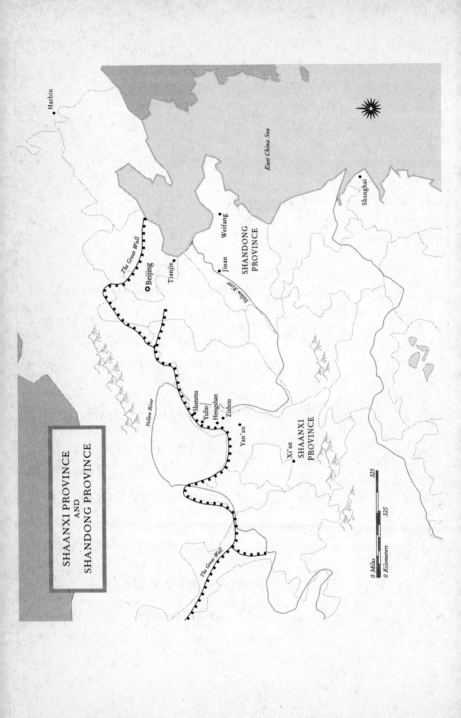

SHAANXI PROVINCE AND SHANDONG PROVINCE

The Great Wall

Yellow River

Beijing

Tianjin

Harbin

Weifang

Jinan

SHANDONG PROVINCE

East China Sea

Shanghai

Shenmu
Yulin
Hengshan
Zizhou

Yan'an

Xi'an

SHAANXI PROVINCE

The Great Wall

0 Miles   325
0 Kilometers 325

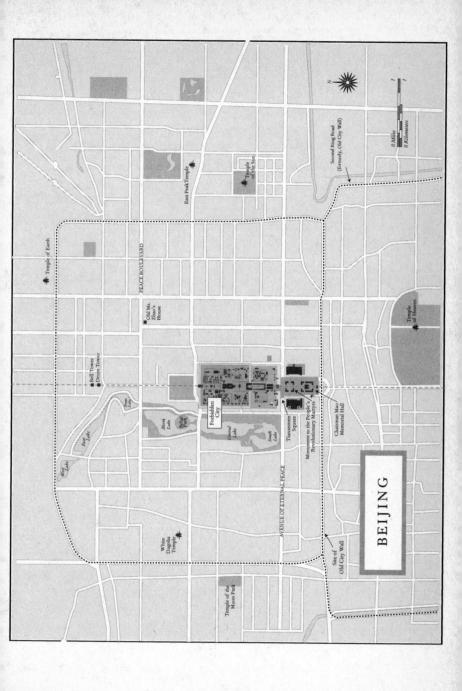

BEIJING

Temple of Earth

PEACE BOULEVARD

Old Mr. Zhao's House

Bell Tower
Drum Tower

East Peak Temple

Temple of the Sun

Second Ring Road
(formerly, Old City Wall)

N

0 Miles
0 Kilometers

Temple of Heaven

Jade Lake

North Lake

Beihai Park

Bell Lake

West Lake

White Dagoba Temple

Temple of the Moon Park

Forbidden City

Central Lake

South Lake

Tiananmen Square

Monument to the People's Revolutionary Martyrs

Chairman Mao Memorial Hall

AVENUE OF ETERNAL PEACE

Site of Old City Wall

wild grass

Prologue:
One Hundred
Battles a Day

China's rulers have developed a bad case of the nerves. Unemployment is high, corruption permeates daily life and relations with the outside world result in recurring crises. Often these tensions erupt in small protests, sometimes against the government, other times against outsiders. They usually end after a few days, often crushed, sometimes petering out when a few ringleaders are arrested and the protesters' demands partly met. But they are never resolved, surfacing like a corpse that won't stay under.

When the anniversaries of these protests come around a year later, commemorations are held and petitions delivered. Some of these grudge dates are intensely local: a family's memory of its house torn down to make way for a corrupt real estate project, or a village that commemorates a local leader arrested for standing up to abuse. Other commemorations are shared by millions: the killing of students or the banning of a popular religion.

The government, ever watchful for challenges to its rule, tries to keep track of them all. Protests, arrests, detentions: each year the victims try to commemorate these disasters, and each year the government tightens up around these dates. Slowly, the country's mental calendar has become a series of overlapping scabs and sores.

Beijing, the country's political and spiritual capital, where most protests take place, is especially affected because petitioners from around the vast republic ultimately make their way there. Each sensitive date is accompanied by increased police patrols, roundups of dissidents and tapped phones. The signs are not always obvious, but once they are known, they are unmistakable: the triple-teamed soldiers that cordon off diplomatic compounds, late-night police roadblocks, roving patrols on trains heading for Beijing, the sealing off of the cavernous Tiananmen Square, accessible only to those who present their identity cards for inspection.

China's government wasn't always so unsure of itself. Shortly after taking power in 1949, the Communist Party enjoyed some popular success. It united China for the first time in a century, put people to work and redistributed land. Even when the disasters came—and they came fast—the party didn't have to worry too much about unrest. Famines and persecution were regular occurrences during the party's first three decades in power. But China was frozen by totalitarian rule. Even small protests to mark these misdeeds were difficult.

Then, the totalitarian dictatorship of Chairman Mao Zedong collapsed with his death in 1976. Weakened by thirty years of failed policies, the party tried to win back popular support by withdrawing its control over people's personal lives and by allowing capitalist-style economic reforms. Over the past decades this looser form of control has succeeded in raising living standards but hasn't helped the party win deep-rooted legitimacy.

With the government no longer micromanaging their daily lives, people now have time to travel, to reflect and, slowly, to demand more. With prosperity and better education, Chinese people have begun forming independent centers of power outside government control—trade unions, religious organizations and clubs. It was the development of this "civil society" that helped bring about the downfall of communism in Eastern Europe late last century. Now, these groups are eroding the power of China's Communist Party.

It would be unfair to say that this cacophony of demands has paralyzed China's leaders. On key economic issues, which they view as vital to their survival, the mandarins can push through reforms. Hence, China's admission into the World Trade Organization, a sign that whatever its name, the People's Republic of China practices little in the way of communist economics. China now has stock markets, labor markets and a more open economic system than some developed countries.

But politics intrudes even in this relatively neutral sphere. This is because economic reforms have progressed to the point that a true market economy is only possible by adopting political reforms—which, put simply, means some sort of an end to the Communist Party's monopoly over power. Only this step can pave the way to a real market economy, which requires a fair judicial system, less corruption and transparent regulations. Despite the government's best efforts to separate the two, economics and politics make the same demands on the government. Political reform now tops every Chinese thinker's agenda. It is widely discussed, even by the party. But in any meaningful sense of the word, it is taboo.

Like other governments under stress, China's has reached for nationalism as a solution. In this it is similar to nineteenth-century Germany—an economic juggernaut run by a backward-looking oligarchy, its masses partly satiated by prosperity and nationalism. This manifests itself in periodic displays of national outrage at perceived slights. Generations of Chinese have been taught that the world is out to belittle their country, and many believe it to be true. That allows the government to win support by presenting itself as the defender of China's best interests.

But nationalism is a temporary salve. The true source of unrest—the Communist Party's poorly checked powers—continues to breed unrest. Problems continue to rise up, forcing leaders to juggle an increasing number of demands. The effort seems to exhaust the government; unable to lighten its burden through political reform, it resembles a person carrying an ever-heavier weight, its gait slowing to a shuffle, its stoop growing more pronounced.

It is a slow battle of attrition that the government is loath to lose. The police state remains, from the labor camps in China's far west to the toy soldiers in downtown Beijing. The message is clear: we are nervous, possibly even weak, but do not meddle; we can still crush you.

These subterranean tensions are the subject of this book. I do not presume to predict when the crust will crack. Such forecasts are usually wrong, and I believe that China's current political system can probably survive for many more years. But tectonic shifts are grinding away, making change inevitable and giving rise to eruptions felt in China and abroad.

These pressures come mostly from thousands of ordinary Chinese who in small ways demand more from their government than the current system can accommodate. We often expect that history will be made by people like us. Academics think change will come from daring thinkers, journalists look to brave writers, while politicians are eager to meet China's Gorbachev. Such people, except perhaps the Gorbachev figure, all exist in today's China.

But the push for change comes mostly from people we rarely hear of: the small-town lawyer who decides to sue the government, the architect who champions dispossessed homeowners, the woman who tries to expose police brutality. Some are motivated by narrow interests of family or village, others by idealism. All, successful or not, are sowing the seeds of change in China, helping to foment a slow-motion revolution.

Although I have met scores of interesting, brave and forward-thinking people in China, this book focuses on the three most remarkable ones, people representative of the tremors shaking the land. When the current government falls or changes into something more democratic, it will be because of the efforts of this sort of people. Each, wittingly or not, has pushed to change the country's ossified politics. Each represents key problems facing China: the crises in its villages, cities and its soul.

Not surprisingly, the three stories also touch on the country's nascent legal system. For the first three decades of their rule, the communists had little use for laws or the legal system. Disputes were mediated by the party, with little recourse to courts. Economic reforms, however, made laws necessary: people and companies need clear, enforceable rules if they are going to engage in economic relationships. Indeed, the first law promulgated after reforms began was a 1979 law that regulated how foreign and Chinese companies could form joint ventures.

But China's leaders are more ambitious—they want a legal system that can keep order nationwide. This stems from the chaos of the totalitarian era, which made the Communist Party realize that the country needed laws as a bulwark against disorder. So the government has set about "constructing" a legal system. It wrote a constitution in 1982 and since then has promulgated laws at a dizzying rate: General Principles of Civil Law, Contract Law, Intellectual Property Law, Insurance Law, Property Law, a new Criminal Code and even a Marriage Law. Law schools have been established, with tens of thousands of judges and lawyers trained.

A sense of justice is universal, and Chinese people have enthusiastically tried out their new legal system. On purely economic matters it sometimes works: companies find that contracts can be enforced in the courts, and in some narrow areas the government can even be challenged successfully—for example, for failing to follow a certain procedure in making a decision. But overall, law in China is not neutral. Courts and judges are part of the government, not independent of it. Communist Party committees regularly instruct judges on how to rule. Even the constitution gives a nod to the party's supremacy. So when the party feels challenged by a suit, it uses the courts to its ends. Instead of allowing laws to rule the land, the government uses laws to rule.

Still, living standards continue to rise. Education spreads. Knowledge of rights increases. Try as it might, the party can't put a lid on the demands that people are making for change. The result: China's legal system has become a microcosm of the tensions percolating up, a revolution brewing from below.

This book is an attempt to portray this untenable situation and hint at the sort of more open, fairer country that Chinese people want. Over two millennia ago, the Chinese philosopher Han Feizi wrote a treatise on political philosophy. In it he described the tensions inherent in an autocratic system: "Rulers and ruled wage one hundred battles a day." As these stories show, the battles still rage.

1 THE
PEASANT
CHAMPION

The photo of Ma Wenlin fluttered in my hand, catching the attention of the man sitting across from me on the train.

"He's a lawyer," I said. "I'm looking for him."

The man was silent for a moment and then said, "He looks like a peasant, not a lawyer."

The black-and-white picture showed Mr. Ma staring straight into the camera, his face expressionless except for his faint eyebrows, which arched slightly in a quizzical expression. His hair was short, almost crew-cut, and he had a light stubble above his lips. He wore a plain white dress shirt, buttoned to the neck but with no tie. There was no effort to engage the viewer, no grin, no smile. It was an old-fashioned photo of a man who didn't pose for the camera as modern people do, a man who in the first half of his fifty-nine-year life had been photographed just once or twice.

"He represented peasants," I said. "In a lawsuit against the government."

Like all second-class sleepers, ours had six bunks and no door, allowing people to wander freely down the car, poking their heads in to visit friends and see who else was on board. But we were alone: the only other person in our compartment, a man in a middle bunk, was snoring lightly and the other passengers bustled back and forth in the corridor, concerned only with finding thermoses of hot water to make tea.

"Those kinds of lawsuits are complicated," the man said ambiguously.

Then he paused and collected his thoughts. He had a shock of gray hair that hadn't receded an inch from his tanned, creased forehead. His suit was Chinese style, the sort worn by the founder of modern China, Sun Yat-sen, and popularized by Mao Zedong, or Chairman Mao, communist China's first leader. Like Mr. Ma, the man wore his shirt buttoned up to the neck, with a fountain pen sticking out of the left breast pocket. It was the outdated uniform of Communist Party cadres from a decade ago, one rarely seen in the country's prosperous areas. But here, in a slow train leaving a remote county seat, it didn't look quite so out of place.

"I'm sure he won't be successful," he continued, looking at me carefully. "This is a poor part of the country."

I nodded but disagreed, casting a glance outside for confirmation. The windows of the train were streaked with rain, and through the blurred glass the denuded hills and earth-colored villages of the Loess Plateau rolled by. Once, this had been fertile forests and steppes, one of the birthplaces of Chinese civilization. Nearby was the grave of the Yellow Emperor, mythic founder of the Chinese people. Down in Xi'an, where we were headed, were the world-famous terra-cotta warriors that had been buried with China's first emperor more than two thousand years ago. He and other rulers had protected this cultural heartland by building fortifications not far from here that later became known as the Great Wall. Seventy years ago the plateau's mountains and gullies had sheltered the Communist Party for a decade, first during China's civil war and later during World War II. It was a region oozing in history and significance but now was exhausted, poor and relatively obscure.

One commonly hears that these parts of the country are where change is least likely to happen. Instead, one is always encouraged to go to the prosperous coastal metropolises, such as Shanghai or Shenzhen, to look for China's future. But the more I learned about Mr. Ma, the more I understood that this region's backwardness had made it a precursor of change elsewhere in China—the poverty, the intransigence of local officials and the extreme environmental degradation bringing to a boil here problems brewing across the country.

"Well," I said. "This was a poor place when the communists were here, and they ended up running China. Maybe it's not so backward. Maybe it's even avant-garde."

We both laughed, relieved that we could safely turn the conversation to something less risky. We blew on our tea leaves, hurrying their descent to the bottom of the cup.

My cell phone went off. "If you want any information about Ma Wenlin, I suggest you ask me now," a man said quickly. "Because by the time you arrive in Xi'an, I'll be in jail. My phone is bugged."

"I'll call you when I get to Xi'an," I said. "I'm sure there will be no trouble. We'll have dinner tonight."

"I won't be around tonight. I will be in jail."

"No, you won't," I said. "Let's talk later."

We hung up and I switched off my cell phone.

The old cadre sitting opposite poured some water from the thermos into our cups, filling them back up. He eyed me curiously.

"Retired?" I asked.

"Yes, going to visit family in Xi'an."

"Your children?"

"Yes, they've moved to Xi'an and work there. I have grandchildren down there."

I liked him, a retired official still dressed for work but on his way to baby-sit. He reminded me of Mr. Ma, who had also been a doting grandfather. It was hard to explain why I had Mr. Ma's picture in my hand, and would probably have seemed incomprehensible to the old man if I had tried. He had been dubbed by locals a *nongmin yingxiong*, or "peasant champion"—a name that conjures up a reckless romantic stirring up revolt among the repressed. It seemed slightly absurd, like something out of a florid South American novel, yet Mr. Ma had scared the government enough to jail him for "disturbing social order." This was a vague, almost meaningless charge, but what I heard about Mr. Ma before my trip only piqued my interest. People said that he had represented tens of thousands of peasants in a lawsuit against the government. Rumors, too, abounded that he'd led protests, traveling from village to village to whip up the peasants against the government. It all seemed a bit hard to believe, so I had come to find out what he had done. I wondered what it meant, at the turn of the millennium, to foment a peasant rebellion, a specter that for thousands of years has haunted China's leaders and hastened the downfall of more than one dynasty. It was his history— the facts about who he was and what had happened to him—that I was after. I wanted to uncover one man's story from the rumors and half-truths that silt up events in China.

We sipped tea and smiled at each other. The old man closed his eyes, trying to sleep. I stared at Mr. Ma's picture, trying to figure out what I'd learned about him.

My eyes, however, kept wandering to the jagged landscape outside. The yellow alluvial soil that covers the plateau runs up to 300 feet deep and is so prone to erosion that geographers reckon it is the most uneven landscape made of soil in the world, constantly shifting and breaking. Grotesque outcrops rolled by, formed when huge chunks of loess soil break off the side of a hill vertically, like slabs of lava falling into the sea. Standing on top of such promontories, which centuries of human effort have inevitably turned into a small terraced cornfield or the site of a small temple, you can see dozens of other miniplateaus and fields, some just a few hundred yards away, but separated by cliffs and gullies that can fall hundreds of feet to a dried-up creek below. A newcomer can sometimes feel a sense of panic after scrambling along a few ridges in either direction and finding only precipices.

The cliffs sometimes gave way to the flat, dry riverbeds and smudgy vistas of hills beyond. Underpinning this monochromatic scenery was a supercharged environmental destruction. Each year thousands of tons of topsoil wash down the rivulets and streams into the giant Yellow River. The river, which skirts the plateau in a giant northern loop of several hundred miles, takes its name and silty consistency from the plateau's discharge.

As our diesel locomotive carefully picked its way south, we were embraced by a warm yellow glow, the color of the soil, the water and, on days like this, even the sky. This had been my fifth trip to the Loess Plateau, and I got back about once a year, drawn by the scenery, the stubborn cultural traditions and the tensions bubbling up from below.

I had set off to find Mr. Ma two days earlier, boarding an 8 a.m. flight from Xi'an to Yulin, a small city of 93,000 that boasts the only airport on the Loess Plateau. It was a Monday and the flight was full, a shuttle ferrying small-time officials on coveted trips down south to the provincial capital and back up with booty bought in Xi'an's relatively swank shops.

Yulin has virtually no private enterprise to speak of, so no one but a bureaucrat or official from a state company could afford the $100 ticket, equivalent to the annual cash income of a Loess Plateau farmer. Unlike the train, there were no retirees on board, no students, no children and almost no women. It was all men, all in two- or three-piece western suits, many lugging consumer goods that were pricier or harder to find up on the plateau. One man had a video disc player in a box bound with twine, another carted a box of apples, a third hauled a wheel rim for a Chinese-made Audi.

An hour later I was in a taxi heading for town. It was only 10 a.m., but in August the sun was already high and we raised a cloud of dust as we raced through the parched streets. After a few minutes we entered Yulin, its roads lined with white-tiled buildings and dusty poplars.

This was a moment I'd rehearsed several times. I knew my driver was going to ask me where to go in Yulin and I knew I'd have to lie to him. What I wanted to do was go to a hotel in town, check in and meet a couple of lawyers who had known Mr. Ma. They had insisted on meeting in a hotel because they were terrified the Public Security Bureau would get wind of our talk if we discussed Mr. Ma's case in public.

Hotels, though, are dangerous places, and I had to stay there for as little time as possible—an overnight stay was out of the question. That's because guests in Chinese hotels are obliged to give their visa number. Mine was a journalist's, with a "J" in front of the number. Each night, hotel guest rolls are handed over to the police and in the morning—depending on the vigor of the local police department—they are checked. The presence of suspicious types, including journalists, is reported to the local government, which then checks if the person has applied to visit its town—or is there illegally. By staying at the hotel for just a few hours, I minimized the chance that the Public Security

Bureau would know of my presence in town; the bureau would have likely completed its morning check for that day, and it seemed unlikely that the hotel manager would call up the authorities and report my presence. After all, the Great Wall is located just a few miles north of the city and tourists were welcome.

But I couldn't tell all this to the taxi driver. Taxis are scarce in small towns like Yulin, and drivers tend to hang around hotels waiting for customers. So, too, do security agents, who lollygag in lobbies watching the people go by. If the driver were to wait for me in front of the hotel, he'd likely get bored and go inside the hotel to chat, possibly with an agent, perhaps telling him about the foreigner he'd just picked up at the airport and taken to a hotel and who intended to go on later today to Yan'an—strange travel plans for a tourist. Another worry was that if the security bureau later checked the hotel rolls and noticed me, they might ask the hotel staff how I'd left town. The doorman or the other taxi drivers waiting at the hotel would probably be friends with my driver. A call to the taxi company would give them the car's license plate and maybe the driver's cell phone. That would allow them to trace me to Yan'an and spoil the rest of the trip.

It sounded paranoid but it had happened to me before, on a trip here eighteen months earlier. I had come to visit a nearby town that had filed a class-action lawsuit against the government. Like Mr. Ma's peasants, the peasants of Peijiawan had been plagued by illegal taxes. Their solution had been to hire a lawyer and charge the government with assessing excessively high taxes.

They did so by taking advantage of China's Administrative Litigation Law of 1990, which allows people to sue the government. The idea is not that you could sue to establish basic rights—for example, one couldn't sue government censors for violating one's right to free speech, which, in theory, is guaranteed in China's constitution. Instead, you were allowed to correct administrative foul-ups—for example, that an official had erred in denying one a permit or license. It also allowed people to file suits together—like western class-action lawsuits—taking the government to court en masse to correct a wrong.

The case had been much celebrated in China in the late 1990s, trumpeted in a government-run newspaper that covers legal affairs, *Legal Daily*, as an example of how China was developing peaceful, modern ways of solving disputes. But it was also controversial inside the government, with some seeing in it a dangerous precedent.

In 1995 the peasants in Peijiawan had suffered a drought and their crops had failed. The local government, however, wanted to squeeze more money out of the local peasants so had raised taxes. One farmer had told me how his cash income had dropped that year by more than 75 percent to the equivalent of $12, but his taxes had quintupled to $25 from $5. He scraped together $20—which he said the officials took without issuing a receipt—and promised the rest at the end of the month. But a few days later when he was out in the fields, they came by again, broke down his front door and confiscated his television.

Infuriated by this and other acts of bullying, villagers met in secret and elected representatives. The sixty-eight delegates studied central government laws regulating how much tax can be collected and concluded that the local officials had acted illegally. Initially, the leaders asked the government for partial repayment of the $75,000 that they estimated had been taken illegally.

When that was rejected, they sued, collecting signatures from 12,688 farmers, or two-thirds of the residents in the township. Chipping in 25 cents each, they hired lawyers, who filed a very cautious lawsuit. In court the lawyers hadn't brought up the officials' brutal tax-collecting tactics, instead focusing on the amount collected and the tax regulations. It was an open-and-shut case: in 1999 the farmers got the full $75,000 returned to them.

News of the Peijiawan farmers' victory spread quickly across the Loess Plateau. Farmers in a village one valley over from Peijiawan felt that they, too, had been overtaxed and had hired a well-known local lawyer, Mr. Ma, hoping to duplicate their neighbors' success. So Mr. Ma filed an almost identical lawsuit to the Peijiawan case. But in late 1999, just a few months after the Peijiawan peasants won their suit, he ended up in jail.

When I heard about his case from outraged lawyers in Beijing, I wasn't entirely surprised. When I had left Peijiawan, I had noticed some people standing on top of their houses, glaring at the farmers who had talked to me. Two guides who had accompanied me there started getting nervous and urged me to get out of town. I figured they were exaggerating the risk: after all, the Public Security Bureau couldn't have a post in this tiny village.

But I was wrong. When I returned to Beijing a couple of days later, a message was waiting for me to call the two guides. I did so, and they told me that police had been waiting for them upon their arrival back home in Yulin. They had been let off with a warning, but their story inspired caution: village officials had found a phone in a neighboring village and called to tell the police about our visit, even giving our car's license plate. Meanwhile, police in Yulin had received the hotel register from the night I'd spent at the hotel and noticed my journalist visa. They were quickly able to trace our route, from Yulin to Peijiawan and then on to my next destination. It turned out that I had narrowly escaped being detained in Peijiawan; the police had turned up just an hour after my departure.

That experience and Mr. Ma's fate had made me extracautious. Before leaving Beijing, I obtained a map of Yulin and found some landmarks near the hotel where I was to meet the lawyers. A hospital was located right across from it, and I had decided to tell my taxi driver to let me out there.

As we drove through town, I told the taxi driver that an old classmate of mine was now living in Yulin and was sick. I wanted to go visit him for a couple of hours before we headed down to Yan'an. Sure, he said, no problem.

I wondered if I wasn't being unreasonable. The driver had told me that he was a former factory worker who'd been laid off and was trying to make ends meet by driving. And even if he were buddies with the security agents, chances are he wouldn't bother to give them a call or even mention me—one should never underestimate human laziness and inertia. It was always a problem in China to figure out the line between excessive caution and carelessness, not only for foreigners like me but for people like Mr. Ma. After all, he'd only done what others had done by representing peasants in a lawsuit. Now he was in jail. What line had he crossed? It seemed like this was the crux of modern China: On a daily level people are quite free to do as they please. But still firmly in place are the old restrictions devised by an authoritarian government. The regime might be dying, but will use these powers when it feels even a little threatened.

We pulled up to the hospital, and I told the driver to go home and pack a bag and a thermos of tea for the trip down south. He thanked me for my consideration and headed home. We agreed to meet back at the hospital in two hours.

After waiting to see him drive out of sight, I walked across to the hotel. Despite my precautions, this was still the trickiest part of the trip. The manager might be very cautious and immediately report my presence to the police, not waiting for the daily visa check. Or a security agent could be killing time in the lobby and go to the Reception out of curiosity, ask to see my registration form, notice the "J" prefix to my visa number and wonder what a foreign journalist was doing in town.

Entering the hotel, I noticed a couple of men sitting on a red leather couch in the lobby. Dressed in polo shirts and tight polyester slacks, they looked every bit the part of public security officers detailed to check out the local hotels. Men like this seemed to be a fixture in hotels around China: chubby guys, doing nothing, chatting on cell phones and waiting for the karaoke lounge to open. Every time I saw them, I dreamed of a revolution that would sweep them out on the streets where they'd have to earn an honest living.

Well, this town had a tourist draw, I figured, so nothing wrong with me being here. I stopped before a giant plastic relief map of Yulin with the Great Wall marked north of the town. I studied it for a minute and then went to the front desk. A few minutes later I was in my room, waiting for Mr. Ma's colleagues to arrive.

Few other issues are as sensitive as the right to take someone's money. The problem in China started in the mid-1990s, when protests against heavy taxation cropped up repeatedly. The government responded by tinkering with the existing system, hoping to use old-style authoritarian threats to make it work. But it became pretty clear that the government's efforts were inadequate, and taxes remain one of the friction points between rulers and ruled.

When the Chinese Communist Party took control of China in 1949, taxes weren't an issue. The party collectivized agriculture and banned private enterprise. All profits from any enterprise, rural or urban, remained with the state, and these profits were the government's chief source of revenue. It was a classic communist system, similar to the one in the Soviet Union or Eastern Europe.

As in most communist countries, this system bankrupted itself within a few decades. But while in Eastern Europe communism's economic problems led in the late 1980s to political revolt, China's communist leaders were able to stay in power by reforming the country's economic system early on—in 1978, less than thirty years after taking power. The first and most successful step was abolishing collectivization. Farmers were given control (but not ownership) over plots of land, which they could do with as they pleased as long as they paid taxes, often in grain, to the government.

That led to stunning economic growth—free to profit by their own labor, China's peasants reverted to the hardworking entrepreneurial class they had been before 1949. Other reforms followed, such as lifting the ban on small privately run businesses. Suddenly, small factories sprouted up across China, quickly putting an end to the lack of consumer goods that plagued other communist countries.

Overall, the government benefited from these changes. It recovered some measure of support, which had almost completely dissipated during the first thirty years of disastrous policies. People were so busy getting prosperous that calls for political change were small, albeit insistent. But the changes did have one unforeseen downside: the government had a tough time raising taxes.

The old system of skimming profits from state-owned enterprises was no longer adequate. State enterprises had begun to face competition from new privately run factories and foreign competitors, who had been allowed in the marketplace. In addition, the government needed more money than before. It had ambitious social projects, such as eradicating poverty and enforcing a limit on the number of children allowed per family. It also embarked on a costly modernization of its armed forces, raising salaries for soldiers and buying costly weapons systems from abroad. Since the mid-1990s, for example, annual military budgets have risen by double-digit figures. In addition, corruption continued to siphon off billions of dollars each year, much of it to well-connected party leaders, their friends and offspring.

The peasants' taxes helped, but because they were mainly in the form of grain, they didn't alleviate the fiscal crunch. The grain did allow the government to sell subsidized grain in the cities, helping to buy itself support there, but it was not a substitute for cash.

So Beijing was left with a problem familiar to many governments: how to get more money. Many countries would see this as a political problem—will people accept paying more taxes? If so, raise taxes. If not, cut expenditures or take on debt. But in China the problem was mistakenly seen as simply a technical one. In officials' eyes, the issue wasn't whether people were willing to pay taxes but simply how to collect them. This was reinforced by advice the government got from abroad: the World Bank, for example, supplied the government with plans on how to set up a new tax system, advising it to implement a national income-tax program similar to the ones that exist in other countries. What was rarely discussed is how people would feel about paying more taxes to a corrupt, unaccountable government.

One of the central misconceptions about China is that because it is an authoritarian system it can do anything it wishes. Actually, China lacks the institutions and credibility that allow modern bureaucracies to function effectively. While Beijing can crush a peasant rebellion or student protests, enforcing a fair and reasonable tax system is different. There the question isn't one of sending in soldiers to shoot off guns but of establishing and running a complicated bureaucratic structure, one that relies on people's trust in the government and a belief that things are fair enough in society so that average citizens feel a sense of duty to pay. Threats can force individuals to pay taxes, but collectively it is belief in the government's legitimacy that allows a tax system to work.

The economic reforms gave the government new legitimacy, but by the turn of the century its biggest successes were a couple of decades old. Gradually, the party's definition of success had become too meager for wider and wider swaths of the population. Having enough food to eat is a wonderful accomplishment, but it's also a bare minimum that a government should offer its population.

Beijing's drive to raise taxes took little of this into account. It launched a massive effort to increase revenues through a simple method: user fees. It was basically the toll-road concept—you use it, you pay for it. It had the advantage of simplicity—money could be collected on the spot from the user—and a semblance of fairness. The disadvantage, of course, is that it falls heaviest on the poorest. A typical tuition fee of $30 per semester for elementary school might be bearable for a prosperous farmer but would be out of reach for a poor farmer. It also was ripe for abuse by local officials, who could slap a fee on everything—and who are held accountable by no one for their decisions.

User fees suddenly began appearing for everything. Farmers could pay a bewildering number of taxes: a vague "village" tax, an agricultural tax, a general education tax, a school repair fee, a market management fee, a head tax, a hygiene fee, an irrigation tax and twenty days of unpaid labor a year for government projects—not to mention special levies, such as the second irrigation fee that caused the furor.

With no checks or balances, farmers suddenly faced huge tax bills. By the mid-1990s, protests had become daily occurrences. The government responded by tinkering with the system. Taxes, it announced in 1991—and has repeated every year or two since then—would be limited to 5 percent of farmers' annual income. That sounds like a great rate—most developed countries tax citizens between 30 and 50 percent—but Chinese farmers have little cash, so 5 percent is still significant. Plus, that rate didn't take into account the user fees—hundreds of local governments simply declared these special taxes exempt from the 5-percent rule.

The central government wasn't blind to the problem and responded with sometimes ingenious solutions. The government, for example, issued a national tax checkbook that farmers were to carry around with them. When a farmer paid a tax, the book would be stamped, and then the farmer could prove that he'd paid his taxes and was exempt from more. But these patchwork solutions were often bypassed by China's tax-starved government. Special fees and surtaxes were still levied and peasants continued to suffer—and protest—despite the regular pronouncement that this time the government was really serious about reducing the peasants' burden.

The rural protests had interesting echoes in Chinese history. Then, as now, uprisings often started against local officials who abused power. When the imperial government supported the officials instead of the victimized peasants, the rebellion often spread and anger became focused against the center. One of the most famous peasant rebels was Chen She, who started the rebellion that led to the downfall of the Qin, which was the first dynasty to unite China. In the summer of 209 B.C., Chen failed to deliver prisoners to a penitentiary on time and faced the death penalty for his tardiness. So he incited a rebellion among peasants unhappy with local conditions. The rebellion quickly spread and ended up toppling the government and setting up a new dynasty, the Han.

Similar examples can be found throughout Chinese history. Sometimes the peasants' role has been exaggerated or romanticized—for a while it was fashionable to see them as an amorphous arbiter of power in Chinese history, a primordial force that rose up occasionally to topple evil governments. While that is an exaggeration, it is true that some of China's earliest political philosophers saw the populace (which then was almost all rural) as a sort of judge that decided legitimacy. If the government is corrupt, they argued, people had a right to rebel. This has imbued ordinary people with a moral power to choose their rulers. It also helps to explain why the government today treats the countryside with such contradictory policies, at once seeking to raise standards of living but also treating any sign of rebellion with extreme brutality.

Messrs. Zhao and Shao walked gingerly into the whitewashed room, which reflected the morning sun like a floodlit stage. Mr. Zhao strode forward and grasped my hand. He was forty years old but appeared to be in his early thirties, a trim, dapper man who could have been at home in any of China's modern metropolises like Beijing or Shanghai. I couldn't quite place it when I first saw him, but later I realized that he looked a bit like a member of China's Uighur Muslim minority group, with a pencil-thin mustache and a sharp, angular nose. He was dressed in light green trousers, a beige shirt and vented brown leather shoes. Instead of the usual brush cut, his hair was a bit longer and neatly parted down the side. With a gold chain around his neck, he was something of a Loess Plateau dandy.

"Welcome," he said in English. "You are welcome."

"Thanks," I said. Then I switched back to Chinese. "Yulin is a beautiful town."

Mr. Zhao looked at me quizzically, gave a quick shrug and laughed. I liked him already. Most people are intense local patriots, but Mr. Zhao seemed as unimpressed with the dusty little county seat as I was.

"Let me introduce you. This is Lawyer Shao. We are colleagues."

I took one look at Mr. Shao and wished he hadn't come along. Sweaty and bald at age forty-eight, he wore a tight blue polo shirt that hugged his paunch and made him seem the caricature of a lazy official. He looked at me distrustfully, probably thinking that this whole exercise was a dangerous waste of time.

"Ha-ha," Mr. Shao said nervously. "Ha-ha. Ha."

I thought he would keel over from nerves, but instead he plopped himself on one of the beds and wiped his brow with a handkerchief.

Mr. Zhao wasn't ready to sit down yet. With a dramatic flourish he pulled a stack of documents from a plastic shopping bag and dropped them on the bed where I sat.

"You read this and you'll understand everything you need to know about Ma Wenlin. The court transcripts, his self-defense, his appeal, the letter to the governor—it's all here. All except the most recent peasants' petition."

Mr. Shao sat back nervously, as though the documents were a bomb. He kept one eye on them and glanced at me with the other.

"Ha-ha," he said. Then he wiped his brow and cleared his throat. "I have a suggestion: I suggest you leave Yulin immediately," he said, now looking up in my general direction. Still not comfortable about talking to a foreigner, he preferred instead to address the fan behind my head. Then, turning to Mr. Zhao, he motioned to go.

I jumped up.

"Here," I said, thrusting paper cups filled with green tea at them. "Mr. Zhao. You must be familiar with the Peijiawan case. Why was that different from this case? Just from a legal point of view."

Mr. Zhao wasn't ready to go and accepted a cup of tea, sitting down on the bed next to his colleague, who fidgeted nervously and waved away the tea.

"They're basically the same," Mr. Zhao said, ignoring Mr. Shao. "Both cases are from the same area and involve the same principles. Peijiawan has been handled okay. The government paid the money, and the peasants got what was coming to them. But the government can't accept that such a suit could happen again. If all the peasants in China file class-action lawsuits, then the Communist Party is finished. So Ma Wenlin's case couldn't be allowed to succeed."

Mr. Shao sputtered and his eyes twitched. He looked over at the fan, started to say something and then caught himself. Thinking that he might be the cautious bureaucrat type, I clumsily tried to calm him by imitating what I figured to be the government line.

"Ma was probably also a bit radical," I said helpfully. "Didn't he accompany the peasants to Beijing and help them file an appeal to the central government?"

Mr. Zhao looked at me as if I were a fool, and even Mr. Shao cocked an eyebrow skeptically.

"What you're saying is wrong. That wasn't his problem. No, from the government's point of view his problem was that he linked up the farmers with the legal system. This shouldn't be a crime, but that's what he did. Isn't that right?" he said, nudging Mr. Shao.

Mr. Shao looked over sternly at Mr. Zhao. Discussing Mr. Ma's crimes seemed to have made him even more wary. He mumbled something about the court documents being secret.

"Nonsense," Mr. Zhao said. "They're not. They're from the courthouse. Anyone can access them."

None of us believed what he'd just said. Criminal court documents in China weren't public, certainly not those regarding as sensitive a case as Mr. Ma's.

Mr. Shao cut in, tapping his watch and looking expectantly at Mr. Zhao. He looked at the fan behind me. Then he finally looked at me and, looking me straight in the eye, spoke: "I have another suggestion: Don't go to Zizhou. The public security is too tight. They've arrested a peasant representative who organized the petition for Ma. It's dangerous. You must not go there." Mr. Shao was speaking fast, as if by spilling out all this information his guilt would be less. He sat back, red in the face.

I sat back, a bit concerned. I had planned to go to Zizhou, the county where Mr. Ma had organized the peasants. It was halfway between Yulin and Yan'an, which is where Mr. Ma lived. I knew that Mr. Shao was ultracautious, but he seemed earnest and I knitted my brow in thought.

Mr. Zhao smiled and lit up a cigarette. Everyone sat thinking for a moment. I looked at him and wondered why Mr. Zhao stayed on the Loess Plateau. Probably, it was simply the fact that Chinese can't easily move from city to city. Without friends or connections it was hard to leave and set up a new life, so he remained here, a small seditious element spreading modern thinking in this backwater.

Outside the window a two-stroke tractor roared by, a small

contraption that looked like a ridable lawn mower. They were ubiquitous in rural China, used to plow fields or haul produce. I was suddenly reminded of the peasants whose fate had so concerned Mr. Ma.

It was time to go. We drained our cups and stood up, shook hands and the two walked out. Mr. Zhao left last, turning to me and saying firmly: "Shao is cautious, but he's right. Don't go to Zizhou. There are police everywhere. I wouldn't even overnight in Yulin if I were you."

I quickly remembered the petition.

"What's that petition you mentioned?" I called out to Mr. Zhao.

"Ask the peasants," he said, turning his head to answer as he walked down the hall.

I ran after him, and he stopped to talk to me as Mr. Shao continued down to the elevator.

"But you said to avoid the countryside," I said.

"They'll find you. It's hard to avoid Ma Wenlin when you get down there."

I stood for a second puzzled, trying to formulate one of the many questions buzzing in my head. But Mr. Zhao had already turned, and was hurrying away after his colleague.

I checked out of the hotel after just ninety minutes, mumbling an excuse to the receptionist, and called the driver on his cell phone. I crossed back over the road to the hospital and waited, eager to be away from the hotel and the men loitering in the lobby. The driver pulled up, I hopped in and we headed south toward Zizhou.

The road was only two lanes, but it was smooth and we started overtaking trucks and tractors as our driver found his pace. I felt giddy as we gained speed and left urban China's orbit. The valley that spread out south from Yulin zipped past, and I contemplated what had happened. Mr. Zhao's answers had left so much unclear. He said Mr. Ma had linked the peasants to the legal system, but hadn't the other lawyers done the same thing a year earlier? Why weren't they jailed? And the petition was also unusual. How had the peasants organized it, and what did it contain?

The valley around Yulin soon gave way to the Loess Plateau's distinctive hills. The road started to wind around the huge earth and stone outcroppings, their crumbling faces evidence of the unending erosion and decay. Precarious terraces, sometimes marked by slapdash wooden fences, clambered up the hills, which were occasionally dotted with pine and willow trees. Groups of schoolchildren in bright red caps walked past cannibalized trucks and cars, which lay scattered every few miles at the side of the road.

Along the way, cave dwellings would appear halfway up a hill. Many mistake these dwellings for caveman-type accommodations, imagining that the inhabitants are modern versions of Peking Man, living a primitive existence in dark hollows. In fact, as the locals somewhat defensively say, the caves are warm in the winter and cool in the summer. They're practical to build because wood is scarce, but the earth is loose and easy to excavate. Floors are hard-packed or sometimes tiled. The homes usually have one wooden or adobe room that juts out from the hill, giving their homes at least one bright room with natural lighting. Romanticizing this life would be wrong, but a good cave truly is warm and snug, even if sometimes a bit malodorous.

We passed by old cave dwellings, most abandoned for newer ones. The more modern versions were better because they had higher ceilings, 7 or more feet, made possible by better engineering techniques such as braces and crossbeams. In the older caves one often had to stoop or worry about hitting a beam—often just a tree branch braced against the walls. But the older ones did have exquisite windows, the glass fronted by delicate handmade wood lattice. In the past the lattice wouldn't have had glass behind it; instead, paper would have been glued on. The lattice was to a degree functional, preventing the paper from tearing or blowing in during a storm. Glass made this unnecessary, so the new houses dispensed with the lattices. Probably from a cave-dweller's point of view this was an advantage because the new windows were cheaper and gave more light. Somehow, though, the lack of decoration made the newer homes bleaker, the one bit of frivolity stripped away. Inside the homes, people owned more possessions than in years past—televisions, quilts and fans weren't uncommon, even in this poor region—but from the out-side it looked as if the plateau's residents couldn't be bothered to beautify their homes anymore. After centuries of poverty and a progressively deteriorating environment, the region seemed to be hunkering down, concentrating only on material survival.

At noon we reached Zizhou, the county seat just twenty miles north of the center of the rebellion. It was the closest town to the area of unrest, and Mr. Ma had been here numerous times to visit officials on behalf of the farmers. Surrounded by villages that were home to 260,000 farmers, Zizhou's 30,000 residents lived on a small island of urban China. It was typical of hundreds of small cities across China, with almost no structure older than a couple of decades. Buildings were concrete, covered with white tiles. Small shops lined the main road. Government offices hid behind steel gates and high walls. Peasants drove ferociously through town, their two-stroke tractors barreling past like ancient Industrial Age machines on wheels, belching out smoke and raising clouds of dust in the midday heat.

I stopped at a small noodle restaurant and ducked inside to avoid drawing attention. As I ate lunch, I debated whether to go into the hills where Mr. Ma had been active. Transportation wouldn't be a problem. The roads would be dirt or gravel and steep, and I knew from experience that they could turn to mud, requiring hours of pushing to get a car up them. But the weather was cooperating, and I figured I could probably spend the afternoon in one of the villages and still reach Yan'an by midnight.

The epicenter of Mr. Ma's peasant rebellion was in neighboring Tuo'erxiang Township. A farmer there, Wang Xingwei, had grown rich trading grain and had installed a telephone. His number was among the materials that lawyers had given me earlier in the day, so I decided to give him a call.

I walked out back toward the outhouse, switched on my cell phone and called. It was a bit of a risk to turn the phone on because its signal could be used to track its user. But it would be even riskier to go blindly into the mountains without making a call first. Mr. Wang didn't seem surprised to be talking to a foreign journalist. He said local media had contacted him, but nothing had appeared in the press recently because the case had become too sensitive to report.

"The government has repressed the farmers again and again, but we can only dare to be angry and not say anything," Mr. Wang said in an accent so thick that I had to ask him to repeat every other sentence.

We talked about the local economy, which had suffered from the chronic drought that was affecting swaths of western China. "The natural conditions aren't good. About seventy to eighty percent of us have to borrow money just to eat. If you want to make ends meet, you have to go out and work as a laborer in the big cities."

What if I came and visited, I asked him. "Sure, come on over," he said quickly. Then he paused and thought better of his offer. "But they'll arrest you. The Public Security Bureau has stationed officers in the village."

He said that the peasants had recently held secret elections and elected several dozen leaders. Like other villages in China, Tuo'erxiang was supposed to have democratic elections—indeed, such grassroots democracy has been the subject of intense study by western academics and funding by western aid agencies. In some model counties these elections do in fact work as a safety valve: although the candidates are screened by the party, outsiders sometimes get in and end up influencing the party's programs. But like most of these elections, the votes in Tuo'erxiang had only resulted in the same clique of party officials winning the posts in the village councils. Mr. Wang had been elected by a real vote, one conducted with secret ballot and multiple candidates. In his view and those of his neighbors, he and the other delegates were their real leaders.

That exercise in grassroots democracy, however, had brought the police in from Zizhou, who arrested or placed under house arrest the village's newly elected leaders. Police, he said, were still in the village, their cars parked in the center of town. It sounded impossible to visit the village—even for Chinese reporters, let alone a foreign reporter. I told him my travel plans, and we agreed that I'd try back in a few hours. I returned to the table, finished my noodles and walked back out onto the street.

I squinted at the town, trying to find something recognizable in the jumble of white-tiled buildings and small shops. This was where I had left my Peijiawan guides eighteen months ago, but already it had blurred into the other village towns I'd visited. We were now at a crossroads, with a line of stores that sold travel goods: snacks, fruit, alcohol and dried goods, most of them packed in bright red boxes so they could be given as presents. Most of the buyers were farmers who lived elsewhere as laborers and needed to stock up on presents before heading back home into the countless villages that lay in the mountains beyond.

I had a pressing decision to make—to go into these hills or not. I was eager to go because it seemed the best place for me to find out what had happened to Mr. Ma's quest. I had counted on talking to farmers and learning about their problems, what Mr. Ma had done, how they'd been organized and what actions they'd taken. If I didn't go, it seemed impossible to get to the bottom of the rebellion.

But then I ran through the likely outcome of a visit to Tuo'erxiang, the center of the rebellion. The village had just a few hundred residents and I'd be instantly pegged as an outsider. I could hide my appearance, for example by crouching in the back seat of the car and jumping into a peasant's home upon arrival. If the car had dark windows, that could work; I'd done it in other situations and had managed to talk to farmers that way. But this village was so small and controls were so tight that our out-of-town license plates would be instantly recognizable and give me away. The town was probably just a few dozen caves carved into the side of a mountain with everyone in sight of everyone else. If police were already there, I stood no chance.

A bit depressed, I got in the car again, and we continued south, bypassing the rebellion's epicenter. Now I was heading for Yan'an, the communists' headquarters from 1937 to 1947 and Mr. Ma's home for thirty-five years.

When the communists lived here, they relied heavily on peasant support, not just for food but as a way of legitimizing themselves. By living among peasants here on the Loess Plateau, they showed that they were different from the corrupt Nationalists. The communists had been purified by the soil and unified with the lowest class in China. This played well among some of China's intelligentsia and especially among a group of foreign China-watchers, who saw peasants as strong, earthy figures with ample common sense and a quick smile. Unlike the Nationalists, who took over China shortly after the emperor was overthrown in 1911, the communists would put peasants first.

In fact, Chairman Mao showered money and benefits on China's cities. Rural life might have been celebrated in song and dance, but benefits went to the cities, where health care was free and the capital accumulated through agriculture invested in heavy industry. Peasants had none of that and were seen mainly as food-making machines, best symbolized during the Great Leap Forward when famine-stricken counties were forced to send their last kilos of grain to the cities.

Still, in the official mythology, this part of China was the forge that created the communists. I wondered if living near such a historically important place made peasants more assertive. Being a part of revolutionary history might have raised locals' consciousness, leaving them with the feeling that the revolution was supposed to have been fought for them, not the bureaucrats who ran the country. This was certainly the feeling one got talking to the Peijiawan farmers who had filed the initial, successful lawsuit against high taxes just a year before Mr. Ma's ill-fated suit. I remembered how one farmer had said that Chairman Mao had compared the communists to fish swimming in the sea of peasants.

On the other hand, the peasants' bold actions weren't confined to this one region, with protests occurring across the country. Recently, a national newspaper had published a letter by an official working in a township in central Hebei Province, a part of the country more prosperous than the area we were now driving through. The letter, "The True Feelings of a Township Party Secretary," was written by Li Changping, a thirty-seven-year-old economist who'd worked in the countryside for seventeen years.

Mr. Li said his district had a population of 65,000, although 25,000 had found conditions so difficult that they'd left to find work in the city. Taxes for a family of five amounted to an astounding $310 a year, virtually wiping out every family's cash income. Despite that, the village governments that collected the taxes were under such pressure to keep channeling money to higher-ups that each village in the township owed on average a staggering $500,000 in back taxes.

The newspaper had been able to print the letter only because of the happy ending tacked on to the bottom. Mr. Li's letter had reached central authorities, who had sent an inspection team to the township. Later, the province convened a meeting and reduced taxes by $6 a person, or $30 for the five-member family. But it wasn't much of a happy ending—the cut amounted to just a 10 percent reduction, which would still leave an average family with a backbreaking $280 a year in taxes. In addition, the inspection team had not only confirmed Mr. Li's analysis but said the situation he described was common across the country. Although this one success story had been written up, most cases were unresolved, or else they, too, would have been trumpeted by the government-controlled media.

We'd been driving now for several hours, and Yan'an was approaching. The plateau's corroded hills came in relentless waves. The sun was now falling, and the hills, which had been tan-colored through the day, now began to soften, turning slightly yellow.

As we bounced down the road, I'd only been able to glance through the court documents that the lawyers had given me back in Yulin. Still, I couldn't help but be amazed at Mr. Ma's audacity. He hadn't just represented the peasants by typing up a dry lawsuit in his office. He'd also canvassed the peasants for support, traveling from village to village trying to find peasants willing to join his lawsuit. He reminded me of U.S. lawyers who filed class-action lawsuits on behalf of victims of industrial pollution. Unlike them, however, he stood to gain little, since legal fees were low.

And even if only part of the files were true, he had led protests and tried to storm the local government offices in Yulin. It seemed bizarre and almost suicidal; the outcome of such actions had to be clear: jail and possibly death. I knew a lot of young people who were sometimes naïve, thinking that the government surely wasn't so brutal as to jail people for expressing their beliefs.

But Mr. Ma didn't fit into the category of young romantic. Born in 1942, Mr. Ma was fifty-five at the time he filed his lawsuit. He had spent almost all his life under communist rule; there had been no overseas education for him, no familiarity with English, no real knowledge of the outside world. In a country where many people retire at sixty, Mr. Ma was an old man born of an old system. I couldn't imagine what could cause such a person to challenge the system, setting in motion a massive lawsuit and, if I believed the court documents, protests and demonstrations across the countryside.

I remembered, too, that Mr. Ma had been shaped by the Cultural Revolution. During that period of totalitarian excess from 1966 to 1976, Mr. Ma had been an enthusiastic member of the Red Guards, Chairman Mao's fanatic followers who roamed the countryside, destroying temples and humiliating people they didn't like.

Such an experience would affect anyone, leaving them either contemptuous of the law or its fervent supporter. In Mr. Ma's case it had been the latter. Many people who'd survived the Cultural Revolution were intensely self-confident: not necessarily very savvy about the outside world—after all, contact with it was rigorously banned—but many were also unafraid of authority.

A more typical product of his time was Wu Hanjing, whom I met on my first trip to the Loess Plateau, in April 1996. He was the head of Gushui village, which like most villages in the plateau was a series of caves dug up the side of a loess hill. He'd put up me and two friends in the town's official guest cave, which Mr. Wu had set aside for official business and entertaining visitors. The night before, we'd feasted on potato and carrot stew, later playing cards and drinking grain alcohol under a 40-watt bulb. The air in the cave reminded me of a saying—that villagers here bathe but three times in their lives: at birth, at marriage and at death. We had been unlucky enough to catch them in between these auspicious occasions.

After spending a sleepless night in the oxygen-starved cave, I got up early and walked over to our car, an old Czech Skoda that we'd rented in Baotou, Inner Mongolia. When we'd set off, the driver had been terrified that his little car would be splashed by mud. But by the end of the trip, he was just glad that he hadn't broken an axle. I walked over to the car, gray and battered in the morning light, and fished a bottle of water out of the trunk. Above me was a small hill, and I started up it, hoping the water would clear my head.

At the top was a cluster of five temples: four small ones and a big one in the middle. The four smaller temples were fairly routine affairs, one-room, one-story buildings dedicated to popular Taoist gods: the God of the Earth, the Jade Emperor, Lord Guan and the Lady Who Registers Births. But they were just a buildup for the main temple. Two stories, with a slate-gray tiled roof and curving eaves, the building was called the Pavilion in Memory of Heroes. It was a temple to communist China's founding father, Chairman Mao.

Worshiping Mao was a nice twist on his legacy. Although he cultivated the image of a traditional thinker—composing poems and practicing calligraphy—one of his chief hatreds was traditional culture. His goal was to replace China's religions with the cult of the leader—himself. Worshipers were honoring a man who had tried to forbid worship.

A weak early spring light filtered into the temple. Three women prostrated themselves before Mao, a papier-mâché statue about twice his real size, seated with giant hands resting on armrests. The women did three kowtows in quick succession and then got up. Usually, people praying in a Chinese temple will plant three sticks of incense in a burner in front of the god. But the women left after their kowtows. I turned around. Mr. Wu was standing in the doorway watching me watch the women pray. I greeted him and asked about the incense.

"That's superstitious," Mr. Wu explained. He pulled out a cigarette, lit it and stuck it filter side down between Mao's index and middle fingers. "That's how we show respect. He liked to smoke."

Next to Mao were two other oversized statues, one of his premier, Zhou Enlai, and the other of his top general, Zhu De. Cement walls were painted with cartoon scenes of Mao's life. Everything was covered with a light layer of yellow dust.

The second floor of the temple was empty—more shrines were planned, Mr. Wu said, but the village had to raise more money first. We stepped outside and surveyed the valley and the miniplateaus in the distance. Gushui lay below us, a town of 1,200 people who earned on average the equivalent of $100 a year. In the distance were three other villages, all scraping an existence from the worn-out land. The fields were planted with millet and wheat and gradually we could see people moving toward the fields.

Dressed in a Mao suit with a round white cloth cap of a type favored by local farmers, Mr. Wu viewed others suspiciously, preferring to chain-smoke and listen. He'd run the village since the Cultural Revolution, the final and one of the most destructive of Mao's campaigns. He'd got his job in 1952 because his father had died as a "martyr" for the communists in the civil war against the Nationalists. Then he set about doing what every good cadre should do: blindly follow the party's directives. In that era this meant aping absurd government policies. His biggest adventure was a trip to a model village, Dazhai, where he learned how to terrace fields up the sides of steep hills, a costly, backbreaking technique of reclaiming land that requires thousands of hours of labor. Like Dazhai, Mr. Wu's village also had fields that precariously climbed slopes of more than 25 degrees. Those extremely steep terraces, soil conservation experts now reckon, are responsible for about half the plateau's topsoil runoff each year—a prime reason why the environment has worsened so quickly in recent decades.

Mr. Wu had even been to Beijing in 1977 to shake hands with Chairman Mao's ill-starred successor, Hua Guofeng, who lasted just a couple of years before being supplanted by Deng Xiaoping, the leader who implemented economic reforms and ended the Mao cult. But even then, Mr. Wu had kept his job in this conservative neck of the woods, carefully following the party line as it embraced reforms, all the while not-so-secretly pining away for the good old days. Mr. Wu had one year of schooling and usually expressed himself with grunts. But then I brought up Mao.

"Mao fought on the Loess Plateau for thirteen years. He was one of us for all that time," Mr. Wu said, suddenly eloquent. "Who could forget Mao Zedong? He was first among a thousand emperors."

In 1980, Mr. Wu began building the temple. Or, rather, he began to order his peasants to build it. On his own initiative he forced locals to "volunteer" their free time in the winter to the project and he invested the equivalent of $20,000 of the village's money in the main building. He knew that the peasants were eager to rebuild the other temples, which had been destroyed in the Cultural Revolution. Farmers liked praying to the local God of the Earth, for example, and asking for sons from the Lady Who Registers Births. So he rebuilt those. But he made the centerpiece of the complex the new Mao temple, integrating it into the old religion.

"Who runs these temples?" I asked.

"The temples are controlled by the Taoist Association," Mr. Wu said, referring to the national association headquartered in Beijing.

"Do they have a representative here?"

"That's me. It's one of my duties," he said, suddenly mumbling.

Mr. Wu had a lot of duties. He was party secretary and village chief of Gushui—ostensibly two jobs, the latter of which is supposed to be elected by popular vote.

"What about this new idea from Beijing of holding elections for the village chief. What do you think of it?"

"Oh yes," Mr. Wu said, his voice trailing off again, as though distracted by a memory. "We had elections here."

Like many other elections in rural China, Mr. Wu's had been rigged. He had been the only candidate and the electoral commission, which is charged with vetting candidates, consisted of himself and a few other party members. The talk of modern inventions bothered him and he hurried off to the caves. One had three signs out front nailed from top to bottom on a beam: "Party Office," "Village Council" and "Taoist Association." He unlocked the door and went inside.

Mr. Wu's work had been influential. Farther down the road to the west were the towns of Dingbian and Jingbian. They both had Mao temples built in imitation of Mr. Wu's. We set off to see them, but Mr. Wu didn't come to see us off. He gets a lot of visitors, an aide said, and is very busy.

After arriving in Yan'an at dusk, I checked into a hotel and gave Mr. Ma's wife a call. She invited me over, and I decided to stroll through town to her apartment.

I'd expected that the communists' wartime base would have been pampered, boasting good roads and bleached into an antiseptic cleanliness favored by Chinese urban planners. This usually involves concrete buildings covered in white tile and blue glass, a main street lined with thirsty saplings and a large public square decorated with a few strips of fenced-off grass.

Instead, Yan'an was a chaotic, dirty little city of 300,000. Like the rest of the communists' former strongholds, it had been poor before the revolution and was still plagued by its natural conditions, which left it isolated and surrounded by inhospitable mountains. A few signs of government largesse lay strewn around town. A massive five-story party headquarters dominated the downtown, its streaked concrete walls slowly cracking in the summer heat. During the Cultural Revolution, Yan'an had been a pilgrimage site for youths hoping to imbibe the old revolutionary spirit, and from that era the city had inherited a gargantuan railway station. Now, four of its five platforms lay unused and its giant waiting hall busy only when the train from Xi'an arrived in the morning and departed at noon.

Out on the streets, aggressive beggars accosted passersby, demanding money. Itinerant peddlers hawked cheap shoes and slacks. Streets drained poorly and no one obeyed traffic regulations. Of course, this didn't really matter too much; the town's few streets were permanently jammed with trucks and cars, tractors and horse-drawn wagons. Nothing moved at more than walking pace.

As with most of the Loess Plateau, part of the problem was geography. Unlike Yulin, which was built on a plain, Yan'an is jammed into three valleys. One is along the Yan River, from which the city gets its name. (The suffix *an* means "peace.") The other two valleys follow small streams that feed into the Yan. The confluence of the biggest stream and the Yan is the center of town, basically just a bridge over the river. Rising up from the banks are hills dotted with caves where the communist leaders lived between 1937 and 1947. The hills had been turned into parks, with a Buddhist pagoda atop one hill the city's symbol—an odd choice given the communists' rejection of traditional culture.

Mr. Ma and his wife lived on the campus of the No. 3 Middle School, where Mr. Ma had worked as a teacher and his wife still taught. It was an arrangement not unusual in China. Before economic reforms took hold, most people in China's cities lived in housing provided by their employer, and even now that is still often the case. The housing is often surrounded by walls, meaning visitors have to pass a security guard even for social visits. I was lucky because it was suppertime and the guard wasn't on duty. The gate to the school was open and I walked in.

I had thought Yan'an was a dump, but as I had walked through the gates, the stark beauty of the plateau suddenly overwhelmed me. In front of me was a hill that rose up sharply behind the school yard. Most hills on the plateau are denuded, but this one was dotted with dozens of newly planted willows. As the setting sun caught the hill, the wispy green leaves and yellow soil glowed ethereally, blurring like a watercolor that hung behind the pockmarked school.

The school yard was mostly empty, the students and teachers at home eating dinner. A couple of people out for a walk stared. I went up to the second floor of the building where the teachers lived, and knocked. Mr. Ma's wife greeted me at the door.

Cao Pingfen was a stout woman of fifty-six with short hair parted on one side. She smiled broadly. "Thanks for coming over," she said, ushering me into their living room.

I sat down on a giant black leather sofa and she in a matching easy chair. Ms. Cao pushed a pack of cigarettes across the huge glass coffee table that separated us.

"Have a smoke," Ms. Cao said, her eyes downcast as she made the perfunctory offer.

The pack of Yan'an-brand cigarettes was unopened. She didn't smoke and had bought them to offer the people whom she met on her husband's business—judges, lawyers, journalists and any others she thought worth cultivating with small gifts. I smiled in thanks but didn't pick up the pack.

"Let me get some tea," she said. I had been traveling all day and was exhausted. I thought of the thin green tea leaves slowly sinking in a mug of boiling water, releasing their steady stream of caffeine. I nodded and she got up to boil some water.

I got up and looked around while she busied herself in the kitchen. The apartment was probably twenty years old, a shabby concrete structure with low ceilings and small windows. Mr. Ma and his family had invested a bit of money in fixing up the inside, a sign that, for all the region's problems, living standards had risen. The floor had once been bare concrete but now was covered with big white tiles. The walls had light-colored plywood paneling that ran up from the floor to waist-level. Beige wallpaper covered the rest. The furnishings were black and massive. Up against one wall was a varnished pressboard entertainment center that held an enormous Panda-brand color television. A one-piece desk and chair requisitioned from the school stood up against a wall. The windows were guarded by steel burglar bars—the apartment was on the second floor and crime was a concern. Before sitting back down on the sofa, I studied a giant poster. It showed an enormous flower garden, probably computer-generated but meant to look like the orderly French gardens of Versailles. It was ubiquitous, hanging in countless restaurants and homes around the country.

Ms. Cao returned and quietly put down two paper cups filled with hot water and a few wispy green tea leaves. We were sitting across from each other; I waited for her to finish drinking from her cup. Ms. Cao held the cup gingerly and took a sip. Her face was square and pudgy, with almost no eyelashes and the faintest of eyebrows. She was dressed plainly in a plaid shirt tucked into blue cotton trousers.

I wondered if I should suggest that we go out to get something to eat. Her apartment could be bugged and I was worried about what the lawyers had said. If she was under surveillance, then my arrival might have been noticed. But I knew she was most familiar with her situation and didn't want to create an unnecessary sense of paranoia. She put down the cup and began to talk.

"Teacher Ma," she said, using his old job title, "was arrested in Beijing on June 7, 1999, and put on trial on November 8 of that year. He was sentenced to five years in jail."

"And you appealed that?" I said.

"Yes, Teacher Ma's lawyer was excellent and he filed a rebuttal to the intermediate court two days later," she said, continuing on with a legal summary of his trial and imprisonment.

I thought it odd that she referred to him so distantly, by a title he hadn't used in years. But as she continued, I could see that she knew his case inside out and had an astounding command of legal vocabulary. She must have spent countless hours reading court documents and even more time recounting Mr. Ma's plight to people who might be of help. Slowly, I realized why she referred to him as "Teacher Ma." She'd dedicated her life to securing his release. The title was a way to keep his imprisonment factual and abstract, as though it were a stranger's fate. I interrupted her.

"How long have you been married?" I said.

"Thirty years."

"How did you meet?"

"We knew each other since childhood. We grew up in the same village up north."

Up north. The county where the peasants lived was north of here—the place I'd stopped for lunch. They came from there?

"In Zizhou County?" I asked.

She nodded.

"Of course. Our families were peasants. We went to elementary school together and junior high. We got married in 1962, when he was still in college. We've known each other all our lives."

Ms. Cao's voice trailed off and she looked down hard. I followed her glance downward and stared at the floor, allowing her to compose herself.

I noticed her shoes. She wore the kind of women's cotton shoes that few wear anymore. They were black, with brown plastic soles and a single black strap that goes over the top of the foot, fastening with a snap. Sometimes the shoes have flower embroidery but hers were plain. I hadn't seen a woman wear such shoes since I had first been in China in the 1980s. They were so old-fashioned they were almost ridiculous. But a different word came to mind, a Chinese word: *laoshi*. It means "honest," "truthful" and "good."

"So you've known him all your life?" I said. I wanted to say something more personal, like "you've loved him all your life," but it wasn't necessary.

"Yes. He's always been very naïve and stubborn. We went back to our hometown for New Year's and the peasants talked to him." Ms. Cao was now speaking in a torrent. "You know, I tried to make some arguments against taking the case, but he's stubborn, so stubborn. . . ."

Before she started crying, her daughter entered the room, carrying a tray of watermelon slices. She was tall, with short hair, thick lips and an angular face. Dressed in a long, tight lime-green dress, she looked eighteen. She put the plate down in front of us and then sat on a wooden chair in the corner by the window, staring intently, almost hostilely, at her mother.

"This is your daughter," I said to Ms. Cao. A boy ran in and picked up some toys that lay scattered around the room and ran over to the daughter. "And this is your son," I said to the daughter, quickly revising my estimate of her age.

The daughter smiled thinly. She looked at me skeptically and I didn't blame her. Maybe I was trouble. At the very least, I was probably a waste of the family's time. I felt a chill of helplessness in the air and tried to turn the conversation back to a more neutral narrative of facts.

"How did your husband get involved in legal issues?" I asked Ms. Cao.

Ms. Cao picked up her story. She hadn't gone to college, but her husband had attended teacher's college in Xi'an, the provincial capital. He graduated in 1962 when he was twenty and was sent back up to the Loess Plateau. But instead of returning to his village, he went to Yan'an to work in the city's "Foreign Affairs Office." This is a typically communist institution, a committee that coordinates relations with the outside world—defined as anything beyond the narrow confines of the town or even the factory. This meant that officials from other parts of China visiting Yan'an would have their Foreign Affairs Office contact the Yan'an Foreign Affairs Office and arrange lodgings, meals, entertainment and all manner of appointments.

Mr. Ma worked there during the Cultural Revolution, when millions of young Red Guards descended on Yan'an to learn about the communists' legendary wartime base. But in 1978, when China embarked on capitalist-style reforms and Yan'an returned to being a backwater, his office was downsized and he was assigned to teach at a school run by the old Ministry of Post and Telecommunications. He joined the Communist Party in 1985, a normal move for a teacher, especially for someone who owed his education and job to the party.

"He'd always liked to write and did well teaching writing," Ms. Cao said, watching her grandson out of the corner of her eye. "He wrote a few essays on local history for the Yan'an newspaper and this launched his career."

In 1992 the provincial government asked him to write the Yan'an volume in a series of local histories it had commissioned.

That increased his fame, and the local government transferred him to the No. 3 Middle School in 1993 so he could teach Chinese and history instead of the basic-level engineering that he'd taught at the postal ministry's school.

Slowly, Mr. Ma began branching out into law. This might seem odd, but as in imperial China, a mastery of written Chinese is seen as essential for people who want to come into contact with the government. As China started to develop its legal system in the 1980s and 1990s, this is how people saw the law—as a modern form of petitioning that has existed in China for hundreds of years. Who better to work in the legal field than a gifted writer? This is especially true because in China's legal system lawyers rarely make grand speeches as they do in western countries. Juries do not exist, and cases are decided by a panel of judges that—if it hasn't been explicitly ordered to decide a certain way by the local branch of the Communist Party—bases its decision largely on the documents presented. Flowery rhetoric is rare, but a well-crafted letter could be helpful.

"People came by our home all the time, asking Teacher Ma for help writing lawsuits," Ms. Cao said. He bought books on the law and taught himself about it. In 1994 he passed a national test that gave him a Legal Service Work Permit, China's answer to its dearth of fully trained lawyers. Legal workers are allowed to handle civil cases and draw up court documents but not to defend people in criminal cases. Ms. Cao said her husband scaled back his teaching commitments and eventually quit to work as a legal worker for a local law firm, South City Legal Services.

Later, I talked to a representative of that firm who told me that Mr. Ma had been one of its best-known attorneys. Although he didn't have the title of lawyer, he was the firm's star. "People used to ask for him," the lawyer said. "That's uncommon. We usually just assign a lawyer to a case. It's especially uncommon because he wasn't a lawyer but a legal services worker. But people thought he was the best and wanted him. He had a good track record."

Mr. Ma handled many economic contracts, but he excelled at civil suits, where a descriptive turn of phrase or dash of eloquence could be especially helpful in distinguishing one case from another. He was even allowed to handle the odd criminal case, although as a legal services worker he wasn't technically permitted to do so.

In fact, one of his biggest cases involved murder. It concerned a man whose wife had committed adultery. The two lovers plotted to kill the husband, who learned of the plot and, in a rage, stabbed his wife to death in their kitchen. Mr. Ma was asked to defend the husband and did so. The family was poor and Mr. Ma did it for free. Faced with the death penalty, the man got off with fifteen years in a labor camp after Mr. Ma pleaded extenuating circumstances—jealousy and self-defense.

"Everyone was sure it was execution," the lawyer at South City Legal Services said, making a pistol out of his hand and pointing it to the base of his skull. "But Old Ma pointed out the adultery and that it had been in a fit of rage. It took place during the high point of an anticrime campaign, but he still got the charge reduced to manslaughter. He really had a natural talent."

We took a break from our talk as Ms. Cao and her daughter got the young boy ready for bed. It was dark outside and the weather was changing. Hot and dry since the morning, the air was now damp and heavy. A cicada started to chirp. Others joined in and the buzz swelled into a deafening crescendo, broken only by the roar of two-stroke tractors that drove by every few minutes.

I got up to stretch and walked into an adjacent room. It was the master bedroom and doubled as Mr. Ma's study. A small desk and bookcase were crowded into a corner. The bookcase had glass doors and I gingerly opened one. As I read the titles, it slowly sunk in that every single book in this bookcase was related to China's legal system. Among others, I saw *People's Republic of China Practical Guide to the Law and Legal Principles*, *Testing Material on the Law* and the *1998 Legal Yearbook*, filled with statistics on cases, rulings and the number of legal personnel in each city, province and territory. Mr. Ma had one shelf devoted to legal dictionaries, while others were stuffed with primers on the legal system, textbooks with case studies, books on economic law, civil law, criminal law and, most salient, administrative law, which Mr. Ma had used to sue the government on behalf of the peasants.

His desk was stacked with newspapers, the topmost dating from December 1999, by which time Mr. Ma had already been in jail for six months.

"I stopped ordering his newspapers then because I thought he wouldn't need them for a while."

Ms. Cao had walked in. There was a long silence and I fingered the yellowing stack.

"Everything he had was related to the legal system and to rule of law," Ms. Cao said. "All his books. All the newspapers that he read. He was obsessed with rule of law."

I pulled a photo album off the shelf. Inside were grainy black-and-white photos of Mr. Ma's and Ms. Cao's family. Taken in the 1960s, they looked like Mr. Ma in the photo I had of him: stern, formal and lifeless. They also reminded me of photos I'd seen from the nineteenth century, with everyone dour and serious; for many, it was probably the only photo they'd had taken in their lives.

All the men in the photos had white cloth caps on their heads. The caps fitted halfway down to the ears and had flat tops, making the wearers look like health care workers or cooks of some sort. Most men in this dry, barren backwater used to wear these caps, a tradition whose roots had long been forgotten. It was one of the few items of traditional attire that Chinese people still wore, but was found only here in a remote part of the country. It was another reminder that Mr. Ma's people were among the very poorest.

He must have been brilliant to have gotten out. He probably had also benefited from policies, long discarded, that helped find jobs and education for people from "correct" communist class backgrounds—workers, farmers and soldiers—and especially those who grew up in former communist guerilla bases, such as the region around Mr. Ma's hometown. A smart young peasant growing up in the 1950s right after the communists' "liberation" of China could have done worse than to have come from this arid patch of the country.

Few of the pictures were of Mr. Ma or his wife. Some were of his children, but even when they were growing up in the 1970s and the '80s, photography wasn't that widespread, especially in this small city. But his grandchildren—they were represented with dozens and dozens of photos, all in color. Shots of two chubby kids digging into a white-frosted birthday cake, with Mr. Ma peering on tentatively but proudly from the side. Another showing half a dozen adults grouped around a grandchild at a park.

Ms. Cao handed me one to keep. It showed her and Mr. Ma on a sofa with two other grandchildren. Ms. Cao is bouncing the younger on her knee, making him laugh. Next to an eight-year-old, Mr. Ma sits somewhat stiffly in a white dress shirt buttoned up to the top, a cotton double-breasted blazer buttoned up as well. A glass of beer is next to him and a white birthday cake dominates the foreground. "It's my favorite," she said. "Take it."

I hesitated for a moment and decided to keep it. Then I pointed to one of the old grainy photos. "People like this— peasants—asked him to represent them, didn't they?"

"It was in early 1997 when he went back home to the countryside, up near Zizhou, to visit his mother," she said, sitting on the edge of the bed. "That's when it started."

Mr. Ma's hometown is a small village, Lijiaqu, which is located in Tuo'erxiang Township, which in turn is about seventeen miles from the county seat of Zizhou, the same town where I had stopped for lunch earlier in the day. Every year Chinese try to go back to their old home for Lunar New Year, and 1997 had been no different for Mr. Ma. Along with his wife, he returned to Lijiaqu to be with his mother and some close friends.

The Mas spent the holiday at home, preparing and eating big meals and relaxing—the television was on most of the time and the occasional game of mah-jongg broke out at a neighbor's house. Over the next few days farmers dropped by to visit the local son who'd made good, and they told him about their troubles. Drought had struck and they had difficulty making ends meet. As Mr. Wang had told me on the telephone when I called him from Zizhou at lunch, farmers who refused to pay—or in many cases couldn't pay—were beaten up and thrown in an improvised jail run by county leaders.

They'd all heard about the successful Peijiawan case. Like those farmers just a few miles away, Mr. Ma's relatives and friends had suffered from drought, seen their crops fail and been overtaxed. The farmers told Mr. Ma about their problems and asked him to help them sue the local government, just like the Peijiawan farmers had. I later met a farmer, wearing the same white cap as Mr. Ma's ancestors, who told me their thinking: "Ma is from this town. He had a license to handle this sort of case. When he came back home, we told him that the township government is corrupt and had set up illegal jails to beat farmers. We begged him for help."

Mr. Ma was touched but refused. "I didn't want him to handle it and neither did he," his wife said. Mr. Ma told the peasants that the case was complicated and he was too busy to take on another big case.

Another reason was that his hometown was controlled by a different district government than the city of Yan'an where Mr. Ma now lived. This is a key distinction in China, where courts often take their instructions from the local government. Mr. Ma lived in Yan'an, and his hometown was controlled by the party office in Yulin. He had no contacts in the Yulin party committee, and if he got in trouble, he'd be on his own. Plus, he knew that China's legal system doesn't have the concept of precedents—courts often make rulings that completely ignore the fact that other courts have ruled differently in similar cases. So even though the Peijiawan farmers had won their case in the same jurisdiction as Yulin, he knew that would be meaningless when his case was tried. The whole enterprise seemed very risky, and after the holiday Mr. Ma went home.

But over the next few months the farmers kept calling Mr. Ma. The family didn't have a phone at the time, but the farmers reached him through a neighbor, who recalls Mr. Ma speaking with people from his hometown on the phone. "You could tell he wanted to help out but that he had some worries," the neighbor said. "He kept telling them how difficult the case would be. He understood the law and understood that their case would provoke a lot of political pressure."

But then, in the summer of 1997, Ms. Cao received a letter

from one of their daughters, who lived in Zizhou. Ms. Cao had to read the letter twice because she couldn't believe it. A rumor was rife in Zizhou that Mr. Ma had turned down the case because he'd been bribed by the Zizhou County government. When Mr. Ma came home that evening, she showed him the letter. He blew up.

"First he blamed our daughter and said she was crazy. Then he made some phone calls and realized it wasn't her fault," Ms. Cao said. "She was telling the truth. People really were saying this."

It was early July 1997, and Yan'an was hot and dry, just like today. Usually, it was a quiet time with little work and days spent outside the apartment block, sitting in the shade with neighbors. Those who could would go somewhere cool: a trip to China's distant coast was possible for the wealthy, but most lazed away the summer at home.

The rumor ate at Mr. Ma. Each morning he got up, bolted down a bowl of rice congee and headed over to his law office. He didn't come home for lunch, burying himself instead in his work in his near-deserted office. Back at home in the evenings, he didn't talk at dinner, stewing silently inside. He didn't speak the whole time.

On the fourth day he came home for lunch. Ms. Cao made a bowl of noodles. Halfway through, he looked at her and said, "I'll take the case." Ms. Cao started to object but checked herself. Her husband wasn't listening. Instead, he was intently polishing off his noodles. Two minutes later he got up and without another word went back to work.

"I think one of the farmers started it," Ms. Cao said to me, "knowing it would get Teacher Ma riled up and that he'd be forced to take the case to prove he hadn't been bribed. Others say it was just a silly rumor."

Whatever the truth, Mr. Ma was now the farmers' advocate, and he set about winning for them tax relief just as the lawyers for the Peijiawan farmers had a year earlier. To him, just as to the Peijiawan lawyers, he had a straightforward case: local authorities could only tax farmers 5 percent of their income. But he could produce hundreds of witnesses with hard proof showing that they'd been taxed many times this amount. It was a simple administrative lawsuit. As far as he was concerned, it needn't have political implications. After gathering depositions and evidence, he filed the suit on behalf of several thousand farmers in the Yulin Intermediate Court that autumn. The exact number of farmers is hard to ascertain, since farmers continued to join the suit after it was filed. About 5,000 initially signed up, with tens of thousands more following by the end of the year.

Even though Mr. Ma had been reluctant to take on the case, he proceeded with an assumption that people in China have made for centuries: if only the upper levels knew of the true situation, then everything would be fine; it was all a question of lousy local administrators. The case, he figured, would alert regional leaders in Yulin that that farmers were overtaxed. They would order the judges to reduce the taxes and the farmers would win. Case closed.

Up until now I felt I understood Mr. Ma, but this made me wonder. If only top leaders knew? Top leaders benefit mightily from the current corrupt system: their sons and daughters study abroad, work for companies that pay them extravagant salaries for lending their family name and connections. If only they knew about corruption? If anyone was familiar with corruption, it was China's leaders. I had immense respect for what Mr. Ma had tried to do but wondered how he had clung to this idea. It probably explained why China's rulers had stayed in power for so long.

"In the early stage of the case he was naïve," Ms. Cao said. "He didn't know the complexity of society. He thought that the farmers had these difficulties just because the upper-level government didn't know the facts about the real difficulties in the village. He thought he should represent these facts to the upper level. Teacher Ma has always trusted the party and the government, even though he's in jail. He thinks that it's only that people conceal facts."

Over the next two years Mr. Ma was slowly disabused of this view. After preparing his case in the summer of 1997, he went to Yulin and filed. But just six months after it had judged in favor of the peasants in the almost identical Peijiawan case, the court refused to even accept, let alone hear, Mr. Ma's case. He received no written explanation. Later, when he asked around, he heard that the reason was the government had issued a new order instructing the courts to reject such cases.

"If he'd been from Yulin, anyone could have told him that after the Peijiawan case the courts weren't taking any more peasant class-action lawsuits," a lawyer in Yulin said. "That case shocked the district government and it had ordered the courts that no more cases were to be accepted."

Indeed, even the Peijiawan case had attracted a backlash. As I'd learned upon leaving Peijiawan village eighteen months earlier, some people in power weren't happy with the lawsuit. And although Mr. Ma didn't know it at the time he took the case, those responsible for abusing the peasants in Peijiawan hadn't been demoted or fired. Indeed, according to officials in the Yulin government, some had been promoted.

Unsure what to do, Mr. Ma went back to his home and spent a week in September with his mother. The farmers kept coming by to complain. For thirty years he'd been away, returning only at the holiday season for the annual family reunion, with days spent drinking and feasting. This time around, in autumn, he could see the pitiful harvest that was being wrung out of the cracked fields. The endless droughts were again afflicting the town. And the annual taxes, although not as high as the previous year's, were staggering—on average 100 yuan, or $12, per head.

Many peasants were sure that Mr. Ma had come back to announce his decision to quit. It was a reasonable assumption. After all, the courts had rejected the case and it seemed hopeless. He stayed with his mother, however, and talked to friends. He didn't announce his plans and the peasants held their breath.

Then, two days before he was due to head home to Yan'an, a farmer came by, a man who had been friends with Mr. Ma's father. The man told of how he'd been arrested and beaten the previous year, in the autumn of 1996. His wife had gone to visit the man in the local jail, hoping to give him a blanket. She was refused permission and told to return home. Her husband was a prisoner, she was told, and didn't have a right to a blanket, even though it was below freezing at night and he was being held in a makeshift jail in a pigsty. Angry, she cursed the government official. He struck her. "What's the world coming to when they do this," the peasant told Mr. Ma.

"I remember him sitting in his mother's cave, listening to the story. His face had no expression, but his eyes were wide open, angry like a demon's," the neighbor said. "The government said Ma tried to stir up our sentiment, but it was we farmers who stirred up Ma."

Something changed. Mr. Ma, who had been a legal worker, an amateur lawyer and lover of the law, decided that the law wasn't able to protect the farmers. What was needed, he thought, was some political pressure from below to break the logjam in Yulin. Lawsuits hadn't worked. He decided to arouse leaders' attention by leading a few small protests.

Naïve, or figuring they had nothing to lose, Mr. Ma and his farmer clients decided that autumn to set up an organization to promote their cause: the Tuo'erxiang County Farmers Anticorruption and Reducing Tax Burden Volunteer Liaison Small Group. Quite a mouthful, the title was meant to convey the group's apolitical and nonthreatening nature. It was simply "anticorruption" and for "reducing the tax burden"—two officially recognized national priorities. In addition, it was made up of volunteers and its function simply one of liaising—not of "organizing," an action that authorities dread the most. Even the odd term "Small Group" was meant to convey a sense of informality. It is a communistspeak word that means a body that is a step down from a more formal committee or commission and thus not menacing to the government.

Like the Peijiawan farmers, Mr. Ma's farmers elected representatives, who met several times that autumn and collected money. And just like the Peijiawan farmers, who had collected the equivalent of 25 cents from each farmer, the Tuo'erxiang farmers collected roughly the same amount from the 40,000 residents in their township. Authorities later accused the farmers of "United Front tactics"—a reference to a communist strategy of minimizing radical policies and winning support from moderates in society. Authorities consider this dangerous because the Communist Party often preaches United Front tactics—moderation, in other words—as a front for its own radicalism. To a government accustomed to such devious tactics, the peasants' moderation seemed like a cover.

The fateful plunge occurred on November 2, 1997, a Sunday and a market day in the township. A farmer in Mr. Ma's village donated his belching two-stroke tractor. The men draped it with white cloth banners, writing in red and black calligraphy slogans calling for taxes to be reduced. One of the farmers sat up front on the single seat, grasping the long handlebars that control the steering, speed and braking. Attached to the back of the two-wheeled tractor was a small cart draped with the banners and two large speakers that blared out a tape recording of Mr. Ma reading the central government's directives on tax reduction. It was a primitive version of the small trucks with loudspeakers and banners that you see during elections in Taiwan and Japan. The group drove their "propaganda vehicle," as the government later called it, from Mr. Ma's home village of Lijiaqu to the village of Tuo'erxiang, the seat of Tuo'erxiang Township.

At the end of the ten-mile trip, the farmers and Mr. Ma handed out central government documents on taxation. They took the banners off their wagon and hung them up. Hanging limply in the dusty haze, they read: "Reduce Peasants' Burden" and "Taxation According to Law."

Standing underneath the banners, with his propaganda tractor parked nearby, Mr. Ma gave a speech that attracted several hundred onlookers, who crowded the denuded slopes. The market closed down and people roared their approval as Mr. Ma spoke, easily mixing the modern terms of the law with the local dialect.

"All we are asking is that the local government follow the central government's directives," Mr. Ma said. "Our fields have suffered from drought, but officials treat them like they're heavy with corn. They're trying to squeeze oil out of chaff."

About four hours later, the farmers dispersed, heading back to their villages flush with Mr. Ma's ringing rhetoric and clutching material that explained the government's official tax policies. Unwritten on the flyers but circulating quickly was the story of how Mr. Ma had tried to file a lawsuit but had been rejected. The "liaison small group" believed they had failed because they hadn't garnered the thousands of signatures that the Peijiawan farmers had a year earlier. This rally, they figured, would fire up the farmers and make them willing to sign a petition that would later be circulated.

The next day, the Public Security Bureau contacted Mr. Ma, who was holding a strategy meeting with delegates in a nearby village. Officers asked Mr. Ma to go to Zizhou for questioning. In its charges against Mr. Ma the government says he told the farmers: "We should go together, otherwise I won't go. I won't talk by myself. If we want to talk, we should talk together. If one says something wrong, the other can correct it. They'll take notes. We should take notes as well."

I am not sure why the government put that citation in its charges against Mr. Ma. Perhaps prosecutors thought this showed his devious nature. For example, his advice on taking notes could be construed as giving the peasants clever, lawyerly advice that they wouldn't have thought of themselves—the sort of thing the government must have hated about Mr. Ma. To me it just showed common sense and his desire, even at this stage, not to take too direct a lead in the proceedings. He didn't want to be pegged as the ringleader and wanted to protect the movement against government efforts to split it, perhaps by offering some leaders a bribe to disband.

Agreeing with Mr. Ma's suggestion, about seventy delegates accompanied Mr. Ma the next day to meet with the Public Security Bureau in Zizhou. Some of the farmers saw this meeting with the police as a big victory: at last they'd have a chance to state their case to someone other than the corrupt officials in their township. Others, probably Mr. Ma himself, realized that this was a dangerous new phase to the confrontation.

The Public Security Bureau occupies one of the best buildings in Zizhou, a five-story white-tiled building off one of the main streets. It is surrounded by a 10-foot wall and has an accordionlike antiterrorist gate that moves from right to left along tracks—the sort of gate designed to stop mobs and suicide bombers driving a truck. I don't think China has ever had such a suicide attack, and it always struck me as incomprehensible why so many government offices in China, from museums and hospitals to schools and welfare offices, had installed this sort of gate. It seemed a mixture of paranoia and fad—the latest way for unaccountable officials to waste people's money.

The seventy farmers followed Mr. Ma through the front gate and into the courtyard. A dozen accompanied him farther inside, where they met the head of the local office over tea at a conference table. Even though some farmers had accompanied him, Mr. Ma was clearly the spokesman. He sat at the center of the table and was the only one capable of speaking the security bureau's language of laws and regulations.

Mr. Ma and his supporters asked for the security bureau's help in righting their wrong, while the bureau insisted they disband and "go through normal channels." Mr. Ma was polite, agreeing that he should have asked for a permit to hold his small rally on market day. But he also said the farmers have a right to protest and appeal—rights enshrined in the constitution, although not taken too seriously by the government.

After an hour the meeting broke up and Mr. Ma returned to the village to spend the night. At first the group had been elated that the government officials had deigned to meet them. But the meeting had been unproductive and the farmers were now angry. Mr. Ma, too, was a changed man. His caution had gone, and he saw that the government structure in the county—not just the lower-level officials in the village and township—were corrupt and working hand in hand. "Ma asked if we should push forward," one farmer recalled, becoming excited at the memory of the meeting. "And we all said 'Yes, yes, yes.' "

Mr. Ma and the delegates decided they'd have to appeal to the district government in Yulin. This way they'd go over the heads of the county courts and government, in hopes the higher-ranking officials in the district government would order the local courts to accept the case. After all, the Peijiawan case had been tried in Yulin, so judges and their party overseers must be more enlightened there, the farmers figured. They needed to rent trucks to carry the farmers the ninety-miles north to Yulin, so Mr. Ma suggested raising some more money—the equivalent of another 25 cents or so from each farmer should do it, he figured.

On November 4, 1997, the day after the meeting with the Public Security Bureau, Mr. Ma again met with his delegates and planned the trip to Yulin later that month. He was now working closely with two delegates, Ma Quan and Ma Dengde, who despite sharing the same surname weren't directly related to him or each other. The three of them easily raised the money and agreed to expand their publicity campaign to neighboring Nanchuan Township, which also fell under Zizhou County's jurisdiction. Representatives from that township soon pledged support.

On November 19, Mr. Ma and about two hundred farmers traveled to Yulin to submit a written appeal to the district government, asking leaders to reverse their ban on local courts from hearing the farmers' case. A relic of the imperial era, submitting written petitions and appeals has been preserved as a safety valve for those who have lost everything. Many bureaus accept petitions and appeals in China—from district and provincial offices all the way to the State Council, China's quasi-cabinet that runs the day-to-day operations of government in Beijing. Few petitioners win, but many of China's dispossessed see it as a last hope.

The crowd went to the center of power in Yulin—not the courts or the district government but to the district's Communist Party headquarters. This is the office that holds sway over the courts, appoints government leaders and directly controls the police and security apparatus. For three days the farmers stayed in Yulin, assembling every morning in front of the party headquarters, holding up banners, many of which had already flown about two weeks earlier during their initial rally in the market town.

According to the government, the rallies were gigantic demonstrations that disrupted the city and government. Mr. Ma, in his defense statement, portrayed the days in Yulin quite differently:

> The truth was that only four or five farmer representatives and I were broadcasting recordings on the street and reading the central government's documents and policies. But the prosecutor doesn't care about testimony or evidence and distorted the facts, even saying I was stirring up the masses to confront the government. Isn't this a deliberate distortion of facts and claiming black is white and white black?

Indeed, the government's charge sheet did seem to be stretching things:

> The appellants created disturbances in the courtyard of the prefectural Party committee. They blocked up the

traffic in the lanes to the courtyard of the prefectural Party committee. They grabbed the food from the prefectural Party committee's cooking stove and beat up the cooks and administration people. They stopped the county leaders. They stole local residents' coal and made a "pagoda pyre" of the coal. The normal work order of the prefectural Party committee was disrupted by them until they left on November 22.

It is possible to imagine that the farmers were running out of money, desperate and hungry—so perhaps they asked for a meal. I wondered if the cooks had refused to serve them, or maybe they were just incensed at the food being served to the party cadres while their families went hungry back home.

As for stealing coal blocks, the lawyers I'd talked to in Yulin, even those who thought Mr. Ma probably shouldn't have led the appeal, shook their heads in disbelief. "What would the farmers do with coal blocks?" one lawyer told me, rolling his eyes. "They just had a few trucks so could barely fit all the farmers on the trucks. They weren't about to start carting coal back to the hills."

After two days the peasants and Mr. Ma headed back to the hills. From a hesitant participant, Mr. Ma was now a *nongmin yingxiong*. The term *yingxiong* is often translated as "hero" but I thought that "champion" captured the way that people there viewed him: as someone fighting for their cause. The ambiguities of the Chinese language also allowed for different ways of looking at Mr. Ma. He could be a "peasants' champion" or simply a "peasant champion"—the possessive is often dropped or unclear in Chinese. Probably the former was more accurate because he wasn't, strictly speaking, a peasant anymore. But his roots were in the countryside, and he took on the case because of his rural pedigree. He was a peasant who'd obtained an education and now returned to the corrupt countryside as its champion.

In December of that same year, Mr. Ma began to spread the word throughout the county. In yet another township, Zhuanmiao, he and peasants held rallies. According to the government documents and interviews with farmers, Mr. Ma was now far beyond his role of passive advocate for farmers' interests. While most of the banners they hung up still had plain, unemotive language such as "Taxation According to Law," new slogans began to appear urging wavering peasants to participate. "What Are You Afraid Of?" hung at one meeting, a elderly farmer recalled.

"We'd been afraid for years, afraid of the government and its police," the farmer said, tugging at the white wisps of a beard growing from his chin. "But Ma's point was that what we wanted was legal. There was nothing to be afraid of."

On January 3, 1998, during what the government called an "illegal" gathering—all meetings must be approved by the government in one way or another—two farmers were detained. Mr. Ma was back with his family in Yan'an but called up the delegates, the government claimed, and "stirred up the people to go to the Public Security Bureau and obtain their release." Mr. Ma said in his written self-defense that he had simply advised the farmers to go to the police and ask for the farmers' release. He didn't participate himself.

Throughout 1998, Mr. Ma devoted more and more of his time to the farmers' suit. Indeed, his family recalls that since taking the case in 1997 he had largely given up other suits, sacrificing his steady income for what at best would result in a meager return. The Peijiawan farmers had won just $75,000 and the legal fees amounted to just 10 percent of this for a team of lawyers, including their expenses. Mr. Ma would have been lucky to cover his expenses and earn a tiny profit.

Far from shielding Mr. Ma from charges of being motivated by greed, his willingness to do basically pro bono work appeared suspicious to the authorities. "They asked me in 1998 what Ma was up to," said a lawyer from the South City Legal Services firm. "If he wasn't making much money on this, which I agreed he wasn't, then they wondered if he wasn't just a troublemaker trying to stir things up."

To make things worse, in the government's eyes, Mr. Ma began spreading his organizational methods to other farmers. In Miaojiaping, a township about ten miles down the road from Tuo'erxiang, peasants set up their own "Anticorruption Liaison Office" that drafted its own plan of action, including propaganda cars, banners and speeches. "Ma planted seeds across the county," a farmer said, scratching his white skullcap. "We were learning about our rights."

The government saw it differently. In assessing blame for crises it creates, the communists like to find "black hands" to blame. In Beijing's myopic world, its inherently corrupt and unstable system of government is never to blame; instead, instigators whip up the innocent masses. This allows the government to avoid confronting the real causes of unrest. This was the way the 1989 Tiananmen massacre was dealt with (a few troublemakers had riled up the students) and how the Falun Gong protests that started in 1999 were explained (a few organizers were to blame). And this was how Zizhou's peasant uprising was seen.

In its charges against him, the procurator laid the blame squarely with Mr. Ma, resorting to subjective, flowery language that reflected the government's anger. "On November 18, 1998, Ma Wenlin even personally attended an illegal gathering in Wancha [village]. He made speeches and his abominable influence radiated to every village and town in the county, seriously affecting the stable unity of Zizhou."

Reading the charges, one gets the feeling the government was searching for something to pin on Mr. Ma. Up until now his actions hadn't been all that radical. Boiled down, they amounted to publicizing government tax policies. Some of the meetings might have been illegal, but it would have been hard to jail Mr. Ma—who after all was a member of the same legal profession as the courts and judges that would try him.

In China, urbanites are afraid of the country's 800 million peasants because of this gut feeling that, once aroused, they can't be controlled. For the most part, this is bunk. Farmers in China are by and large cautious and only do what they figure is in their best interests. But mass action does have its own dynamic, and sometimes things can spin out of control. Maybe this is what happened next. In any case, it was exactly what the government needed to jail the peasant champion.

Ms. Cao and I stopped talking for a moment. We sat facing each other, I on a chair and she on the side of the bed, her face framed by the yellowing white wall behind her. The room was lit by an electric bulb, which hung from the ceiling, its dim rays searching the four bare corners for shadows. It was late and she was tired, the creases on her face made harsher by the crude lighting.

This was the hardest part of the story for her, the event that she'd gone over in her head time and again, trying to re-create a different outcome. She looked at me pleadingly. "I regret that I let him handle this case," she said, carefully putting her hand palms down on her lap as if to straighten out the sequence of events. "But we couldn't prevent him. You know, he found those farmers really pitiful. He tried to be careful. We always urged him to be careful."

On April 8, 1999, the county sent a senior official named

Zhao Liang to Laoshanmao, one of the centers of activism. According to the government, he was sent to check the village's books—in the government's words to "learn about the opinions and come up with an analysis." It sounded as if someone was finally listening to the peasants.

Mr. Zhao arrived late that afternoon and immediately conferred with the local village secretary. They had dinner and then around 10 p.m. went into the local village committee's office to look over the books. After a couple of hours the two men went to sleep in the office, intending to pick up first thing in the morning.

It seemed an odd time to audit the village's finances, and word spread through the village about the odd audit. Seven senior men, all surnamed Ma (but not related to Mr. Ma) walked down to the office, a small one-story building in the center of the village. They conferred outside for about five minutes. They didn't trust Mr. Zhao. He worked in the county seat of Zizhou and oversaw all villages' finances as head of the Village Basic Level Organizational Rectification and Construction Work Team, a powerful body that reported directly to the district's Communist Party. In that capacity he already had copies of the villagers' finances. He must be there to doctor the originals and cover the tracks of the wrongdoers. Their precious evidence was about to disappear.

The seven men decided to act. They threw themselves against the flimsy wooden door, breaking the lock off cleanly. Mr. Zhao and the village party secretary leapt up, the books behind them. The seven men asked for the books. Mr. Zhao refused, saying he still had not finished.

The seven insisted and moved forward. Mr. Zhao swallowed hard and handed the books over. Under the dim bare bulb the nine men huddled over the books. Look at the incomes ascribed to various farmers, they said; such incomes were impossibly high for poor loess farmers. How could they pay 5 percent on such figures? Mr. Zhao squirmed through the lesson and admitted he had no answers. The farmers' decision: detain Mr. Zhao until he provided satisfaction.

The next morning, April 9, Mr. Ma came to Laoshanmao on one of his now regular semimonthly trips to the countryside. The government says the farmers asked Mr. Ma what to do about Mr. Zhao. Should they release the official? Quoting one of the farmer delegates who oversaw the kidnapping, the government claims that Mr. Ma said, "Don't release Zhao or what we've done for the past two years will be in vain." Mr. Ma supposedly asked for two copies of the village's books and then organized villagers to watch over the official.

This version of events is impossible to corroborate and it was never proved in court. According to Mr. Ma's written self-defense, he never instructed the farmers to keep Mr. Zhao and didn't even know the official was being held. Farmers agreed. "Ma never asked us or advised us about Zhao," one farmer later told me in an interview. "We were just so angry at the idea of him taking away our evidence that we grabbed him."

The government's case is based on the testimony of one of the seven men, Ma Quan, who had worked closely with Mr. Ma over the previous year. He was close to Mr. Ma but also had something to gain by his testimony: the government documents say he had been the chief spokesman for the kidnappers, meaning he faced a stiff sentence unless he cooperated—a decade in a labor camp wouldn't have been unusual. Under many legal systems such potentially biased testimony could have been called into question. But here it formed the sole basis of Mr. Ma's arrest and imprisonment.

Reading through the accounts of events and talking to witnesses, what comes through clearest was the government's anger that this lawyer had taught peasants all this highfalutin legal talk. For example, in describing Mr. Ma's alleged role in the kidnapping, the court papers said he told the peasants to "speak artfully" with officials, as if this were a crime. In one other case the documents said Mr. Ma told a farmer: "If they want to arrest you, give them your hands and let them. Then send someone to me." This sounds like the soundest advice a lawyer can give a client—don't resort to violence, let your lawyer get you off—yet was used in summation as evidence of Mr. Ma's errors.

"Ma never admitted what he did and never regretted it," the indictment concluded. "Therefore according to the law he should be punished severely." It was the millennia-old slogan used by prosecutors in China: leniency to those who confess, severity to those who do not. Stripped down, this means: we'll break you if you stand up for your innocence.

And indeed, the government did break Mr. Ma.

"This was delivered to us in June, shortly after he was arrested," Ms. Cao said, reaching down under the bed and pulling out a black leather attaché case. It was the sort of shoulder bag that many Chinese men carry—most stuff them in the front basket of their bicycles or carry them under their arm like a football.

She got up and walked back into the living room. I followed and we sat down. She put the bag on the coffee table between us. She opened the bag and pulled out a towel caked in blood.

The alleged kidnapping in April 1999 had ended after fifteen days when the government negotiated the official's release. County officials in Zizhou sent a delegation to the village, and after several days of talks the peasants had agreed to let the official go if their concerns were taken seriously. But they knew that the promises were empty—after all, the officials making the promises were colleagues of the official whom they suspected of doctoring the books. "They were all in it together," a peasant later told me. "We needed to bypass the county."

Her husband agreed with the peasants, Ms. Cao said.

"He thought that his only hope lay in getting the central government to pay attention," she said, looking down and shaking her head. "He was so naïve."

But it wasn't completely a move of desperation. Mr. Ma's original efforts to file the case—like the successful class-action case in the next valley—had been reported in the national Chinese media. In 1998 the newspaper that is run by the country's Ministry of Justice, *Legal Daily*, published a favorable article. So, too, did *Focus Report*, the country's leading investigative television newsmagazine, run by the central government's television network.

"He thought that with all this favorable publicity and the fact that they'd accepted the other case, all he had to do was make the central government understand and it would support him," Ms. Cao said.

After talking it over with farmers in June 1999, Mr. Ma was ready to set off with five of the elected delegates to Beijing. Their goal was to file a written appeal with the central government asking for intervention. Local authorities were nervous, and before he left for Beijing, the Zizhou County Public Security Bureau made several trips to Mr. Ma's house.

"They were courteous," Ms. Cao said. "But they didn't want Teacher Ma to go. They said that he had done his best for the peasants and that he'd reached the end of his legal appeals. They said we should all be reasonable and drop it," Ms. Cao said.

But Mr. Ma was beyond making the endless compromises that define life in China. He'd backed off cases before and had always been willing to listen to the party's legal affairs committee when it deemed a case sensitive. This time, however, he felt his countrymen—the families he'd grown up with on the Loess Plateau—were facing an economic catastrophe. This time events would be pushed to their logical conclusion. Mr. Ma listened to the officials and thanked them for the visit. Then he made his travel arrangements for Beijing.

On July 7, Mr. Ma arrived in Beijing with his five companions. The next day they made their way to the State Council's Petitions and Appeals Office. He'd taken farmers to a local-level version of this office in Yulin about eighteen months ago. Now he was at the modern-day equivalent of the emperor's appeal office. Located up an unmarked alley on the south side of Beijing, the office is guarded by plainclothes police, who block people who they think will cause trouble.

Mr. Ma went in and registered. A few minutes later a receptionist came out and asked which of them was Ma Wenlin. Mr. Ma raised his hand, and the receptionist ushered him in for a talk. He was led to a small room where two men sat. They said they were from the Beijing Public Security Bureau. Mr. Ma asked for identification. The two, probably warned by their colleagues in Zizhou that Mr. Ma was a troublemaker, beat him. He lost thirteen teeth and stanched the bleeding with the towel that lay before me on the table.

I picked up the towel. It was caked in blood, but I tried to put myself in the government's position. They'd argue that it could be anyone's blood. Even if it was Mr. Ma's, it could have been from a bad nosebleed.

Then I looked inside the bag. It was filled with legal books, including the *Handbook of Legal Terms* and *Legal Questions*. There was a pair of plastic-framed eyeglasses and a cheap flex-band wristwatch. Tucked into a side pocket was a copy of *Legal*

Daily from June 1, 1998, about a year before he was arrested. A long article on page 3 detailed the Tuo'erxiang case and was critical of the court's refusal to accept it. This must have been Mr. Ma's sustenance—an article published by the Justice Ministry's official newspaper arguing that he was right, that the courts should hear his case. The bag belonged to a dedicated lawyer who mistakenly felt he had the system on his side. Not a hell-raiser or criminal.

I sat holding the cloth like a talisman. For Ms. Cao it was a relic, proof of what had befallen her husband. To a government using laws to rule the country, it was easily refutable evidence. Ms. Cao put the articles back in the bag and walked out of the room.

After the beating, Mr. Ma was taken to a hospital, where he was told that said his injuries weren't serious. He was returned to the Public Security Bureau in Beijing, which held him until July 12. Then the Zizhou Public Security Bureau picked him up—odd considering that Mr. Ma lived in another county—and took him to jail in Yulin. It was only four months later, on November 10, 1999, that Ms. Cao was allowed to see him. She picked up his black bag and delivered some clothes. By then Mr. Ma's fate was sealed: five years in a labor camp.

The trial, though, was hardly insignificant. The outcome was never in doubt, but through it Mr. Ma became even more of a rallying point for the legal community—not just here up on the Loess Plateau, but down in the provincial capital of Xi'an, which is one of China's most important cities. It turned Mr. Ma into a local martyr.

The case relied on the flimsiest of evidence: one witness who had overseen the kidnapping of an official. That gave him a vested interest in fingering Mr. Ma and, indeed, he had received a drastically reduced sentence. In addition, the charges were written in highly unprofessional language. Mr. Ma, for example, was accused of "pretending" to be a lawyer, when in fact he had the legal credentials to handle civil cases, including the peasants' administrative lawsuit.

In addition, the case was marred by procedural irregularities. From the start, Mr. Ma had been vigorously defended by a local lawyer, Feng Xuewen. But Mr. Feng had immediately run up against numerous signals that the trial would be a sham. On October 15, 1999, for example, Mr. Feng went to get a copy of the prosecutor's charges against Mr. Ma and was told he could only copy the first page. The formal list of charges detailing which crimes Mr. Ma had committed were off limits. Only after he protested was he allowed to see the charges.

On October 27, Mr. Feng was told the case would be tried on November 1 and was instructed to hand in his defense statement. Two days later the trial was delayed until November 3 after prosecutors said they wanted to have time to study Mr. Feng's defense plans. On October 31, he handed in his defense statement and the list of witnesses he planned to call. At the top of the list were the peasant delegates who'd hired Mr. Ma.

Police went out and arrested Mr. Feng's six witnesses. Two were released the next day, but four were kept in jail. The next day Mr. Feng asked that his witnesses be allowed to testify in court. The request was denied on grounds that the witnesses didn't want to testify and had also recanted what they'd said in their depositions. Suspicious, Mr. Feng filed another written request to the court, noting that it had the power to require witnesses to testify. Surely, at least those in its custody could testify. Again, a rejection.

The court now delayed the proceedings until November 8. On that day, just before the hearing was due to start, Mr. Feng learned that two of the three judges on the panel deciding the case had participated in drawing up the charges. So intertwined are China's police, prosecutor's office and judicial panels that such events are not uncommon. Mr. Feng asked that at least one of the two be removed from the panel. Another rejection.

The next day, evidence was to be presented to the court. Mr. Feng's six witnesses had now been turned against Mr. Ma, all providing written statements that Mr. Ma was guilty. Mr. Feng stood up and asked that the witnesses give their testimony in court.

"If not," Mr. Feng told the panel of judges, "then one might wonder how the prosecution obtained the testimony."

The allusion to torture wasn't lost on the judges. Infuriated, they ordered him to sit down and not question the evidence. In fact, they said, he had no right to raise questions and must remain silent for the rest of the trial.

Mr. Feng collected his papers and walked out of the courtroom in protest. The trial lasted another day and ended on November 10.

Without a lawyer, Mr. Ma had to represent himself, an irony considering the fact that as a "legal worker" he wasn't allowed to represent clients in criminal cases and had been criticized by the government for overstepping his powers in representing the farmers. As the government presented its case to the judges, Mr. Ma sat in the courtroom in Zizhou and wrote down his thoughts.

What flowed out was an amazing document, a twenty-six-page handwritten self-defense that showed how Mr. Ma had won his reputation. Copies of the document have become coveted among local lawyers. Written on tissue-thin lined paper a bit smaller than regular letter size, the rebuttal cited Chinese law to show how his legal work had been within the framework of China's existing legal system. It is a robust defense of independent legal work, at times eloquent:

> As is my responsibility as a legal worker, I was just explaining the central government's policies and related laws. The farmers grasped this. The burden on peasants is a key issue that can influence reforms and stability. If it isn't firmly solved then it will harm the national economy and development. But if we could solve the problems, the government would love the people and the people would love the government.

To the end he was unrepentant. As he wrote: "Formerly, when peasants met government cadres who committed illegal activities, they didn't dare confront them. Now those cadres don't dare charge farmers randomly or fine them. They won't dare bully them."

Six days later the verdict was delivered: five years, exactly what the prosecution had requested. His sentence started the day he was arrested and beaten in Beijing. He would be released July 7, 2004.

Mr. Feng immediately wrote an appeal and filed it on November 30, 1999. He also began organizing pressure in the provincial capital of Xi'an. In mid-December he held a meeting of two dozen legal experts, including many prominent law professors. Besides roundly condemning the sentence, the experts called for the case to be reheard and overturned.

Shortly thereafter, Mr. Feng filed his defense statement for the appeal. It is a blunt, eighteen-page document that details Mr.

Feng's travails and Mr. Ma's efforts. Reading it, I couldn't help contrasting its factual analysis with the government's empty rhetorical blasts. In its charges, the government alleged that Ma had committed a dozen crimes, yet it furnishes no proof for any of its charges.

Mr. Feng noted that these crimes—disrupting traffic, disturbing the workings of the government and even of the government's canteen—could be objectively proven if they were true. If the district capital's traffic had been paralyzed, why couldn't the government show one traffic report? If protesters had really overrun the district's Communist Party headquarters—an absurd proposition given the security at such locations—why no police reports of disruptive protests?

He answered his own question in another part of the defense. In it he defended Mr. Ma's goal of representing the peasants in their fight for a more just society. It was an idealistic vision, one that challenged the government on its own terms: China's need for "social order." This is a claim heard endlessly from government officials. Democracy and freedoms, they argue, are well and good, but disorder would be a fatal flaw to China. It would be a throwback to the chaos of the Cultural Revolution and disrupt the steady gains in standards of living and political freedoms.

Mr. Feng didn't deny these arguments. No one, he says, wants to see China slip into disorder. But a death grip is not stability. The inability to change may in the short term look like a virtue, but in the long term it is a weakness, suppressing natural change and leading to violent outbursts.

"During this period [of protests], the social order of Tuo'erxiang was an abnormal social order," Mr. Feng wrote. "It was a social order of increasing burdens that farmers couldn't accept. The farmers rose up, struggling hard to make of Tuo'erxiang a good, just social order, a social order where reasonable taxes were paid."

On December 28 the appeals court reached its verdict: The lower court's decision was upheld. Mr. Ma faced five years in prison.

Ms. Cao had been confident that the court in Yulin would reopen the case. One good sign was that *Legal Daily*, the newspaper that is run by the Ministry of Justice in Beijing and which had reported favorably on Mr. Ma's efforts in 1998, had written a report in early 2000 criticizing the local courts. The report was an "internal" article written for leaders only, but it was a good sign that word of Mr. Ma's innocence was filtering out.

"I went to Yulin and talked to a medium-level official about the case. I told him that I will keep suing and suing until I die," Ms. Cao said. "That man told me, 'You already have sued and sued and where do you want to sue now? How will you afford it?' "

It was a good question. Even if the court in Yulin were instructed to reopen the case, Ms. Cao would have to hire a senior lawyer—only they can handle suits brought before intermediate courts. One from Beijing would cost the equivalent of $12,500, and even an ordinary lawyer from Xi'an would cost about a tenth of that—completely out of the question for a schoolteacher like herself making $100 a month.

So, like her husband, Ms. Cao decided to learn the law herself. "I ended up using some of Teacher Ma's books," she said, again using his formal title. "I wrote a new defense statement myself last month (July 2000). When some farmers heard that I was going to try to get it reopened, they sent me three written testimonials saying they'd encouraged Ma and that he'd just been their representative. It was courageous. I sent it all to the court in Yulin."

It was indeed courageous. A few days later police went to Tuo'erxiang and arrested the three farmers who had given Ms. Cao the written testimony.

Ms. Cao now sees her husband about once a week. He is held in a labor camp several hours outside town, where he works printing materials for the government. Mr. Ma had been arrested for spreading what was supposed to be the law of the land. Now he was in jail printing government documents.

"He's not mistreated," Ms. Cao said. "But he has a heart condition and there's no medication for him. We've applied for him to be released on medical parole, but people in Zizhou are afraid of him getting out of jail."

I later learned that the Shenmu Prison, where he was being held, put in two requests in 2002 for Mr. Ma to be released early. Officials said Mr. Ma was a model prisoner, teaching inmates reading and math. He was finally released in 2003, about fourteen months early.

When he got out, he had lost his job as well as his legal worker's license and membership in the Chinese Communist Party. He gets by on his wife's small retirement pension. "They violated my human rights by arresting me like that," he said in his thick Shaanxi accent. "I won't rest until they admit this."

If all else fails, Mr. Ma said he will try to influence public opinion by writing a novel. The plot will revolve around corrupt officials and peasants who rise up against them. I told him it sounded more like fact than fiction. He laughed in agreement.

The heat that had been building up finally broke the next day. I woke to rain and after talking to a few drivers decided to abandon my plan of driving back to Xi'an. A new highway was under construction, forcing drivers to take a long detour through dirt roads. Those roads had now turned to mud, and the trip to the provincial capital would take eight hours by car.

I decided to take the train later in the day and began to pack my bags. The phone rang.

"Come down to the lobby," someone said in a thick accent. "I want to tell you something about Ma Wenlin."

I went down and looked around the lobby. It was small, with a counter over to the left and a couple of sofas to the right. The receptionist looked at me and, with a frown, cast her gaze at a man who didn't belong here: a farmer with a white skullcap and a faded blue cotton jacket. I walked over and greeted him like an old friend. The sofas were empty, so we sat down and chatted. The receptionist shrugged and returned to her books.

"I heard from friends that you were going to Yan'an, so I came to tell you about us," the farmer said, speaking in quick, low tones.

He'd arrived late the previous night and had stayed with friends, bunking in a dormitory at a construction company. He looked around, eager to go. Then he slid over a big brown envelope. "We're still active," he said. "Look."

I opened the frayed envelope and pulled out a thick document. It was a copy of a typed, twenty-one-page petition signed by 30,166 farmers from Tuo'erxiang and the two neighboring townships where Mr. Ma had campaigned for farmers' rights. Local lawyers had been banned from working on the case, but the petition was clearly a lawyer's handiwork: it repeated in legal language many of the points in Mr. Ma's self-defense. Many farmers were under police surveillance but they, too, had participated, providing nitty-gritty details of police abuse.

So the peasants had found me and I finally had the petition, just as the lawyers had predicted yesterday. I put the packet in my carry bag and we sat there in silence. It wasn't the best place for a conversation.

"Just tell people that we're responsible, not Lawyer Ma," the peasant said. "He was just our lawyer."

I wanted to ask the man his name but hesitated. The lobby was small and we stuck out. We both looked outside.

"The rain is good, finally some rain," he said. "I'm a bit worried about the terracing. Our fields aren't used to this much rain and they might wash out."

He seemed eager to make his trip back home and kept looking outside at the weather, which steadily worsened, the rain now falling in sheets. I stood up and we shook hands, glowing like coconspirators.

A couple of hours later I was on the train back to Xi'an. After getting off the phone with the paranoid journalist and talking to the old cadre, I spent the rest of the ride watching the Loess Plateau recede and reading the court documents. A few hours later I was in Xi'an, a vibrant but filthy city that still boasts its ancient city walls. I tried calling the journalist to arrange dinner as planned but got no answer. I thought nothing of it and instead got in touch with a local lawyer who gave me a copy of a petition sent by the provincial lawyers' association to the provincial governor asking that Mr. Ma's case be heard by the provincial supreme court. Only by bypassing the local courts in the county and district, they felt, would Mr. Ma get a fair shake.

I wondered. Mr. Ma had already tried appealing to higher-level authorities but had been burned as badly by them as by the local officials. He'd gone to Beijing to petition, yet it was Beijing police who'd arrested and beaten him before delivering him into the hands of the local police. The central government's policy was stability above all else. No governor would risk that by tacitly appearing to condone the unrest that had consumed one of his counties—and a county of such enormous symbolic importance to the Communist Party.

Still I admired the lawyers. They'd signed their names to the petition. Like all such people in China, they worked either for state-run universities or state-administered law firms—independent schools and law practices don't really exist. As lawyers and teachers, they were expected to toe the government line, not support a rabble-rouser who'd been condemned and jailed by the party. Yet they had done so—more proof, I thought, of the growing courage and independence of Chinese society.

Back in Beijing the next day, I found a fax waiting for me on my desk. It was from a human-rights monitoring agency in Hong Kong, which reported that the journalist who had called me up on the train had been detained a few hours after getting off the phone with me. The journalist hadn't been paranoid. His phone had been bugged. The police had prevented him from speaking to me by detaining him for a few hours. I gave him a call.

"I'm fine now," he said over the crackly line. "It's no big deal. Anytime someone comes here to talk with me about Ma, the police always take me out to the countryside. We had dinner and returned home at one in the morning."

"That was a long dinner," I said.

"Yes," he said. "Great hosts. We even had beer and grain alcohol. At the end of it I realized that the province will never reopen Ma's case. But they are worried. That's a start."

2 DREAM OF A VANISHED CAPITAL

Mr. Luo stepped out from the shadows of the bus stop and walked over to me slowly. He was a good-looking man of fifty-seven, despite dyed hair, a comb-over and bushy eyebrows in need of a trim. I'd met him several times before, and he was always gruff, a bit like a 1930s hard-boiled detective who talked in monosyllables and rarely showed emotions.

He slowly turned his head to the bus shelter and nodded deliberately. His partner, Mr. Feng, stepped out from the shadows, carrying a smart black leather satchel stuffed with documents. He reminded me of a *shutong*, the boy servant to an artist or poet who in ancient China followed behind the great man, carrying his books and works.

Los Angeles detective and classical-era *shutong*, the two walked over to me and we entered our meeting place: a Kentucky Fried Chicken in old Beijing. It was bright and neon-lit, with plastic bucket seats and Formica floors. Mr. Luo motioned for us to go to its upstairs seating area.

"Shouldn't we buy something?" I asked, thinking this would prevent the busboys from throwing us out. "Maybe a tea or coffee?"

Mr. Luo looked at me as if I were the only person in Beijing who didn't realize that this KFC was his private office. In a concession to his foreign guest he nodded to Mr. Feng and said, "Buy some tea." I started to protest that I'd pay but Mr. Feng looked at me sternly and motioned for me to follow Mr. Luo. No silliness, he seemed to say, just follow the boss's orders.

Mr. Feng went to order tea and we walked upstairs to the restaurant's upper level. Mr. Luo surveyed the scene. It was a weekday at 7 p.m. and most of the tables were taken, including his usual spot in the corner. With a grunt he selected a four-person table in the middle of the room. I cringed at the thought of us on display but figured that if we spoke in low tones, no one would hear us over the noise of other people talking.

After Mr. Luo and I exchanged pleasantries, Mr. Feng arrived with three paper cups of Lipton tea. This was the third time I'd met the two, and as usual we started off with small talk, chatting about the weather, places of interest in China for a foreigner to visit and places that the two of them had visited. It always struck me how different they were. Both had grown up in the old part of Beijing, but they seemed to have little else in common. Although Mr. Luo was the leader and Mr. Feng deferred to him, Mr. Feng kept a superior air about him. At sixty, he was three years older than Mr. Luo, which should have made him the leader of the two. And before retiring he'd helped set policy in the Ministry of Culture. That made him a *ganbu*, a civil servant, and thus a prestigious member of society.

Mr. Luo, by contrast, had worked for the past thirty-eight years in the same agricultural machinery factory as a quality inspector, his hands always a little dirty with the sort of machine grease that never quite scrubs off. But Mr. Luo possessed gravitas. Mr. Feng was sometimes nervous, but Mr. Luo had a strong, commanding presence, the mark of a man who had ordered people around on a hot factory floor for decades.

Both men were dressed smartly, if cheaply—Mr. Luo wearing a green plaid jacket, black pinstriped shirt, leather loafers and dark polyester pants with a crease down the front. Mr. Feng also wore polyester dress pants with a green cotton shirt. I wondered why Chinese men, even those coming straight from a factory, looked smarter than American men, for whom dressing like a slob was some sort of casual proof of their wealth.

Slowly, we got to the topic of their work. Beijing's historic old city was being systematically destroyed at an ever-increasing pace. Tens of thousands of people had lost their homes to government-owned development companies over the past few years, and many residents ended up living on the outskirts of town in poor housing. Quietly, mostly unaware of each other because the local media was barred from reporting their actions, thousands of these former home-owners like Messrs. Feng and Luo had taken the city to court, not so much to protect the historic old city as to demand compensation for their expropriated homes. At first I had been interested only in their lawsuits, seeing a parallel to Mr. Ma's suit in the countryside. Over time I began to see in the effort something different: a more sophisticated effort to mobilize public opinion and a slow recognition by Chinese of their vanishing cultural roots. But now I was just learning about the men's lawsuit, and they were still uncertain about me, fearful that I wasn't really clear about their goals.

Mr. Luo yielded the ritualistic part of the talk—the education of the barbarian—to Mr. Feng. Mr. Feng had a thick, friendly face but seemed slightly ill, his pallid skin made pastier by his jet-black hair, which he dyed. He pulled out a handkerchief and wiped his face in one giant mopping motion. Then I hunched forward dutifully and took notes while he spoke.

"During the 1990s, the city confiscated a hundred thirty-eight billion yuan [roughly $15 billion] in real estate," Mr. Feng said in a slow, careful way. "More than two hundred thousand people in the old city lost their homes. They got practically nothing in compensation."

"Who got the money?" he said, picking up the tempo. "The government did. How? The local governments cheated the residents."

The district governments, Mr. Feng said, established real estate companies that were given the confiscated land. The real estate companies provided the home-owners little compensation—only a token amount of money and substandard housing in remote suburbs of the city. Then the government real estate companies sold the land to developers, making a huge profit.

"Who benefited? Not the people," Mr. Feng said. "But the local government, which owned the real estate companies."

Mr. Feng was just winding up, but Mr. Luo leaned forward and cut him off, bringing us quickly to the point: "We filed the suit on behalf of twenty-three thousand other home-owners like ourselves. We claimed that the government had forgotten to compensate us. But the administrative hearing officers rejected our case, as did the intermediate courts."

Mr. Feng and Mr. Luo had been brought together by personal tragedy. Both men's homes had been confiscated in 1994, when China was going through an economic bubble and investment poured into real estate projects. Growth rates for the national economy were double-digit and new buildings went up daily. The boom was driven by easy money lent primarily by state banks. Everybody seemed to have the same idea: build concrete and glass high-rises in the center of town. For dozens of cities like Beijing, that meant getting rid of residents and leveling homes. In Beijing, many of the homes dated back six hundred years to the Ming dynasty.

Mr. Luo had lived his whole life in a fourteenth-century

home that his father had bought in 1943. It was just a few blocks away from our KFC and had been torn down in 1996 to build the city's "Financial Street," a real estate development that saw thousands of Ming-era homes razed. As compensation, he was given a substandard apartment in the western outskirts of town, an hour's bike ride from where we now sat.

Mr. Feng had lived near the Forbidden City and was evicted from his home of thirty years to make way for a ritzy shopping mall built by a Hong Kong developer. It was called Oriental Plaza, a giant mirror-and-concrete monolith that didn't have a trace of the Orient in it. The development had caused a furor when it went up because the government not only threw out home-owners like Mr. Feng, but also well-connected commercial interests. A corruption scandal later came to light that caused a vice-mayor of the city to commit suicide.

That didn't save Mr. Feng's 50-square-meter home. It wasn't ancient—it had been put up in the 1950s as housing for government officials—but he was cheated out of a small fortune by the government. His home was sold to the developer for $2,500 a square meter, or $125,000. His only compensation was a small apartment on the tenth floor of a housing silo with dank elevators and cracking cement walls that probably cost a tenth of the $125,000 to build. The local government pocketed the balance, in violation of laws that require fair compensation.

After their individual suits were rejected, they'd independently come to the same conclusion: strength in numbers. Their early suits, they figured, had failed because they had filed alone. Working together, they collected the signatures of 23,000 people and in 1998 filed a class-action lawsuit. It was a heroic effort that was not strictly illegal, but by many measures dangerous. The half-dozen principal leaders of the lawsuit had all been detained several times for questioning. Although the men were released each time after a few hours, they knew that they were treading on dangerous ground.

Mr. Feng was now surveying the group's finances. Each of the 23,000 participants in the suit had given the equivalent of between $2.50 and $6; the money was used to hire a lawyer. After they lost the initial suits, they used the money to print their materials and try to spread their tale to the local media and government officials, hoping this would pressure the courts to rule in their favor.

"It cost eight yuan [$1] to have a page typeset and then four mao [5 cents] to copy a standard sheet of paper, maybe two mao if you do it in bulk," Mr. Feng said, ticking off their expenses. "Then it cost seven yuan to mail out the packages, seventeen if we had to express-mail it.

"This is what we've produced. What do you think of it?" Mr. Feng said, putting an 8½-by-11-inch book on the table before me. I picked it up and thumbed through it, not bothering to read it very carefully. It seemed to be a collection of their lawsuits. Handy, but I didn't see the point.

"Was this book published?" I said, looking in vain for the *shuhao*, the number given out by the Press and Publication Bureau to every book published legally in China. Then I realized that this wasn't the smartest question. Of course it hadn't been published. It was samizdat, like the Soviet books printed underground to escape censors.

Mr. Feng squinted at me. He was dealing with an idiot. Mr. Feng collected his thoughts, trying to figure out how to simplify the story so that even a slow-witted foreigner would get it. His emotions swirled and then he erupted.

"Corruption—you're familiar with that word, eh? Corruption." If Chinese had an alphabet, he'd have spelled it out, he said it so slowly. *"Fu bai,"* he said again, drawing out the sylla-bles. *"Foo-buy."* I got it.

"This is *fu bai*," he said with a slow drawl and a quick sweep of his arm, covering not just the crooked real estate deals but the whole system of government, one that controlled what informa-tion was published, which lawsuits were heard and whose homes got demolished.

"If we could get an honest judge, we'd win the case. The constitution is on our side. We have land-use rights and should be compensated according to a fair price. But they don't accept the case."

It slowly dawned on me that he was indeed dealing with an idiot. Mr. Feng had been trying to tell me from the start that my question—"What's new with your case?"—had been stupid. There was nothing new for them to tell me about their case because there couldn't be anything new. With so much money at stake, the courts couldn't accept the lawsuit. But what he was say-ing was that something else was afoot. The lawsuit might not be going anywhere, but people were organizing. I looked at the book in my hands. The lawsuit might be going nowhere, but something more potent was stirring: public opinion.

"We've given the courts documents this thick," Mr. Feng said, spreading his middle finger as far apart from his thumb as possible. "They've taken away our right to sue. They've denied twenty-thousand people the right to sue."

Mr. Feng stopped for a second to catch his breath, his ashen forehead glistening with sweat.

Mr. Luo now weighed in, speaking with a deep, slightly slurred Beijing accent, a full, manly voice heavy with authority. It reminded me why he was the leader.

"We've filed this suit but to no avail," he said. "The local media can't report on it. We know many of the journalists. They want to help, but they cannot. What can you do to help us?"

Mr. Feng folded and refolded his handkerchief, but the anger boiling inside him forced him to do something. He busied himself wiping the table clean with an empty sugar sachet, sweeping the loose granules into a neat pile. Then he leapt back into the conversation.

"Who dared to say no when they tore down our house? You say no and it's fifteen days in jail just like that," Mr. Feng said. "Do you call that robbery?

"They beat you" he said, jabbing the table with the sugar sachet. "They arrest you. They jail you. Is that robbery?

"You resist and you're a nail sticking up out of a board," he said, hitting the table with the packet. "They smash you down. Is that robbery?

"You file a suit and they throw it out. You lose. They don't even answer you when you file. Is that robbery?"

He flicked the crumpled paper across the table.

"Not one written answer from the courts. Is that robbery? No, it's not just robbery. It's the Mafia."

He was speaking in short, beautiful sentences, in a cadence I'd never heard from any of China's stodgy leaders, with their wooden clichés and pinched voices. Then I looked around. A couple at the next table had long finished their meal and were staring at their plates. I wondered if they were fascinated by the outburst or repulsed that a foreigner was hearing about their country's problems. I looked back at my two hosts, and Mr. Luo picked up the thread in his steady voice.

"You write it. You write something of value. You seek truth from facts. You report this and you'll have lots of friends, ten thousand friends." Mr. Luo sat back, pleased with himself. A foreigner with 10,000 Chinese friends. That was a generous offer.

Mr. Feng, always eager for the rhetorical trump card, chimed in: "Yes, not just ten thousand friends. We only filed on behalf of twenty-three thousand homes, but two hundred eighty thousand households have lost their homes. They have on average four persons to a household. That's a million friends. You'll have a million friends."

I grinned awkwardly, trying to get their voices down. "That's a lot of friends," I said. "Great, thanks."

I thumbed through the book. I noticed a chop on some of the pages that read, literally, "Ten-Thousand-Person Mass Lawsuit."

"Is this your chop?" I said.

"It's not a chop," Mr. Feng said in an exasperated voice, making sure I understood, once again, that they were on the up and up. "Only the government has the right to issue a chop. A chop is for official use only. This is a stamp, made of rubber. Chops are round and usually made of stone. This is a square rubber stamp. It's just our insignia."

Then I began to flip through the book again, paying more attention. After a minute I looked up at Mr. Feng and shook my head in disbelief at its audacity. He smiled in satisfaction. I seemed to be getting it. The book was 108 pages long, handsomely printed with a color cover and photos throughout. The front was bright blue with a title in red characters: "A Compilation of Materials Concerning the Demolition of Beijing Residents' Housing Administrative Lawsuit in Accordance with and Under the Protection of the Law."

The compilers wanted the title to be as nonthreatening as possible. The "in Accordance with and Under the Protection of the Law" phrase was a reminder to the reader that what was being done here was legal.

The rest of the cover, however, dispensed with caution. In the upper-right-hand corner was a red box with black characters:

"Demolition of the Capital, No Law—No Heaven." Scattered randomly across the cover were tiny phrases, parenthetical ideas that the authors also thought worth getting on the cover but didn't want interfering with the bigger-type title. They read: "Corruption of Distribution and Leasing of Land"; "Should People's Rights Be Protected and How?"; "Should Power Be Controlled and How?"; "The Trans-Millennium Lawsuit of the Capital"; "The Expropriation of 23,000 People from Prime Real Estate" and "In Broad Daylight Plundering 138 Billion Yuan." Written at the bottom was the name of the publisher: The Demolition of Beijing Residents' Housing Administrative Lawsuit Group. I liked the use of "group." In Chinese it implied something economic, like a group of companies, but was also vague enough not to imply the legal registration needed for a corporation or association.

What was especially striking was the use of color photos. During the Tiananmen student uprising in 1989, copy machines were still tightly controlled by the government. They were seen as a dangerous weapon that people weren't allowed to use without permission. Now copy shops with modern color printers were on every other street block of Beijing, and the result was obvious by looking at this little booklet, with color snapshots on the inside and back covers. One showed Messrs. Feng and Luo and five other representatives of the 23,000 residents standing before the Beijing Municipal Second Intermediate Court, where the lawsuit had been heard. Another showed them presenting the case to an official, while another focused simply on the stack of 23,000 signatures. The inside back cover hinted at what prompted the lawsuit. One snapshot showed a bulldozer leveling an old brick home in September 1996. Another was of an old lady in the rubble of her home, leaning sadly on a tree that used to be in the center of her courtyard. The back cover was even more revealing: people's belongings strewn through the rubble, a sign that they hadn't left voluntarily. Another showed crowds confronting riot police who were protecting the workers as they went about destroying the homes.

Inside, the book laid out what the compilers said were the two huge scandals to have afflicted Beijing during the 1990s: the corrupt redevelopment of the old town and the corruption of the judiciary. The latter, the authors said, was especially destructive because "this is the largest judicial law incident in the People's Republic of China's history. The corruption of the judiciary legalizes the government's ignoring of the law, which exerts baneful social influence." In other words, if the government ignores the law, others will, too, and society will lose its moral order.

It was incendiary not only because of its contents, but because of the ordinary people who had produced it—people like Mr. Feng and Mr. Luo, not dissidents who'd spent years reading political tracts. As I read through further, I was amazed at the careful research that laid out government corruption on a grand scale.

"These ideas," I said. "The numbers, the analysis of the government's corruption, where did you get them?"

Mr. Luo sat back and smiled. "Fang Ke," he said. "Have you heard of him? He's one of the smartest men in China."

I hadn't but they quickly filled me in. Fang Ke was a young doctoral student at Beijing's elite Tsinghua University who had gathered material throughout the mid-to-late 1990s on Beijing's real estate market. What his meticulous research made clear was the depth of government corruption and its destruction of the old city, which he argued could easily have been avoided with some sensible urban planning.

"We thought the demolition mostly affected us," Mr. Feng

said. "Fang Ke's studies showed how the problem was bigger. Our heritage is at stake."

As I later noticed when reading through Mr. Feng's and Mr. Luo's book, Fang Ke's ideas had provided the intellectual underpinning for their suit. The precise analysis of the real estate companies' transactions, the sale price of land and the resale to other government-owned entities—all this was the work of painstaking research.

Mr. Luo motioned to get up. Mr. Feng gathered the material and stuffed it into his black briefcase. The audience was over.

We walked downstairs and out into the warm night. Across the street was a twenty-story Bank of China building, a blackglass structure built on the site of several dozen fifteenth-century homes. The street was lined with thick, knotty scholar trees, but they couldn't prevent the bank from overwhelming everything else, ruining what had once been a neighborhood of one- and two-story buildings. The rest of the street was lined with stores selling hardware and stands hawking pirated videos. As far as one could see were restaurants, mostly one-room joints with tiny stools, peeling walls and a bucket of greasy, soapy water out front to wash the dishes.

"I lived just behind there," Mr. Luo said, pointing to one restaurant.

"Poor Luo," Mr. Feng said. "He had a beautiful courtyard home."

"Isn't this an odd place to meet?" I said to Messrs. Feng and Luo, pointing to the Kentucky Fried Chicken where we'd just spent a couple of hours.

"You don't like fried chicken?" asked Mr. Feng.

"No, I mean it's a symbol of westernization and the destruction of the old city. Wasn't it a funny choice?"

Mr. Feng looked at me quizzically.

"KFC didn't tear down a building to build this restaurant," Mr. Feng said. "Plus, it's safe. No one is a regular there and the attendants are all students." He stepped closer to me to make sure I heard him clearly: "Those people who overheard us, we don't know them. We'll never meet them again. It's safe. I like KFC."

We shook hands and they left. I hopped into a taxi. I lived in a new part of the city on the other side of the densely populated old town. The driver was about to take a ring road built on the site of the old city wall that once encircled the old town. But just as we set off, I remembered that a couple of years ago Beijing's urban planners had blasted a six-lane highway through the old city, another in an endless string of egregious wrongs done to the old town. It was called Peace Boulevard. I suggested to the driver that we try that road. The driver was dubious, but I argued and he gave in.

We ended up flying through the old city, speeding over leveled palaces and six-hundred-year-old homes. If we'd taken the ring road, the trip would have taken forty-five minutes, but we pulled up in front of my apartment block in twenty minutes. Even though it was shorter and meant less money, the driver was ecstatic.

"This is when you're happy to pay taxes," the driver said as I got out. "I'd even pay a toll to ride on a road like that."

Up until the 1950s, Beijing was an architectural wonder, an almost perfectly preserved metropolis from the preindustrial era. Many ancient towns and cities exist around the world, but Beijing was enormous: 62.5 square kilometers (25 square miles) large including lakes, parks, palaces and of course the Forbidden City, the emperor's home. Surrounded by some of the greatest fortified walls of antiquity, it was a microcosm of ancient China, a city that symbolized the political and religious ideals of a system that had existed for twenty-five hundred years.

Beijing was not a historic center of Chinese culture; for centuries it had been a backwater compared to other ancient Chinese capitals, such as Xi'an, Luoyang, Nanjing or Hangzhou. It was primarily the capital of kingdoms of northern nomads, such as the Khitan, the Jürchen and of course the Mongolians, whose dynasty lasted from 1279 to 1368. But in 1403, the Ming dynasty's Yongle emperor usurped the throne and decided to relocate the seat of government from Nanjing to Beijing, where his power base was located. Suddenly, Beijing was home to the emperor, making it the center of the Chinese world.

Becoming the capital meant more than building palaces and other symbols of political power. It meant turning this unremarkable site into holy ground. Unlike many other great cities of antiquity, Beijing was not built near the ocean or a major river. Abutting the Mongolian foothills on the north end of the North China Plain, it was flat and almost featureless.

This made it easy to superimpose China's cosmological system over the new city. Legend has it that Beijing's spiritual underpinnings were drawn up by a geomancer, who handed the Yongle emperor plans for his new capital. The layout of streets and boulevards followed the typical Chinese love of symmetry and clear, square designs. But it was also seen as a spiritual whole, too. Over the city's landmarks was traced the body of Nazha, a young god credited with taming the waters of the Beijing plain. Like an astrological figure drawn over the stars, Nazha's eight-armed body was made the basis of Beijing's layout. His head lies in the south of the city and his feet in the north—south being the most auspicious direction and most Chinese maps pointing south, not north. His head was represented by the Zhengyang Gate, two wells inside that gate were his eyes, the Gate of Heavenly Peace (Tiananmen) was his brain, the pathway to the Forbidden City his gullet. His right hand was the Chaoyang Gate, and in that hand rested the East Peak Temple. Each body part, each organ had its counterpart in the city.

Over time, the city became dotted with other links to heaven—temples. In 1911, the year the emperor abdicated, the city had well over one thousand temples—Buddhist, Taoist, Confucian—and a handful of mosques, excluding innumerable tiny shrines that weren't included in official counts. Almost every street had its temple. The guts of the city were its alleys, or *hutong*s. This is a Chinese word that some historians believe stems from an ancient Mongolian word for "well," since water was crucial to such an arid part of the country. Rainfall isn't just sparse: the city abuts the foothills to the Mongolian Plateau, making it susceptible to dry, withering windstorms. Many *hutong* names have the word "well" in it, but others are purely descriptive: "Wei Family Hutong," "Master Wu Liang Hutong," "Vegetable Market Intersection Hutong," "Great Tea Leaf Hutong" and "Green Bamboo Hutong." They are intensely local names, helping to reinforce the identity of those who live in there.

The *hutong*s were also the city's capillaries, carrying traffic the final few hundred meters from the city's major arteries to its final destination. Because few *hutong*s were through streets, most were quiet, almost traffic-free pedestrian zones where people could sit out front of their homes and talk and watch their children play. They were not like European streets, lined with trees and leading to large public spaces. Instead, they were lined with walls—most traditional homes in China are surrounded by walls—and the trees planted inside those walls grew out over the streets, making the city look from the air like a giant park.

Such a cityscape, though, could have its darker side. In the early 1980s, the writer Bei Dao wrote a Kafkaesque short story,

"13 Happiness Street," about a boy whose kite flies over one of these walls. When he climbs the wall to retrieve the kite, he disappears, as does a family member who goes to search for him. The story was claustrophobic and paranoid, but it was easy to see how streets made of walls could breed such feelings.

Encasing the city was the biggest of all walls: the city's fortifications. Up to 62 feet thick at the base and 34 feet thick at the top, the wall dominated Beijing in every respect. Invading nomads faced 50-foot buttresses with crenellated parapets, while local residents knew that they only came and went through the wall's gates with the permission of authorities. Chinese wrote poems about the wall—and the refreshing view when going outside it—while foreigners wrote obsessively about its size, measuring and mapping it in excruciating detail. The city wall gave Beijing its square shape and continues to do so today. Now a series of concentric ring roads enclose the city, each one roughly following the wall's course in wider and wider circumambulations around the old city.

When the imperial system collapsed in 1911, the city slowly rotted. Over the next thirty years, it was ruled by a warlord, a president and a foreign invader. Amazingly, though, Beijing stayed intact. What it couldn't resist, however, was the self-loathing and lack of confidence that had been afflicting China.

For about a hundred years, from the mid-nineteenth to the mid-twentieth century, China was under attack from abroad. Western countries forced it to import opium and agree to a series of humiliating treaties that carved up the country, giving colonies and special legal rights to foreigners. Efforts at gradual reforms were undercut by foreign powers, which continued to carve up China, culminating in Japan's invasion in 1937. As often happens in crises, moderation was supplanted by radicalism. A crisis of confidence swept China, and people began to doubt that the country's traditional culture had anything of value left. After a four-year civil war, the communists came to power in 1949, advocating an almost complete break with the past.

That applied to urban planning—especially to the country's capital. Like the Yongle emperor, China's new rulers had their own geomantic system, but this one saw progress in the form of oversized squares and boulevards, with smokestacks dotting the horizon. It was a communist vision of urban planning, a particularly radical view of traditional European cities. Reproduced from Ulan Bator to East Berlin, it called for most ancient buildings to be torn down, not in spite of their age but because of it. Temples were closed en masse, with many converted to offices or factories. Today, despite some impressive efforts at restoration, the city of roughly 12 million has just twenty functioning temples.

The most dramatic blow was struck against the city's pride, its walls. China was in the grip of the totalitarian Mao era, but, amazingly, people fought in defense of the city wall. Architects, intellectuals and ordinary people protested, writing petitions and letters to local newspapers. Plans were put forward to reconcile historic preservation with the need to modernize, for example, by preserving the historic core and locating a new government center nearby. But the new government would hear nothing of it. The wall had to go. It took years to destroy the wall, but by the early 1960s it had vanished—almost.

Besides a few gates that were preserved in the center of traffic circles, the wall lived on in street names. It had been punctured by sixteen gates, and from them ran main streets from one end of town to the other, giving the city a gridlike street pattern. Those streets still exist and are still named after the gates that they ran through, with the suffix *nei* (inside) and *wai* (outside) reminding the traveler whether he is outside or inside the old gate. Nowadays, for example, one still travels along "Inside the Noble and Refined Gate Street" (Chongwenmennei Dajie), and, when one has passed this gate, which no longer exists, one drives on "Outside the Noble and Refined Gate Street" (Chongwenmenwai Dajie). The street where I met Messrs. Feng and Luo in the KFC was Fuchengmennei, or "Inside the Gate of Abundance." A few steps away would have been the gate, and through it the street still changes to "Outside the Gate of Abundance," as if the gate still stood. It was an interesting way to experience Beijing, traveling along streets that announced gates and walls that no longer existed, a virtual walled city that existed only on street signs.

But except for the loss of the wall in the 1960s, the essence of the old city remained—the hundreds of *hutong*s that weave between the lakes and parks, lined with courtyard homes and the occasional palace. Those probably would have been destroyed next, except that China again slipped into chaos. But instead of fighting foreign invaders, it was now consumed with itself, leaping from one failed version of communism to the next. For much of that time, the city continued to deteriorate, with the courtyard homes that lined the *hutong*s turning into noble slums. But all in all Beijing remained intact, its lost walls a reminder of what could come next.

Lawyer Wu got excited when I pulled Fang Ke's book out of my bag.

"Ah, Fang Ke's book!" he said. "Of course, I know it. I know him well. What a treasure that book is."

Two cell phone calls later and Lawyer Wu had arranged for us to go visit Fang Ke, who was living on the other side of town. We hopped in a car and drove over.

Wu Jianzhong was one of the few lawyers who seemed to

have any chance of successfully suing the city for expropriating residents' property. He was forty years old, quick-witted and eager to try out any new legal technique that came along. At one point he favored U.S.-style civil suits calling for high-priced settlements. When Chinese courts inevitably rejected such cases, he dabbled in real estate law, representing clients hoping to redevelop the city. Now he was on the other side, supporting an administrative lawsuit against government-owned real estate developers. With large glasses, a round face and neatly combed hair, he dreamed of international fame.

He represented an old man named Zhao Jingxin whose house was due to be torn down. Unlike the lawsuit by Messrs. Luo and Feng, whose case hadn't even been accepted by the court, Lawyer Wu had got his case registered by the court and even had had a hearing. After learning of his success, I had decided to meet him and brought with me a copy of Fang Ke's book, which I'd tracked down after hearing about it through Messrs. Luo and Feng.

I wasn't surprised that Lawyer Wu had heard of Fang Ke and his book. After meeting with Luo and Feng, I had begun to look into the destruction of old Beijing. I soon found that everyone had heard of or met Fang Ke and had read his book. In fact, his book was so popular that its press run of 2,500 had rapidly sold out and I'd had to photocopy a friend's copy.

As we headed to see Fang Ke, we sped past buildings that the August smog and heat turned into a concrete blur. Lawyer Wu began to explain the legal steps he had taken on behalf of his client, Mr. Zhao, whom his friends respectfully called Lao Zhao, which could roughly be translated as Old Mr. Zhao.

"The new constitution was written in 1982. That means the constitution was adopted after the [capitalist-style economic] reforms started in 1978," Lawyer Wu said. "But the new constitution isn't less socialist than the old one. Actually, it's more socialist because it says that all urban land is owned by the government. But it does say that use of the land is private, so people do have land-use rights," Mr. Wu said, counting his legal points off on the fingers of his hand.

"Then what about the suit filed by Luo and Feng?" I asked. "Why hasn't their case been heard?"

"Easy," he said. "Their case was too big. They were suing the entire Beijing city government and had, how many, ten or twenty thousand signatures? The courts had a hard time accepting this. It's too broad. It calls into question too much."

"But when they sued individually, they lost, too," I said.

"Yes, but my impression is they weren't specific enough. Basically, they're challenging the government's right to do with the land as it wants. We aren't doing that with Old Mr. Zhao's case. We're attacking their decision on two very narrow and very specific fronts. First, that they didn't adequately compensate him for his land-use rights. His rights are absolutely clear because his father bought the house in 1948 and they have the bill of sale. So we're suing the Property Management Office for inadequate compensation. Second, we're arguing that his home is a protected cultural property and that the local Cultural Affairs Office failed to designate it as such. If it's designated, then it can't be torn down. So you see we have two very specific arguments that allege that the government didn't do its job properly. But we aren't challenging the government's right to expropriate land. The courts wouldn't hear that."

Despite Lawyer Wu's finesse, the suit was still hung up in courts. The initial hearing in a low-level court had gone the government's way, with the judge ruling simply that the government had the right to set compensation as it saw fit and to designate cultural property as it wanted. It could even violate its own guidelines, the court said, since it set the guidelines. Lawyer Wu had quickly filed an appeal, which hadn't been heard yet.

"Look out the window," Lawyer Wu said. "The destruction is only going to pick up if we win the bid to hold the 2008 Olympics. They're just going to blindly tear down the old city and build new roads and new buildings. Somebody has to put a stop to it. Hundreds of years of culture, being torn down in a decade."

Later on, when Beijing's ultimately successful bid for the games was in full swing, I thought back to that talk. The city had hung banners around town extolling itself. In Chinese and English the banners read: "New Beijing, New Olympics." Then someone in the Olympic bid committee realized how odd that might seem to foreigners. Why a new Olympics? What was wrong with the old one? And why do we want a new Beijing? Wasn't the point of China's bid that it was offering its beautiful old capital as the site for the games? Later the English version of the banners were changed to "New Beijing, Great Olympics." The Olympics might not need renewing, but Beijing apparently did.

"This being the capital, however, perhaps they don't have to pay compensation?" I said.

"That's exactly what the government here argues. But there's a new federal law from January 1, 1999, stating explicitly that all expropriated land must be compensated. There's no exemption for the capital. So now they argue that they've never paid compensation so they don't know how to implement the new law. Imagine how ridiculous that is. The capital government doesn't understand the government's laws so says it should ignore the law. Of course, we didn't say that. We said, fine, then you can't tear down Old Mr. Zhao's house until you figure it out. They say, no, they want to tear down first."

We soon pulled up to the grandly named Movie and Television Mansion, which was actually a rather plain five-story building made of concrete and covered in white tiles. It was the summer break from university and Fang Ke was living in a friend's empty dorm room at a small college nearby. We met in the mansion's cafeteria and sat down in a booth.

Fang Ke looked more like a computer freak than an agent provocateur. He was lanky, with a mop of hair and big glasses. I could imagine him in a suit, but he looked more at home in what he was wearing: an MIT T-shirt, baggy shorts and fat, synthetic rubber sandals that had become an unfortunate global fashion trend. He was vigorous and in shape—twenty-eight years old but gave the appearance of an undergraduate. Talking with him was a joy. He had a winning smile and practical, pragmatic answers to any question. He was someone who'd thought hard about the subject and didn't hold back.

Fang Ke and Lawyer Wu sat down and chatted like old friends. I had figured that Lawyer Wu had become active in the cause of saving old Beijing only because he'd been hired by Old Mr. Zhao to save his house—the latest legal experiment that the curious attorney had undertaken. But as I got to know him better, I saw that although that might have been the case to start with, the case had opened his eyes, turning him into a committed defender of the old town. He and the young doctoral student shared the same friends. They also shared a schoolboy sense of humor.

"I heard you had a hard time getting my book," Fang Ke said, pushing two copies across to me. "Take these and give one to a friend."

Lawyer Wu nodded, smirking at the thought of someone

getting Fang Ke's book as a present. "It's not easy reading," he said with a giggle. "Now you've got two."

Fang Ke laughed and continued. "But I'm actually happy that people are interested in this book. It took a while to write and research."

Seven years, in fact, since he'd first started looking into the old city. His teacher at Tsinghua University, Wu Liangyong, had asked him to do a research project on an alley in the old town called Chrysanthemum Hutong (Ju'er Hutong). His interest had slowly grown until he took on the entire old city's redevelopment as his doctoral thesis. He began to look at things a little harder than most people and found some strange contradictions in government policy.

"The first thing I noticed is that all the top leaders live in the traditional *siheyuan* [courtyard] homes. They don't want to live in high-rises, but they try to convince people that the courtyard homes are terrible and old-fashioned. That struck me as odd," he said. "I began to wonder why they were so eager to tear down the old city."

The turning point for old Beijing, Fang Ke said, was in April 1990, when the city announced a new law allowing "dangerous and dilapidated" buildings to be torn down. In October of that year it also promulgated a vague rule to protect twenty-five areas of the old city. When property prices starting rising astronomically a couple of years later, the protected zones were ignored and the city began designating huge swaths of the old town as dangerous and in need of development. They included, for example, Niu Jie, or Ox Street, the center of Muslim life in Beijing. Almost the entire street was leveled, including one of the few ancient mosques in China that was used only by women. The area around the Summer Palace was also meant to be conserved, but developers won exemptions to build high-rises that now mar the view of the sky from the park. Throughout the 1990s, the city lost more famous buildings than in any of the decades past.

It was a process being repeated across China, with historic sections of cities such as Kunming and Shanghai gutted in favor of slapdash concrete commercial districts. Only in a couple of cities where tourism played a key role, such as Xi'an, could historic preservationists win their arguments.

"They reminded me of Napoleon III of France," Fang Ke said as he sipped a Coke. "He wanted to tear down the old city of Paris and build a new one. He didn't really succeed, but at least he had good architects working for him so that what he built was beautiful. Do you see anything built recently that's beautiful or lasting? It's all ugly."

Lawyer Wu and Fang Ke laughed and then sighed. "Their idea of keeping Chinese characteristics is to put a little pavilion on top of a skyscraper," Lawyer Wu said. "And that's all that's left of Chinese architecture."

"People say it was a death by a thousand cuts in the previous years," Mr. Fang said with a halfhearted grin. "But what has now happened its more like a big blow to the head.

"All I argue is that we should turn the 62.5 square kilometers of the old city into a protected area and then decide what needs to be developed inside it. The urban center of the city has 1,050 square kilometers, so I'm not saying the city should be turned into a museum. Right now the city has a protection plan, but it's only for 5.6 square kilometers, most of which is simply the Forbidden City and Beihai Park.

"Beijing's value is as a whole. Its urban design is unique. Just saving a few streets or buildings doesn't save old Beijing. In 1949 it was complete. The Japanese handed it over peacefully in 1945 and so did the Nationalists in 1949. It was like Jerusalem, a complete medieval city."

I'd heard the comparison before. At first it seemed odd, but the more I thought about it, the more perfect the comparison seemed. Like Jerusalem, Beijing had been a holy city, the center of the Chinese religious world. The two also shared challenges for modern-day urban planners, with the Middle Eastern city showing how an ancient city could be modernized without sacrificing its essence. Proponents of gutting old Beijing liked to argue that its narrow lanes and alleys made it impossible to install telecommunications cables and sewage and water pipes. While conceding difficulties, people like Fang Ke argued that Jerusalem showed that by and large the demands of the modern world could be reconciled with ancient structures. Pipes and electric cables could be laid without destroying everything. The population density had to stay low but there was no need for it to be a medieval slum. On the contrary, living in the old city would become chic, much as it is in scores of western cities.

"None of their arguments make any sense. The city did a survey in 1950 and found that five percent of the buildings were dangerous or dilapidated. Then in 1990 they found that fifty percent were. Of course, nothing had been done to the buildings for forty years, so they became dilapidated. But if they'd give the property rights back to the residents, they'd look after them and fix them up. Instead, the solution is to level everything."

Lawyer Wu had sat silently during his young friend's exposition of his ideas. Occasionally, he gave a theatrical sigh or shook his head sadly.

"There you have it," he said after we had been sitting quietly for a few minutes, absorbing the rush of ideas. "The only thing you haven't mentioned is how much money the officials can make off all this."

Fang Ke looked up cautiously.

"I can't prove individual corruption, but I can show how

much ordinary residents got as compensation and how much the city-owned real estate companies sold the land to the developers. The difference was billions and little of it ended up in the city's treasury. I've calculated it by going through the projects one by one and tallying the numbers. To me there's no doubt that officials were motivated by greed. First, they don't really believe in protection. Second, it's in their financial interest to tear down the city."

We finished our meal and got up. Fang Ke said he had something important to show me, and we agreed to meet in a few days.

At first glance, Fang Ke's book seemed sure to lull even a sharp-eyed censor to sleep. It was published by the China Architecture & Building Press, a publisher hardly associated with radical tracts or investigations of corruption. Its design was smart and modern but nonthreatening. The cover was colored dull turquoise with a sketch map of greater Beijing at the bottom. Above it was the title *Contemporary Redevelopment in the Inner City of Beijing*, with the yawner of a subtitle in lowercase letters "survey, analysis and investigation." Its ultimate protective talisman was stripped in small letters across the top of the cover: "Edited by the Academician Wu Liangyong: Science of Environmental Habitat Series."

The involvement of Mr. Wu, Fang Ke's teacher and adviser, was crucial. Although he sometimes took up popular causes, such as the historic preservation of an old town in a remote province, he was a prudent man. His caution had been rewarded with a post on the Chinese People's Political Consultative Conference, a powerless assembly of prominent academics, artists and non-Chinese ethnic groups, such as Tibetans and Uighurs, whose role was to make it seem like the Communist Party consulted with a broad range of people. A book published under the auspices of such a man, a censor would reckon, couldn't be that radical.

Despite all this, it was probably only a measure of how many books are published and how cursory censors have become that the book wasn't banned. Its cover might have been cautious, but the book burst with bold ideas and criticisms. One striking point was that it was loaded with pictures. Poorly reproduced black-and-white pictures, perhaps, but photos that couldn't help but grab one's attention. On page 85, for example, was a photo of a deputy in the national parliament who was questioning the government about the tearing down of old Beijing. Below it, in the text, was the statement that the amount of money the deputy believed that developers had misappropriated was in excess of 10 billion yuan, or $1.25 billion—a staggering amount in any country but especially in a developing one where prices are low. To put it in context, during the 1990s, developers had ripped the city off the equivalent of an entire year's worth of economic output, as if every man, woman and child, all 11 million Beijingers, had simply given away everything they produced in one year.

Complementing the pictures were descriptions of the lost buildings, such as the home of China's greatest novelist, Cao Xueqin, who had written the classic novel of manners, *Dream of the Red Chamber*. His home was to be leveled to make way for a wider road. Others were left to rot, such as the homes of two of China's great reformers, Liang Qichao and Kang Youwei. One could imagine that soon they, too, would be leveled as "dilapidated and dangerous" buildings.

The last third of the book was taken up with surveying other Chinese and foreign cities that also had historic centers and discussing how their efforts at preservation could be applied to Beijing. One soon realized that this was something unprecedented and desperately needed, a careful, factual study of how to stop the destruction of one of the greatest architectural treasures of the world.

As I read along, what gave me the most pleasure were the facts and figures. Usually, books filled with such ballast aren't fun reads. But for years I'd worked in a country where the adjective *chabuduo*—"more or less"—seemed to preface every number, every fact, every figure. One began to realize how one takes for granted straight, factual answers to questions. In China, by contrast, round numbers were so common they were ridiculous. I'd been to innumerable factories or government offices where I'd hear answers like "We have a thousand workers and our output last year was a million yuan." Exactly a million? "Yeah, well, *chabuduo*," followed by the inevitable suspicious glance at me. Why did I want to know that? Nobody knew that number, except the people who needed to.

Here, though, was a book filled with tables and figures, facts culled from documents and endless interviews with developers. Numbers showing the square-meter purchase and sale price of land in different parts of the city—all revealing the fat profits that developers earned by dispossessing people of their homes and tearing down the old city. As a young Ph.D. student, Mr. Fang had had an easier time obtaining the numbers. He wasn't treated with the arm's-length caution given to local journalists or statisticians. Forget about a foreign journalist; few of the developers he surveyed would have given a foreign journalist an interview. What for? They would never list on overseas stock markets and rarely do business with foreign companies. They were engaged in almost inevitably corrupt deals that involved twisting zoning rules, tearing down old buildings and slapping up new "luxury" development. They wanted zero publicity, especially from the outside world.

As a student, however, Mr. Fang could ask questions and use

letters of introduction from teachers to obtain interviews. And as a trained architect, he could work with the raw figures he saw on the construction plans to calculate density and height. Later, he could compare that with the zoning requirements that are not easily obtained by the public but which his connections through classmates and teachers made possible.

For example, he investigated the construction of Financial Street, a real estate development that wiped out 4,000 homes, hundreds from the fourteenth and fifteenth centuries, including the home of Mr. Luo of the Ten-Thousand-Person Mass Lawsuit. He found out, for example, that the buildings exceeded the 70-meter height restrictions by up to 46 meters.

That was a number I'd struggled to get. In 1997, I'd interviewed an official from the government-owned company that was building the street. The two useful facts I got out of the interview were the figure of 4,000 homes being leveled and that 12,000 people had lived there. When I asked about heights or zoning, I got the same blank stare and the platitude that it "was being done in accordance with relevant city regulation. Those were dangerous and dilapidated homes."

Fang Ke's book showed how the city was abusing this argument that much of old Beijing was dangerous. In 1991, he noted, the city claimed that 3.4 million square meters of land was occupied by dangerous housing. During the next eight years, however, it tore down 3.6 million square meters of "dangerous" housing—and still its appetite was insatiable. A new eight-lane boulevard was being built south of the Forbidden City to complement Peace Boulevard to the north. Tens of thousands of residents were being expelled to substandard housing in the suburbs. They, of course, were living in newly discovered "dangerous and dilapidated" housing.

What thrilled many Beijingers about Fang Ke's book was

that he laid out all the lawsuits opposing the redevelopment. He reckoned that between 1995 and 1999, 13,000 residents had filed fourteen class-action lawsuits against the city, in addition to the suit filed by 23,000 that I had heard about from Messrs. Feng and Luo. The suits were listed in a table, and on the facing page was a photo of a man protesting the fact that he'd lost his home to developers.

He also explained the problems that resettled people faced: commutes to work of three or four hours each way in crowded buses; the elderly who had to take buses for hours on end to find a hospital; unhygienic conditions in the new slums and the increase in people living in "temporary housing"—shanties for those who lost their old homes but didn't get new ones. There were 4,900 in 1991; by 1998 the number had increased to 32,000. It was a modest number compared to Beijing's total population of over 10 million, but it showed that despite redevelopment made ostensibly in the name of improving living conditions, they were actually getting worse.

Mr. Fang didn't advocate a political agenda. The logical conclusion, of course, was that a system in which the government is judge and jury, buyer and seller, can't be fair. He never made that argument or drew that conclusion. But his book was still a challenge to the system. He wasn't simply arguing that good rules had been improperly applied or circumvented by a few greedy people. Instead, he was showing that the rules themselves were bad, which he argues are designed to allow the entire old town to be torn down. For example, the city classifies buildings according to their quality from first (best) to fifth (worst) class. According to the regulations, if 70 percent of a district is made up of third-, fourth- and fifth-class buildings, it can be torn down in its entirety. As Mr. Fang points out, these rules mean that almost any district in the city can be redeveloped. What few monuments are saved will be isolated fragments shorn of the alleys and ordinary courtyard homes that once gave them context.

To some degree what Fang Ke described was universal. Developers around the world try to bypass local governments' urban plans. They ask for exemptions and waivers of zoning rules, always in the name of jobs and progress. In Western countries, historic buildings are under threat, too, but the more common pressure is outward, with agricultural land on the fringes of cities being rezoned for low-density housing that sprawls on endlessly.

In China, urban sprawl is increasing as well—as one can see on the outskirts of any major Chinese city. But suburban life hasn't caught on in China. The wealthiest people, by and large, do not live outside of the city. That's because the high population density makes it impossible to build adequate highways that could make a commute bearable. Rather than commute for hours, the wealthy prefer to live near where they work and shop—as Fang Ke noted early on in his research how senior leaders all like to live in the old town because of its convenience. Thus the pressure to rezone and redevelop is in the center of town, exactly where China's old towns are located. Without any checks or balances to protect the old districts, their fates are sealed.

Another difference from other countries is the intimate relationship between business and government, which is so close that the two are almost synonymous. As Fang Ke bluntly put it early on in his book: "Planning offices cannot say 'no' to the developers. City and district government officials are the senior managers of the developers and the planning offices. When these governments face the problem of choosing between the 'overall interest of the whole city,' represented by the planning offices, and the 'economic interest of the city,' represented by the developing companies, they often choose the latter one. The planning offices are ultimately always asked to compromise."

Fang Ke's research had got to the core of China's economic and political dilemma: the government's desire to control too much of not only the political field but the economic arena as well. In a country where the government ran large chunks of the economy and was its regulator, corruption and mismanagement were inevitable.

A generation ago, China had a planned economy. In a planned economy, developers didn't exist; instead, the Ministry of Construction simply had "units" that went out and built a building, road or whatever, according to the government's need. Reforms have transformed these "units" into incorporated companies. Although owned by the government, they're charged with making a profit, something that wasn't much of a consideration before. Profits mean that the main shareholder, the state, earns money. If a developer can argue that a project will be profitable, his owners (the state) will make sure that other state offices don't hinder the company's plans.

For example, Fang Ke showed how developers bully the cultural relics bureaus and city planners into giving permission. When the city planners are asked to assess the percentage of dangerous buildings in a district, they only do so after the developers have applied for permits. Since cultural and planning authorities are weak, they're under pressure to come up with as high a percentage of dangerous buildings as possible, making it easy to level the neighborhood, sometimes even with government subsidies. "The so-called examination is just a formality. Once the area is chosen by developers, regardless of its buildings' quality, it can still be listed in the dangerous-building list. The tag 'rebuilding dangerous buildings' just provides an excuse for the developers to have more preferential policies and to cover their desire for profits."

Another feature spurring destruction is the money pumped into projects by outside investors, mostly from Hong Kong. In the 1980s, only 200 million yuan was invested in rebuilding the old city. From 1990 to 1997, the figure jumped to 17 billion yuan. Hong Kong's richest man, Li Ka-shing, for example, poured billions into the Oriental Plaza, which had cost Mr. Feng his home. In all, outsiders poured in 11.6 billion of the 17 billion total. According to Mr. Fang's figures, the returns on many projects are astronomical as well—on average about 60 percent.

What hurt the most in reading the book was the thoughtlessness of the destruction. It was captured perfectly in an article that a newspaper in a distant city had published on the destruction of a famous bridge in Beijing called Rufuli. Beijing newspapers were strictly forbidden from carrying such news, but the journalists for the *Yangcheng Evening News* in faraway Guangzhou had managed to record the poignant scene as a team of migrant laborers from the countryside wrecked the bridge.

Under those farmers' hands, the bridge turned to rubbish.

"What should we do about the bricks, tiles and wood?"

"Sell them."

"The bricks can fetch a lot."

"No, they can't. They are too old, nobody wants them. Even fewer will want the wood. The tiles can only be sold for four to five fen [half a penny] each."

"I've worked in Beijing for eight years. I've pulled down many such houses. Two or three months ago, I pulled down a temple near the Directorate of the Imperial Academy. That was a big one. But it doesn't matter. As long as the demolition office gives me money, I can pull down anything, even the Imperial Palace."

A few years earlier I'd come across another book on Chinese architecture. But unlike with Fang Ke's book, I didn't realize the value of Liang Sicheng's *Pictorial History of Chinese Architecture* until it had sat on my bookshelf for a few years. At first I was attracted by Mr. Liang's drawings. He had been a gifted drafts-man and the book was punctuated with skillful cutaway sketches of temples, mausoleums and pagodas.

What I hadn't realized is that Mr. Liang had been the first to systematically study Chinese architecture. People knew China had a long history, but most knowledge came from ancient books, which were often based on hearsay and the biased views of one dynasty writing the preceding dynasty's history. Basing history on empirical study was something western civilization had developed as an offshoot of the scientific revolution. Almost no one had applied these new methods to China's architectural heritage.

The idea to do so stemmed indirectly from Mr. Liang's father, the great reformer Liang Qichao, the pending destruction of whose home Fang Ke had noted with distress in his book. The elder Liang had been a loyalist of the imperial system, trying fruitlessly to preserve some of Chinese culture and tradition as the country careened toward revolution.

Mr. Liang's father had been schooled in the millennia-old Confucian system of rote learning. But he soon realized that part of the West's immense advantage over China was its educational system and scientific method. This was how it had developed such sophisticated weapons that allowed a handful of ships and a few thousand soldiers to seize vast amounts of Chinese territory. It wasn't so much the West's hardware that accounted for such victories, the elder Liang realized, as the software that had developed the material advantage. Most reformers at the time held the opposite view, saying China only needed to buy some up-to-date hardware to catch up to the West. But the elder Mr. Liang was adamant that education was paramount and applied his theories at home. His son was well grounded in China's classic literature, but he was ultimately sent abroad for a modern education.

In 1924 the younger Mr. Liang left for Philadelphia, where he attended the architecture school of the University of Pennsylvania. It was a choice made by his fiancée, Lin Whei-yin, a gifted writer whose marriage to Mr. Liang had been arranged by their parents when they were young. It had been a good match, and they had fallen in love with each other and decided to go abroad together to study. Both were brilliant students and in 1928 returned to China with degrees in hand from the U.S. university.

At the time, no one saw any need to study Chinese architecture. Mr. Liang's father thought it was a waste of time, casually noting that most old buildings were falling down anyway from neglect and the turmoil that had engulfed China since the Opium Wars of the mid-nineteenth century. Instead, he encouraged his son to turn his attention to Chinese painting and encouraged him to write a modern history of Chinese art. Mr. Liang, however, was determined to study China's architectural past and use modern field-research techniques. In traditional China, Confucian scholars worked mostly out of their study, poring over books and writing. No one got dirty by doing fieldwork. He decided to be the first to use the scientific method to catalogue and date the vast trove of buildings that China's thousands of years of history had left scattered across the land.

Mr. Liang made numerous field trips in northern China in

the late 1920s and 1930s. He found examples of architecture dating back one thousand years and identified the different styles, putting them in historical order—all of which were firsts for the history of Chinese architecture. But in 1937, as he was preparing to write a book detailing his work, war broke out with Japan.

The war brought to an end a small renaissance in intellectual and civilian life. Mr. Liang had been part of an educated elite that flourished during the Republic of China, which was founded in 1911 as the last imperial dynasty was being overthrown. (The last emperor abdicated in early 1912.) The new government's capital was Nanjing, a large city near Shanghai, and the dominant political force was the Nationalist Party.

It has been historical orthodoxy for decades to criticize the Nationalists' short time in power on the mainland. They were corrupt and not very successful in resisting Japanese aggression. Some of their leaders frequented Shanghai opium dens and consorted with organized criminals. Famines were common, and most of the country remained hopelessly backward, untouched by modern conveniences like running water and electricity. The communists have been successful in painting them as one of the worst governments China has had, a simplistic view that has taken root in the West.

Yet there were seeds of a modern China sown around that time that look progressive even today—and especially in contrast with the famines, corruption and purges that accompanied communist rule. Large, successful businesses were established and the makings of a modern economy were laid. Organizations independent of government control flourished—as they largely do not today—and academics like Mr. Liang made groundbreaking advances in understanding their own country and the world around them. Literature hit a high point with novelists like Lu

Xun and Shen Congwen (both would have been shoo-ins for the Nobel Prize had it not been so ethnocentrically western back then), while, like Mr. Liang, thousands of young people went abroad to study.

During World War II, the Nationalists fled to Chongqing (better known as Chungking), and it was to this area that Mr. Liang journeyed along with thousands of officials, teachers, writers and patriots of many stripes. A few others joined up with the communists in Yan'an, the dusty mountain town where Mr. Ma the peasant champion later lived, but most went to Chongqing, where they set up universities and research institutes, trying to keep the embers of Chinese intellectual life burning until the war was over.

When World War II ended, Mr. Liang returned to Beijing. When the civil war with the communists started up, Mr. Liang stayed in Beijing. He went abroad—as China's representative to help plan the new United Nations Building in New York—but not as a refugee. While in the United States, he also taught at Yale and traveled to other universities, receiving honors for his work, which had been published in overseas academic journals during the 1930s and '40s. It was a triumphal tour, and his spirits were lifted further by the prospect that China's civil war between the Nationalists and the communists would soon be over.

He ended up returning sooner than he expected. His wife, whose health had been fragile for several years, contracted tuberculosis. He rushed back to be by her side. The Nationalists' fortunes were slipping, and many of Mr. Liang's fellow intellectuals fled with the Nationalists and 2 million of their followers to Taiwan in 1949. Mr. Liang, however, stayed on to be with his wife, also sure that the new government wouldn't be too radical. At first he simply taught at Tsinghua University's new architecture department. Then, after the communists established control, he was elected to several honorary positions, as well as made vice director of the Beijing City Planning Commission.

Like everything else he did, Mr. Liang threw himself into his job. He drew up a series of principles that he thought should govern the capital's development. It should be a political and cultural center, he said, not an industrial one. The city had never been an industrial center and its old streets and alleys would be inadequate for the demands of modern factories and transport. The Forbidden City should be preserved and surrounding buildings limited in height to a few stories. Most controversially, he called for a new administrative center to be built outside the old city walls—a new center for the city away from the emperor's palaces, which were once the center of the Chinese world.

The communists rejected all these suggestions. The city was industrialized—Chairman Mao was alleged to have said as he stood on the Gate of Heavenly Peace and surveyed the city that he wanted "the sky to be filled with smokestacks." The Forbidden City was only partially preserved, with leaders like Chairman Mao moving into an adjacent palace and much of the rest allowed to fall to pieces, a condition it remains in today. And, most crucially, the administrative center was built in the center of town, forcing the ancient city to bear the weight of a modern bureaucratic state, with old buildings leveled to make way for makeshift ministries and dorms for the huge influx of bureaucrats.

Doggedly—in hindsight one would say foolishly—Mr. Liang stuck to his guns. Every government plan to wipe out the past was met by one of his reasonable and sensible counterproposals. Instead of destroying the walls, for example, Mr. Liang said holes could be punched in them or tunnels built below to allow automobile traffic. The top of the walls, meanwhile, could be turned into a public park. An apolitical man at heart, Mr. Liang couldn't recognize that the communists brokered no opposition on any question. He was relentlessly attacked, charged with being wasteful and reactionary. His friends were forced to disown him and no one dared stick up for his ideas.

By 1955 his wife had died. During her last months, he lay in a nearby hospital room himself, trying to recuperate from a breakdown caused by overwork, nerves and his own case of tuberculosis. After a partial rehabilitation in the early 1960s, he suffered again during the Cultural Revolution, which Chairman Mao launched in 1966. Red Guards tormented him daily and he was forced to burn his drawings and letters. He was expelled from his apartment and forced to live in a drafty shack. Already suffering from a recurrence of tuberculosis, he was hospitalized and died in 1972 at the age of seventy-one, the last two decades of his life wasted.

Mr. Liang was lucky, however, in his friends. In the 1920s he and his wife befriended John and Wilma Fairbank, two pioneers of Chinese studies. They went on a field trip together and corresponded about Mr. Liang's plans. Mrs. Fairbank later tracked down copies of the photos that he had intended to use in his *Pictorial History of Chinese Architecture*. A maid who had worked for the family also saved some of his writings and notes, providing Mrs. Fairbank with some texts. She published the text in 1984 with the Massachusetts Institute of Technology Press (using a different romanization of Mr. Liang's name, Liang Ssu-ch'eng). In 1994 she came out with a charming biography about Mr. Liang and his wife called *Liang and Lin: Partners in Exploring China's Architectural Past*. It was published by Mr. Liang's alma mater, the University of Pennsylvania.

Mr. Liang's historical work was published in China in 1998 (although of course with no mention of his fate or Mrs. Fairbank's role; that would have been seen as unnecessarily dwelling on the party's dark history and an embarrassment that foreigners had saved his work). It was this Chinese version of Mr. Liang's book that I had come across while browsing a bookstore. I had used the book several times when planning outings near Beijing. His description and crystal-clear drawing of the Temple of Solitary Pleasure (or Dulesi) inspired me to visit that temple several times.

One drawing and Mr. Liang's vivid description particularly intrigued me. The drawing was of China's oldest surviving wooden pagoda, built in 1056 in Yingxian, Shanxi Province. Mr. Liang had documented the structure's age, which had an electrifying effect on many Chinese—here, at last, was the scientific method being applied to China's civilization, in this case a discovery that made verifiable previous claims of the pagoda's antiquity. Sure, people knew that this pagoda was old and had existed for centuries. But to be able to prove by use of documents and archives that this structure was nine hundred years old was a milestone. Once, when traveling to Datong in Shanxi Province, I made a special trip to see it. As I drove through the flat, dry Shanxi countryside, the pagoda rose up like a relic from a vanished civilization. I remember thinking how exciting it must have been for a young Chinese researcher to be rediscovering his own people's history. It was like bringing something back to life.

Mr. Liang's work has inspired a new generation of intellectuals to fight to save Beijing. Mr. Liang's brightest student was Wu Liangyong, Fang Ke's adviser. Mr. Liang's son, Liang Congjie, was also active in the movement, although he is mainly known for his work in the environmental field, having founded one of China's few truly nongovernmental organizations, Friends of Nature. And Mr. Liang's idea of moving the ever-expanding government out of the old city remained the current-day activists' prime demand.

In a widely reprinted article, for example, Fang Ke noted that the construction of Peace Boulevard—the one that had so delighted the taxi driver that evening when I had zoomed home from the evening meeting at the Kentucky Fried Chicken—had once again made Mr. Liang's ideas current. A modern, commercial and industrial city were just not possible in an old city like Beijing, he wrote.

> The suggestion of Mr. Liang was denounced for being "nostalgic, conservative and out of date." It's a tragedy that those who support protection today are given the same label. Today they see the result of placing the administrative center in the old city. One cannot help grasp the far-sightedness of Mr. Liang. It is incomprehensible that even today some people are still unable to grasp this idea.

Old Mr. Zhao, Lawyer Wu's client who was trying to save his courtyard home from demolition, was the descendant of another prominent family that had refused to flee to Taiwan when the Nationalists were defeated. His father, T. C. Chao (whose name could also be Romanized as Zhao Zezhen), had been a president of the World Council of Churches and had obtained an honorary doctorate of divinity from Princeton University in 1947. T. C.'s daughter, Lucy Zhao, a Ph.D. from the University of Chicago who translated Walt Whitman into Chinese, even took the last plane into Beijing in 1948, so determined was she to stand by her family and country. With the city encircled by the communists, she arrived in a C-46 on Temple of Heaven Road—the airports were already in communist hands.

Old Mr. Zhao and his father shared her optimism, believing that a clean, new government dedicated to social justice was what China needed. Few imagined the horror that would await people like them, with their suspicious foreign degrees and previous allegiance to the republic.

Old Mr. Zhao was eighty-two and had lived in his home for fifty years when I got to know him in the summer of 2000. His father, like Professor Liang in the 1950s and his student, Professor Wu today, had been asked to serve on several powerful "consultative" bodies and was allowed to keep his home. It wasn't the most beautiful courtyard home I'd seen, but part of that had to do with the vicissitudes of the past five decades. During the Cultural Revolution two wings were given to other families and an archway between the two halves of the building were bricked over. The Zhao family, like most Chinese, was reduced to poverty, and upkeep was minimal.

T. C. Chao died in 1979 at age ninety-one, and Old Mr. Zhao continued to live in the home. He'd been a teacher for most of the postwar era after working at a U.S. Army language training center in Honolulu. He still had the ramrod bearing of a soldier, and his square jaw, short silver hair and piercing eyes added to the feeling that he'd live at least as long as his father and remain mentally alert to the end.

He had installed a modern toilet and glass windows and had tiled the floors. He loved the house in his stubborn, blunt fashion. "I lived here for fifty years, why should I give it up?" was one of the first things he said to me when I went to visit him along with a friend and Lawyer Wu.

"You think I couldn't leave? I have family in the U.S. I have other places to go." Then with a snarly growl he added: "But I'm

Chinese and this is our culture. I am not going to leave this place."

I was a bit taken aback by his ferocity. I wondered if this was some sort of stunt or a ploy to get more money from the city. The area was already mostly leveled, and his house was one of the few left standing. On our way to visit him we'd had a bit of difficulty finding the house. It was No. 22 Meishuguan Houjie, a street that ran north from the Fine Arts Center. Not much of the old street remained; it intersected the broad new Peace Boulevard and was slated for redevelopment, a new north-south axis through the old town to complement the broad east-west boulevard.

We had walked north along the street past a few scholar trees that seemed to be bracing themselves for the bulldozers that would soon be coming their way. A newspaper vendor hawked scores of newspapers from a cart, and people jostled each other as they tried to pass along the sidewalk that had been narrowed by previous road enlargements. On our right was a two-meter gray wall with tiles on top. Such walls were found throughout Beijing and used to separate homes from each other. We came to a small red door with no number above it. It was boarded shut. A few yards farther up the road was another door, also with no number. But it had a doorbell and we rang it. Old Mr. Zhao answered and let us in.

Old Mr. Zhao soon got riled up as he began to recount the facts of his case. What angered him most was the arbitrary nature of every decision concerning the home. A low-level director from the Cultural Relics Bureau had been by in March 1998, he said, and declared that the building didn't date from the Ming dynasty (1368 to 1644) and therefore wasn't worth saving.

"Of course, if they'd said it was a cultural relic then they couldn't tear it down, so they said it wasn't one," Old Mr. Zhao said. He had led us into his home and now we were sitting across from each other on large polished wooden sofas with blue cushions. "But who says a relic is only a relic if it comes from the Ming? There's no rule saying the Ming is the benchmark and everything else can be torn down. It's ridiculous."

Old Mr. Zhao had started his campaign shortly after the official's visit in 1998. He wrote letters and called up his friends in the media. Not much came of it, but the government temporarily backed off its plans. The fiftieth anniversary of the founding of the People's Republic would be celebrated the next year, in 1999, and the government had a "social peace" campaign in force, which called for sensitive or controversial issues to be avoided. Old Mr. Zhao knew a lot of other well-connected people, many of them old-timers with a connection to the old republican era. These people had lived in disgrace for most of the communist era, but now they were seen as useful, besides having some influence through their connections abroad.

In November 1999, a month after the anniversary, the demolition of the neighborhood started. Workers leveled 37,000 square meters of old courtyard homes, including two palaces that had once belonged to princes in the Qing dynasty. Old Mr. Zhao could see that his home would be next, so he and Lawyer Wu filed his first suit, contending that the Cultural Relics Bureau hadn't accurately estimated his home's age. The bureaucrats argued that his house wasn't even on a map of Beijing dating back to the reign of Emperor Qianlong in the mid-eighteenth century and thus wasn't even 250 years old. Old Mr. Zhao, however, pointed out that the name of the street had changed; his home was on the map. The government conceded that point in court but then said it was irrelevant—it still wasn't Ming and still had to go.

"They said in court that it doesn't matter because it was only two hundred fifty years old. That wasn't old enough to be protected. Then they argued that my home is dilapidated and going to collapse, so it has to be demolished," Old Mr. Zhao said, his watery gray eyes suddenly flashing with anger.

Old Mr. Zhao also argued that the cultural bureau hadn't performed any scientific check of its age. The cultural official had been by twice, each time for five minutes. No wood samples had been taken, nor an analysis of the construction of the bracketed eaves, which can help date a Chinese building. "His only comment was the windows had been renovated and the building had lost its historical character," Old Mr. Zhao said.

The initial hearing was before an administrative judge, where the government's word has especially strong sway. The bureau won, but Old Mr. Zhao and Lawyer Wu immediately appealed. Appeals are heard before a normal civilian court, which are presumed to be less in the government's sway than administrative courts. As we spoke, they were waiting for it to be heard by an intermediate court.

I looked around Old Mr. Zhao's home and could see that the official from the cultural bureau had a point. This wasn't a prince's palace and had been restored in a fairly primitive fashion. The new windows were giant steel-framed structures that looked completely out of place. The floor was an ugly faded linoleum and the interior walls had been covered with some sort of pressboard siding.

But these were matters of taste and money. The structure clearly was ancient and in Beijing's bone-dry climate could probably stand another hundred years even if completely neglected. It didn't look dilapidated at all, and in fact the glazed-tile roof was in top shape, while the structure boasted charming details, such as two stone elephant heads that guarded the eaves of the front door. I couldn't estimate the age, but dozens of architects, city planners and historic preservationists had recently signed a petition calling for the home to be preserved. They recognized the home for what it was: a typical Beijing courtyard home. If it could be leveled, the entire old city could be gutted.

I also thought about what other countries had done to make their old towns livable. In Europe, medieval structures now boast insulation, double-paned windows, central heating and other modern amenities. Surely preserving the old city didn't mean that the buildings had to preserve preindustrial patterns of living, such as outhouses, woodstoves and the like. On the one hand, the city said the old town was dilapidated and had to make way for modernization; on the other, efforts to modernize the old buildings were used as proof that they no longer were ancient. Like the policies that Fang Ke had outlined in his book, such arguments seemed designed for one purpose: to allow the city to get on with its lucrative redevelopment.

We got up and walked around.

He pointed to his prized possessions, two room dividers—6-by-3-foot panels of carved rosewood that were hinged together. "What I don't get about the government," Old Mr. Zhao said, "is that it says we have this great and glorious history and culture. We have five thousand years and so on. But in the end we only protect a couple of sites like [the cities of] Lijiang and Pingyao and put them on the UNESCO register of cultural sites. And we think that's good enough. What kind of a policy is that?"

Lawyer Wu's two-pronged strategy for saving Old Mr. Zhao's home included a second suit, the one against the city's housing office. Drawing on Fang Ke's studies of Peace Boulevard, he noted that the city's development code allowed commercial redevelopment up to 70 meters back from the broad new road. But Old Mr. Zhao's home was 100 meters back, he argued, and so should be spared the wrecking ball.

Old Mr. Zhao sat back on the sofa and closed his eyes as his advocate picked up the thread. The city, Lawyer Wu said, had offered Old Mr. Zhao 6,000 yuan (or about $750) per square meter for the 420 square meters of his home. He would get no compensation for his 160-square-meter yard, even though the city-owned real estate office would be able to sell the whole lot to the developers. A few streets over, Lawyer Wu noted, the city is selling newly built old-style courtyard homes for 30,000 yuan a square meter, and buyers had to pay for the yard as well. Using that as a benchmark, the city could pocket well over 3 million yuan, or about $400,000, just by reselling Old Mr. Zhao's yard.

The developer, he said, was the Wangfujing General Commercial Real Estate Development Co., which is owned by the Beijing City East District government. "The buyer of the land is the China Construction Bank, which of course is also owned by the government," Lawyer Wu said. "No one can figure out why they're doing this or why they're allowed to do it. After Peace Boulevard and all the accompanying commercial development opened, occupancy rates fell and the city said no new commercial developments near the boulevard. It's just this blind development. There's no real market functioning here since it's all government money."

Old Mr. Zhao had seemed to be sleeping, but suddenly he bellowed out: "These companies mean nothing. This bank or that construction company—it's all the government. These guys can only make money when they build. They don't care if they rent out the rooms. They only want to sell to builders."

Over the next few weeks I took a closer look at the land deal, and it did indeed seem a bit odd. The bank building that was the ostensible reason for Old Mr. Zhao's move was already under construction. The shell of the six-story building overshadowed the courtyard house and it didn't seem necessary for Old Mr. Zhao to move for the building to be completed.

I couldn't figure out how much the Construction Bank was

paying the city for the land, but I verified Lawyer Wu's statement that one-story homes were selling for 30,000 yuan a square meter. The bank, for a six-story commercial structure, was undoubtedly paying more than that. But even using the 30,000-yuan figure, the city could make $1.6 million by selling Old Mr. Zhao's home to the bank. No wonder they wanted him out.

I called up the city zoning office and found out other odd facts. An official said the new building didn't violate the city's zoning ordinance that commercial buildings were limited to 70 meters from Peace Boulevard. The reason, he said, was that it would be "comprehensive" use, meaning mixed residential and commercial. Later, though, I talked to an acquaintance at the bank who told me it was to be a purely commercial building. Clearly, the "comprehensive" use was a means of skirting the ban on purely commercial buildings in what had been an overwhelmingly residential neighborhood. I also heard from a city planner that the building was only supposed to be 9 meters high, although it was already twice that height.

We had finished walking around Old Mr. Zhao's house and his yard. He'd been through the routine before with journalists. He'd give interviews, we'd write articles, he'd continue to sue and his influential friends would continue to write petitions. One day, he hoped, the city would relent and he'd win. It was like trying to set wet wood on fire.

Overhead, the construction crane swung by and we could hear the migrant laborers yelling to each other. I thought of the newspaper article cited in Fang Ke's book in which some migrant workers boasted that they'd tear down the Forbidden City if the money was right. We tried to take a picture of Old Mr. Zhao and angle the shot so the construction crane would be out of the view. "If you want to know what it looked like before, there have been

some artist friends who took pictures last year," he said. "I'm trying to keep a record of what it was like." We took a shot with the
construction crane hovering over Old Mr. Zhao's head like a stick
about to fall from the sky.

Fang Ke had said he wanted to show me something in the old city,
and we soon set an appointment to meet. We met not too far from
Old Mr. Zhao's street, at the north gate of Beihai Park, part of a
chain of lakes that runs through the center of town. As earlier, he
was wearing sandals, shorts and a T-shirt, this one emblazoned
with "MIT Department of Fine Arts." His wife, Zhang Yan, was
already in Boston studying at the Massachusetts Institute of
Technology and had sent him the shirt and others like it as a gift.
We shook hands. "It's on the other side of the road," he said,
gesturing with his head toward Peace Boulevard.

The busy road roared with traffic. We could cross it only by
taking a pedestrian underpass. As we emerged on the other side,
we were beset by men hawking trishaw tours of the *hutong*s
around the string of three small lakes that spread out to the
northwest of Beihai Park. It was one of the few remaining sections of the old city, one that the city planners had said would be
preserved at all costs. I could believe their intentions if for no
reason other than that the tiny area had become a tourist draw,
one of the few that Beijing had left (the others being the Great
Wall, the Forbidden City and the Temple of Heaven).

We brushed off the pesky hawkers and stood in front of a
large wooden memorial arch on the south end of the lakes. Soon
after we visited, it was torn down, but it used to announce the
start of a famous antique market with bright gold characters
"Hehua Shichang," or Lotus Market. We turned right and

walked up the east side of the Front Lake (or Qianhai), the first of the three lakes called Shishahai, or Lake of Ten Temples, that are connected to three other lakes to the south.

"I wanted to show you how I got interested in Beijing," Fang Ke said as we strolled along a sidewalk that ran up the lake's east side. "I was a student in the architecture school of Tsinghua University and not interested at all in old Beijing. Like a lot of architects, I wanted to build something of my own and put my name on it, something modern. I was really influenced by western theories of modern architecture and that's what interested me, something big and monumental."

But Fang Ke's teacher had other ideas. Professor Wu was the student of Liang Sicheng and carried on his master's work, at least in a very cautious fashion. He had helped redevelop Chrysanthemum Hutong, an alley on which he was allowed to carry out his and Mr. Liang's theory of "organic renewal"—the idea being that instead of clearing out entire neighborhoods, you saved what could be saved and built similar-sized and similar-looking buildings to replace those that truly were hopeless. He made the comparison to an organism that regenerated parts of itself when they died or were injured. The idea was to preserve as much of the old flavor and ways of life as possible while allowing for the fact that some buildings truly were dilapidated and dangerous.

Professor Wu used the same tactics on his students that he used with authorities. He never ordered his students to take up his cause and recognized the fact that most were going to end up building glass and concrete banks. But he did assign them to work on his projects, hoping that some might see his way.

"I still wasn't interested, even after the Chrysanthemum Hutong project. You have to remember that students live up in the university district. We were young and naïve and cut off from the city. I didn't come from Beijing—my home is in the south. None of us even wanted to go into the city. We saw it as a dirty old relic of feudal society. We looked down on the residents of the old city. They were poor, members of the underclass, and we didn't have any connection with them.

Then, in the fall of 1995, Professor Wu took Fang Ke on a tour of the old city. The old professor, then seventy-four years old, must have seen some promise in his young doctoral student and decided he was worth winning over. "I was touched by his concern for the city. I have to say I wasn't convinced that the city was worth saving, but I felt obliged to take on the project of studying the old city for my Ph.D. thesis. After all," Fang Ke said in the best tradition of a Confucian scholar, "he was my teacher and I couldn't refuse him."

At the end of his book, Fang Ke described the walk like this:

I still remember when I started to choose my path of study on November 5, 1995, Mr. Wu, who was seventy-four years old, walked me around old Beijing to investigate and study. At the foot of Prospect Hill, by the Lake of Ten Temples and in front of the Drum and Bell Towers, Mr. Wu was excited and enthusiastic, reflecting on the past in the light of the present. His deep feeling for old Beijing and the people there was from the bottom of his heart and overflowed in his expression, which really moved me greatly. Suddenly, I realized the wide scope of scholarship and the meaning of study. The strong responsibility toward society welled up in my heart. To me, it was a day deeply etched upon my mind. That windy, yet particularly warm, afternoon determined the direction of my thesis and influenced my life over the past few years. What's more, it will influence the track of my journey through life.

We were now walking that same path through the city. After 100 meters, Fang Ke stopped. To our right was a park. The area had been rebuilt recently, and the park was now controlled by some sort of office that barred entrance to the old men who used to go there to play chess.

We looked over the lake. It was around noon, and most people were indoors eating lunch or taking a break from the summer heat. Cicadas, which seem to be everywhere in China in the summer, began to call. In the distance I could glimpse the outline of the Western Mountains, the foothills in a chain of mountains that leads up to the Mongolian Plateau. Yesterday they would have been invisible because the air had been stagnant and the smog had hung heavily over the city. Today, a breeze was blowing, adding a tint of blue to the yellow, washed-out sky and bringing the horizon into a smudgy focus.

I stepped behind one of the willows that lined the lake, allowing a branch to block out the high-rises. From this vantage the city's roofline was still low enough to get a sense of what Beijing had been like for hundreds of years. This is still sometimes referred to as Shishahai, or Lake of Ten Temples, although the temples had long been destroyed. "It's still a pretty lively part of town," Fang Ke said. "People still swim in the lake and go for strolls."

We turned away from the lake and walked up White Rice (Baimi) Street, which used to be lined with rice merchants. The road was only about the width of two automobiles, so car traffic was basically impossible in this part of town. People still drove down the narrow roads, though, and some parked out on the street, making it all but impassable for the flatbed tricycles that delivered goods and picked up refuse.

We stopped at No. 11, a former residence of a provincial

governor in the Qing dynasty, the last dynasty to rule China before the imperial system was overthrown in 1912. The door was open and we walked in. We were in a large yard with a huge plane tree in the middle providing shade and a home for some sparrows.

On the other side of the yard, behind the tree, was a one-story wooden building that would traditionally have been the entrance to some chambers—a reception area, probably—and beyond it to another courtyard with a tree in the middle. The door to that building, however, was closed and signs of construction were everywhere.

Fang Ke's face fell. "An old cadre used to live here. I guess he died and now they've renovated everything," he said. The building had been freshly painted but in a very crude style. Under the eaves wooden beams protruded. Each had the character *shou*, or "Long Life," carved on it and painted in gold leaf for emphasis. But the painting work was shoddy and a bit like a movie set; the closer we got, the worse it looked.

Since we couldn't go in, we walked to the far left side of the courtyard, where there was a passageway to other connected courtyards in the back. Fang Ke stopped for a second and explained our route.

"Western palaces or mansions can have a really intricate number and arrangement of rooms, one here and one there," Fang Ke said. "Chinese courtyard houses are simple. They're like cells that have divided, or replicas of each other."

He took my pen and notebook from my hands and drew a rectangle.

"The courtyard is a rectangle. You enter on the short end and directly ahead on the other end of the courtyard is the main hall. The main hall can be one room, although typically it's made up of three rooms. In the Forbidden City it's nine, the auspicious number. (Ten is the heavenly number, so nine is the next highest, the highest that mortals can attain.)

"On the left and right of the rectangular courtyard are the long wings, usually rooms for attendants. Big mansions simply copy this pattern over and over. Some courtyards have no buildings and are left open for gardens or lakes, but it's all based on a series of connected rectangles. First, they typically add another rectangle behind the first," he said, adding more and more rectangles to the drawing. "Then more to the left and right. It all depends on the constraints of the land or the ability of the owner to purchase land, but this is the basic pattern."

We had entered a courtyard parallel to the main one. It was typical of how run-down much of Beijing's old housing had become. After the communists took over, they allowed many home-owners to stay in their homes but gradually forced them to share their homes. Where once a family had lived, a dozen now competed for space. The courtyards were turned into small slums filled with shacks and sheds. This yard was filled with about a dozen red brick shanties and endless piles of bric-a-brac. Waist-high piles of dusty bricks attested to someone's plans for further construction. A sheet of corrugated iron stood ready to be tossed on the roof in case a leak should appear. A stack of old flower-pots keeled over against a wall.

Saving it all from appearing too bleak, however, was the human scale—everything was one-story high. Plus, plants were everywhere: potted begonias crowned the heaps of bricks, grass sprouted out of drainage pipes and vines crawled up the crumbling walls. Hovering over it all was a giant chestnut tree planted centuries ago.

It was about two-thirty in the afternoon, and the yard was deserted, with most people at work or on siesta. The summer was slowly ending, and the heat wasn't as bad as it had been a month earlier when I had traced Mr. Ma's path through the Loess Plateau. For ordinary people, this was still the center of the world, the capital city that one yearned to visit and, if one were incredibly lucky, to work in. At times like this it did indeed seem one of the most desirable cities in the world.

"The silence," Fang Ke said as we stopped to look at a small cactus growing from a pot. "This is the great success of the old urban planning system. The main roads carry traffic, but the *hutong*s are narrow and perfect for children to play or old people to walk. It almost re-creates village life in the big city, yet there's privacy. Everyone lives behind doors. It's very different from western urban life, which is open and everyone has big lawns showing off their wealth. Here people don't want to show what they have. They're worried about making their neighbors jealous but also just want their privacy."

We walked through another courtyard as crowded as the previous one. As we headed back through the series of side wings, we tried fruitlessly to turn right, back to the main axis of the house, which seemed to be cut off from its former wings. We had now walked about 100 meters from the main entrance and geographically were almost back at the lake. The mansion was coming to an end. As we left the second crowded courtyard, we came upon what was traditionally the deepest and best-protected room in the house: the *xiulou*, or bedrooms where unmarried daughters would have lived. Like the rest, the building was one-story high, with curved eaves and a tiled roof. It looked as if it hadn't been renovated in decades, with the paint peeling off the pillars. It was locked and now was probably someone's home.

We walked back to the main courtyard. A group of government officials materialized: a woman in the center, an important-looking man next to her and three flunkies.

"We're just enjoying the beautiful Chinese architecture," I said, eliciting smiles all around. They were here to inspect the refurbished main halls of the house—the crudely renovated part we had been forced to skirt. The doors were now unlocked for the official inspection and we looked inside as the officials discussed construction costs.

Fang Ke gave a start. "Everything here is new. I thought it looked odd, but I mean everything. Look, the pillars aren't wood, but concrete. The floor is concrete. The walls are concrete. . . ." His voice trailed off.

He looked up and saw another abomination: the roof tiles were yellow, the color of the emperor. But this had never been imperial property. The color was arbitrary, a form of cultural vandalism or exoticism—ancient China lite for the country's new ruling class.

The rooms were empty, awaiting their next high-level resident, a lucky cadre who had been chosen to live in this leafy part of town. We didn't dare walk farther in but glanced into the next courtyard. The earthen ground had been covered with sidewalk tiles, giving it an ugly, sterile feel.

"This would be called *ganjing*," I said, and we both laughed at the word, which is literally translated as "clean" but has a fascist connotation to it as well, this sense of sweeping away the old into an antiseptic sameness that is the hallmark of modern Chinese cities and architecture.

Fang Ke couldn't resist putting in a last word.

"You rebuilt it all," he said to the officials, who looked up and nodded. Fang Ke had a lot he wanted to say, but his anger blocked him up and he chewed on his lip to control himself.

"What was wrong with the old structure? The roof is yellow," he said helplessly.

They said nothing. He was clearly irrelevant. We left and continued up Baimi Street.

"It's so disappointing. Every time I come here, the place changes. Even if all this were saved from the wrecking ball, people wouldn't know how to renovate it."

"You really like the *hutong*s," I said. Then, as a joke, added, "Did you fall in love with your wife here?"

"Actually, you could say that. For my master's thesis I expanded on the work I did for Professor Wu. Zhang Yan was an undergraduate, and she also studied urban planning. We spent several days walking the *hutong*s, looking at the architecture. We got to know each other pretty well."

Zhang Yan had always been a bit more focused than Fang Ke and had been determined to study abroad. Immediately after her undergraduate degree she took the entrance exams to U.S. universities. Soon after they were married in 1999, she went to MIT to study.

Our path led us back to the lake. We walked north and came to a construction site that blocked our way. Beijing's lakes, canals and even the moat around the Forbidden City were once linked and part of a living ecosystem—one of the natural wonders in a city that was on the edge of a desert and extremely dry much of the year. Water flowed down from the mountains through streams that have largely dried up and down into the six lakes that run north to south through the capital. The construction work in front of us was the dredging of a canal that ran eastward out of Front Lake and into the Forbidden City's moats.

"Actually, the canal is just for tourists—it won't be reconnected to the moat around the Forbidden City," Fang Ke said as we skirted the construction site by walking along the canal. But maybe this is a start to repairing the damaged waterways."

We couldn't follow the canal anymore because the area was blocked off for the dredging, so we walked along a street parallel to it. We stopped in front of a doorway and looked at the doors. They were made of wood, painted red and with small flower carvings along the edges. The paint was badly worn and the threshold, which on Chinese doorways is raised 6 inches above the ground, was split and cracked from lack of maintenance— nothing had been painted, it seemed, in fifty years.

One of the doors was partly open, and behind it we saw an intricately carved stone screen, meant to ward off evil influences (according to the principles of Chinese geomancy, or *fengshui*) and give residents protection from prying eyes. Fang Ke pushed the door open a bit, and we stepped over the threshold to look at the birds and flowers carved onto the screen. An old lady appeared around the side of the screen.

"Hello, grandma," Fang Ke said, using a polite address for an older woman. "I'm here from Tsinghua University and am studying Beijing's *hutong*s."

The old woman's face immediately lit up and she welcomed us in.

"The Zhang family lives here," she said. "Come in and have a cup of tea."

The courtyard was even more chaotic than that of the house we had just visited. There, shanties had filled the court-yards that we had walked through, but there was an orderliness and abundance of plants—it was, after all, adjacent to the future home of a senior-ranking leader, and those who lived there were probably relatively well-off state employees. This was the home of ordinary people. A broken washbasin hung from a hook. Bricks were piled haphazardly, and a small garlic plant perched atop a precarious stack of tiles.

"We bought the house in 1950, right after Liberation," Mrs.

Zhang said, using the official term for the communist takeover. "Our family had made money trading goods. It was chaos. All the rich people were fleeing to Taiwan and everything was cheap. It was a great deal. We come from Xianghe and thought we'd move into the big city. I don't know if it was such a good idea."

A decade and a half after they moved in, the Cultural Revolution was launched and the family was targeted as capitalists. They were thrown out and forced to live in slums on the edge of town. The government moved in half a dozen families, allowing them to build shanties on what had been the courtyard. After the Cultural Revolution ended in 1976, the family was allowed to move back in but for the past quarter century had been forced to share their home with the people who had taken it away from them. Tensions were high and people ignored each other. It was a common story in the old city.

Mrs. Zhang was seventy-seven, and she pointed with pride to the beautiful doors and the stone screen. She kept insisting we drink a cup of tea, but we wanted to keep moving, so politely declined. "I'm so happy that young people and foreigners are studying our beautiful old Beijing," she said, running a hand over the screen. "We're so proud of this."

It was a response that conventional wisdom said should be rare. One was always reading from commentators that Chinese are apolitical. They don't care about democracy. They're satisfied with their lot. Chinese people even say so themselves. But what most people mean is that they don't want to get mixed up in some insane government political campaign or power struggle in the party—which is what "politics" means to most people. Ask them if they're happy about corruption or other ways that unaccountable officials abuse their power and you suddenly get the opposite answer: they care very much.

So, too, with urban planning. Ask Chinese people if they'd

like to give up their dilapidated old homes for modern apartments in a high-rise and most will say yes. The conclusion is that they don't care about their old homes.

"That was what I thought when I got started on my doctoral work," Fang Ke said as we left Mrs. Zhang and walked down the alleyway. "I thought no one would really want to live here. But people are really friendly once you tell them you're researching or interested in their old homes. You say that and they love you. They're willing to spend time showing you around their courtyards."

"But it is true," I said, "that many say they are happy to leave for a modern home."

"Yes, but their consciousness is so low. If you give them only two choices—live in this slum or move to a high-rise—most will take the high-rise. But people only think in terms of those narrow choices because the government doesn't allow other discussions to take place. We can't publish articles on other alternatives, such as privatizing the houses and allowing people to renovate them according to historic guidelines. If you sit down with people and ask, 'Would you like to stay here if we could install running water and flush toilets?'—they already have electricity, so that's not an issue—then they almost all say they want to stay."

"But what about the excess population here?" I asked. "What about the six families living with Mrs. Zhang. What do you do with them?"

"Where the property rights are clear, then you have to slowly and carefully return houses to people who own them. We need the high-rises on the outskirts of town, that's undeniable. So we will have to move some people out of the old, crowded areas—just like they did in Europe after World War II. But what we don't need to do is to move out everyone, level the old buildings and put up shopping malls or luxury housing for a few. That isn't fair and we lose our heritage."

We'd now come out onto Di'anmen Street, having walked parallel to the canal for a few hundred meters. In English it could be translated as the Street of the Gate of Earthly Peace, a counterpoint to the famous Gate of Heavenly Peace on the south side of the Forbidden City. (While the Gate of Heavenly Peace still stands, the Gate of Earthly Peace has been torn down.) The street was narrow and bustling with commerce. Shops sold fresh green tea and small earthenware pots. A row of hardware stores offered knives and Mongolian hotpots. We headed north for a few meters and crossed an old stone bridge over the canal. I looked to the right and could see that Fang Ke had been right— the newly dredged canal passed under us but then just stopped, not continuing on its original path to the Forbidden City's moats. We turned left and walked westward, back along the north side of the canal, returning to the lake.

We passed a shopping center designed to look like some generic old China. It had concrete walls painted to look like whitewashed stone and slate-gray eaves that exuberantly curled up at the ends. It certainly looked nice but was somewhat bizarre. That's because it was a mock version of *Jiangnan* architecture from the Yangtze River valley—but built here in Beijing, about a thousand miles to the north, in a failed effort to fit in with the local architecture.

The walk was depressing me. It seemed like an admission of defeat, a few old crumbling buildings, a shopping center designed by someone who didn't know the characteristics of Beijing architecture and corrupt officials driving all the decisions. I couldn't see the magic of the old city or what had inspired Fang Ke to take up his studies. It all seemed hopeless.

We were now back in the *hutong*s and soon arrived at Silver Ingot Bridge, which straddles the two shores at a narrows where Front Lake meets Rear Lake (Houhai). We'd been walking around for an hour and stopped for a break, leaning against the stone balustrades. This view from the bridge northward to the Western Mountains was one of the famous Eight Scenes of Beijing, which had been captured in painting and poetry over the centuries. Low-rises in the foreground spoiled the view of the mountains, but it was still a lovely spot.

Then a small microtruck tried to cross the humpbacked bridge, but its way was blocked by a trishaw trying to head the other way. A bicyclist coming up behind the truck swerved crazily—like most bicyclists in Beijing, his brakes were shot. He fell off. A taxi came up the other side and started honking. The truck joined in. The bicyclist started shouting.

We looked at each other and laughed.

"Let's walk this way," Fang Ke said. "Professor Wu brought me here five years ago on that walk. We ate some *shaobing* (a toasted sesame roll) at a stall right at this intersection, and we walked up this road. It was here that I fell in love in Beijing."

In 1996 he threw himself full-time into his project. The one-hour commute between the old town and the university district became too much, so Fang Ke rented a room in a house near the Confucian Temple.

"I loved it. I realized people there were cultured and knew the old city's history backwards and forwards. For old people it was really convenient for them to live there because the hospitals and everything they needed were nearby."

And the architecture, which he once shunned as old-fashioned, began to attract him, too. "I was amazed at the variety—Qing and Ming mixing together so well. The family I stayed with wouldn't accept rent. They were so excited I was studying the old city and wanted to do something to help protect it, so they put me up."

Next to the bridge where we stood was a narrow street. We walked toward it. "Professor Wu told me that when he walked here in 1950 with Professor Liang Congjie this street was a string of beautiful old buildings, one of the best shopping streets in the capital. Now the entire street has been declared dangerous and dilapidated, but no developer wants to build here because the official height restrictions limit buildings to nine meters. So it's just falling down."

The street was called Yandai Xiejie. The latter word simply means "a small, narrow street." The first word, *yandai*, means "smoky belt" because the street resembles a wisp of smoke curling through the old city. Now, instead of leading the visitor past one famous store after the other, it led past ruins and wrecks that were slowly being converted into bars and nightclubs. A five-and-dime store was housed in one, a shabby video rental in another.

But a close look at the buildings showed how beautiful they could be with a bit of work. One was a small, shuttered Taoist temple with faded green eaves and intricate wooden window frames. Another, No. 24, was a building from the late nineteenth century, an effort to blend western and eastern architecture. It was made of stone—a concession to foreign building practices—but its crumbling friezes of flowers and birds attested to its Chinese creator.

"Once everything was collectivized in the 1950s, no one had any interest in keeping up the buildings anymore," Fang Ke said. We had stopped to stare at No. 24 and a couple of people looked at us suspiciously. I could only imagine the thoughts going through their heads: was that foreigner secretly enjoying China's poverty?

We were now back at the Street of the Gate of Earthly Peace and headed north to the Drum Tower. We looked back down the street toward the way we'd come. Directly south at the end of the street was Prospect Hill and beyond it, straight as the crow flies, the emperor's throne.

"We are standing on the axis of Beijing," Fang Ke said. "This is the pole around which the Chinese world turns."

I closed my eyes and pictured where we were in traditional China's cosmology. Traditional western cities are often built around a church, symbolizing the centrality of Christianity to those societies. Palaces of kings are also often found at the center of cities, showing a ruler's power and might. Many modern cities are formed around banking and sporting buildings, highlighting the role of commerce and entertainment.

But the Beijing that existed a few decades ago went far beyond that. It was a complete expression of ancient China's cosmology, with the very buildings, streets, temples and lakes taking on symbolic importance and fitting into a complex system of religious beliefs.

Imposing a cosmic order on earthly space is a key ingredient of Chinese culture. Temples and houses, for example, are laid out in accordance with *fengshui*. When Taoist priests invoke spells, they open up a window into the spiritual world by walking around an altar, temporarily turning the ground into a miniature re-creation of the heavens that they can enter. And in Chinese medicine the human body is a microcosm of the universe, with organs corresponding with the different elements that make up the cosmos.

Beijing, as the epicenter of China's cultural world for six hundred years, became the purest urban expression of this fascination with attaching spiritual principles to earthly objects. Traditionally, Chinese see a bridge between the heavens and politics—droughts and floods, for example, were expressions that the emperor wasn't fulfilling his duty as the link between heaven and earth. Just as the emperor was the symbolic focal point, the link between heaven and earth, so, too, were his temporal manifestations the center of earthly life. His throne was the city's focus and everything was built around it.

The emperor's throne was located in the Hall of Supreme Harmony, which lay in the center of the Forbidden City, a vast, 178-acre group of 8,700 halls mostly built in the seventeenth century. The popular English name Forbidden City isn't quite accurate and doesn't convey its importance. The proper Chinese name is Purple Forbidden City, with the color purple a reference to a quotation from Confucius in which he said the ruler is like the polestar—the point of reference for the entire country. In Chinese, the polestar is called the "purple pole star" and so the color was added to the Forbidden City's name to show that the emperor was the constant , a reference point to guide the empire.

Likewise, Beijing was fixed on the emperor, not just symbolically or in the sense that all traffic had to stop when the emperor left home, but in a very concrete sense. The main axis or meridian that guided the city's development wasn't a large road or boulevard, but an imaginary north-south line on which Fang Ke and I were now standing. Northward, it ran from the emperor's throne through the center of other halls in the Forbidden City, out through its north gate and over Prospect Hill. The axis then runs north along the Street of the Gate of Earthly Peace to where we stood and continued up to the Drum and Bell Towers, two giant structures whose sounds once regulated the medieval city's life. To the south of the emperor's throne the axis ran out through the Gate of Heavenly Peace and down through two other gates. All the major buildings of the old capital were built either on this axis or just off it on either side.

The axis carried such emotive power that even the communists tried to hitch their pseudoreligion to its power. When they wanted to build the sort of square for mass rallies that every communist capital had, they leveled the houses directly south of the Forbidden City. On it, they built the Monument to the People's Revolutionary Martyrs right on the axis, and when Mao died in 1976, his tomb was built directly on the imaginary line as well. Of course, these structures didn't fit with the traditions. The martyrs' monument is a giant, daggerlike structure that *feng-shui* practitioners say cuts into the energy flow along the axis. The tomb, meanwhile, is a complete abomination—traditional Chinese wouldn't put a dead body on display in the middle of town. Emperors were traditionally buried in the wooded hills outside the capital.

We walked north along the axis to the Drum Tower, a magnificent ten-story structure with a stone base and a wooden top. North of it was a small square and beyond it the similarly shaped Bell Tower. The square in between used to be filled with a warren of small restaurants and market stalls. Stomach indigestion was guaranteed if one ate here, but the chance to eat in the shadow of the two enormous towers was irresistible and several times a year I'd come here to eat spicy tripe, mutton and other Beijing specialties, and then suffer mightily the next day.

Now it was a cobblestoned square with lamps, almost like a European square. A security official lounged on one of the benches set on the square's periphery. His job was to keep people from setting up stalls and hawking things.

"The stalls appeared at the end of the Qing dynasty when the imperial system collapsed," Fang Ke said. "Before then it would have been unimaginable to have disturbed the axis. Even when the stalls were here, you could see a ridge in the center of the square that was right where the axis ran."

It was good that the stalls had been cleared away, but the renovation had been botched. The ridge was supposed to run down the center of the square, but the paving stones had been laid so that the ridge was too far to the right. The square looked lopsided. One couldn't help but conclude that the restorers didn't know the significance of the ridge and had simply repaved the square, not bothering to center it properly.

The buildings along the edge of the square had a Disneyfied look to them. To cover the crumbling stone and rotting wood, the city had put up aluminum siding on the old one-story buildings. The new panels were painted red to look like wooden panels. This was the flip side to destruction: haphazard renovation. As handicraft skills were lost, only a few teams of craftsmen were left to look after an entire city. That meant much of the work was done by people with no idea of how Chinese buildings traditionally looked or were constructed.

Despite all these problems, thinking about the axis—the energy backbone of the city, and in turn, of the imperial system— made me excited that at least this much was left. The buildings around the square had fake façades, but they could be fixed. The fact was that the Drum and Bell Towers still stood, and to the south lay the Forbidden City, its low, sleek buildings testifying to the emperor's broad, vast power. I could see why Fang Ke hadn't given up; the *hutong*s in between these monuments were worth protecting. Together, they formed an ensemble of buildings that hinted at how the Chinese had structured their world for thousands of years.

We walked west from the Bell Tower, weaving through the alleys northeast of the lakes. Walking through a *hutong* was amazingly pleasant, although it can sound tedious if you only imagine a *hutong* as a series of walls. But the *hutong*s' constant turns and twists opened up new vistas every few feet. Trees stretch out over the street from the courtyards, and the doorways often boast small decorations that intimated the owners' power and rank. Sometimes two *hutong*s converge and a few cars might be parked at this mini-intersection or a couple of children might be practicing badminton.

It was late August and still sultry, but autumn was approaching. Flatbed trishaws carted briquettes of coal from door to door, dumping their loads inside the front door. Residents were already arranging the piles into neat stacks that they make under the eaves of their homes or in corners of the courtyards.

We passed by a small hotel on Small Stone Bridge Lane that had become popular with some savvy travelers. It was a former mansion, with a series of courtyards that led to a small garden with an artificial hill. The threadbare accommodations weren't luxurious, but the location in the old town and the courtyards made it fun. Many people staying there would go for a walk in the morning and have a long, leisurely lunch in the restaurant. Sitting under one of the trees in the front courtyard, sipping a beer, one felt transported into another time. Which era depended on how much one knew about the building.

The mansion had been built in the Qing dynasty and been home to a succession of members of the royal family, but its most famous resident had been Kang Sheng, the head of Chairman Mao's secret police and spy network. Kang had lived there for twenty years, coordinating terror campaigns against the populace and becoming a strong supporter of Mao during the Cultural Revolution. It was a measure of just how terrible Kang was that he was expelled from the Communist Party (posthumously, of course) in 1980. After the Cultural Revolution only the very worst of the worst were expelled from the party; most kept their jobs and positions, part of the party's inability to face its history.

Kang was one of those archetypal secret-police heads. He was often compared to the legendary Soviet henchman Lavrenti Beria, but instead of indulging in sexual perversions, he liked to collect artwork, especially his victims'. During the Cultural Revolution, when people like Professor Liang were forced to burn or somehow dispose of their treasured books, scrolls and old wood furniture, Kang was able to amass a huge collection of goods. As an added twist, he imitated the people he destroyed, retreating to this charming location to practice calligraphy and enjoy his antiques.

One person whom Kang Sheng exploited was Old Mr. Zhao, who lost his furniture and library. Fang Ke told me the story.

"When Kang read a book, he stamped it 'Read by Kang Sheng,' and he catalogued the Ming furniture that he stole," Fang Ke said as we walked past the entrance to the hotel. "After the end of the Cultural Revolution the books were returned to Old Mr. Zhao, but he didn't want to see those stamps in the books anymore so he donated everything to the Shanghai Museum." The pieces are on display there today, with a small label underneath the desk where Old Mr. Zhao's sister translated Walt Whitman. No mention is made of the suffering that brought the pieces to the museum.

That explained the lack of old furniture or books in Old Mr. Zhao's home, save for the wooden screen. I wonder how many times one has to have a heartbreaking loss before one simply gives up on possessions. During the Cultural Revolution, Red Guards took a military medal from Professor Liang's mother-in-law. Her son had been an aviator in World War II and was shot down. The medal, of course, had been issued by the Nationalists, not the communists, since the Nationalists were the official government of China and the only one with an air force. But in the zealots' eyes it was a contaminated award and they confiscated it. After losing their books, furniture, home, freedom to think and travel, the mother finally lost the last memento of her son. Did she ever think of giving up?

She hadn't, and neither would Old Mr. Zhao. Like Mr. Liang, Old Mr. Zhao's father had probably made a mistake by not fleeing to Taiwan. There, he could have continued his religious work, instead of being forced to kowtow to the communists' erratic policies. But he was an optimist and had stayed on. The house, purchased in 1949 just after the communists took over, was a symbol of that attitude. Professor Liang's mother-in-law had pulled and tugged at the Red Guards, begging them to hand back the medal as they gleefully held it up as "proof" that the family was secretly allied with the Nationalists. Old Mr. Zhao was fighting for his father's home just as stubbornly.

We headed south to the Rear Lake (Houhai), passing a large courtyard home where Fang Ke had held an impromptu book-signing. He had spent quite a bit of time at that particular home while doing his research and brought over a few books to give to the family and neighbors. When the people heard that Fang Ke was back and that his book was out, dozens lined up. He called a friend who quickly brought over a few cartons of books. That night alone they sold more than a hundred.

"People are interested in their homes and their environment," Fang Ke said as we passed the doorway. We decided not to go in but to continue on. "The big issue now is the home of Cao Xueqin [China's famous eighteenth-century novelist] at the Ciqikou intersection. I got a call saying twenty-two families had sued the government over its decision to destroy that neighborhood and Cao's home."

It was midafternoon, but even though the siesta time was

over, the streets remained quiet. The clouds wanted to burst; a month earlier they probably would have. Beijing gets most of its rain in the summer months and the rest of the year is bone-dry. One could feel that dry autumn approaching. Leaves rustled and the cicadas were silent. Everything felt empty, as though we were the only people in the city.

We stopped at No. 47 Nanguanfang Hutong. It was housing provided to employees of the State Council, an administrative arm of the government—more proof that the government had taken the best homes after 1949 and was still occupying them, while telling everyone else that they had to get out of the old city because it was dilapidated. Some children played hide-and-seek, running from courtyard to courtyard. It was a splendid place to play, and the children shrieked with pleasure as they tore around from yard to yard. Big chestnut and scholar trees shaded the ground, and the children hid themselves in the half-ordered stacks of odds and ends—bricks, tiles, tires and whatever else years of hamster economics had taught people to stow away.

We felt like intruders spoiling the kids' fun so walked out again. The walls along the sides of the alley were red instead of the usual gray. Fang Ke began to explain why.

"These are made more simply than gray bricks. Gray ones have water poured on them when they're hot. These red ones, I think, are old, but for some reason the people back then didn't spend as much time on this segment of the wall," he said, peering at the bricks.

Just as he said that, a man was riding by on his bike. He quickly jumped off and corrected Fang Ke.

"No, no, these are new walls. They were just put up a few years ago," he said with a quick, machine-gun delivery.

He was a thin man, wearing just boxer shorts, brown leather

shoes and white socks. He was shirtless in the summer heat but seemed ready to slip into a pair of dress pants and shirt at a moment's notice.

"Why did they make them red instead of gray?" I asked them both.

"Communists like the color red," the man said. "And it's cheap. No one bothers to make the walls in the old ways anymore. Too much trouble."

With that short lecture on urban construction he hopped back on his bike and headed off.

We'd been walking for several hours and were tired. We decided to head over to a project that Fang Ke had worked on in 1998 with some MIT architects. Originally, we wanted to walk over but we weren't sure we'd make it, so we hopped a cab.

The driver took us through several *hutong*s, and then we were suddenly back on Peace Boulevard. Half the shops on it were empty. Under pressure from developers, the city had argued that leveling the old homes and widening the street wasn't just needed to alleviate traffic flows. The old city, they said, needed big new stores along the street, so it built stores in a mock-old style with concrete walls painted red or gray to resemble an old building. The rents, though, were expensive and too large for most of the mom-and-pop businesses that predominate in this part of town. So they remained mostly empty.

We zoomed west and then cut south into a *hutong*. We were back in old Beijing. The traffic slowed as cars and bicycles competed for the limited space.

"See how crowded it is," Fang Ke said as we suddenly stopped moving. "In 1949, between 700,000 and 1 million people lived here. Now it's 1.7 million. I don't think we need to go back to the old population; we've done studies that show we could reduce the overcrowding and restore most of the old homes if we just moved 100,000 to 200,000 people. That's not that many compared to what's being done now."

We decided to abandon the taxi for the final stretch. We walked south, skirting the White Dagoba Temple (Baitaisi), named after the giant structure shaped like a snake-charmer's bottle. Built in the eleventh century, the dagoba had been frequented by Kublai Khan, who turned it into one of the city's centers of Buddhist worship. The temple was surrounded by six-foot-high walls made of gray bricks that had been gone over with a coat of red paint.

"It didn't look like this originally," he said, running his hand over the flaking paint. They think all old buildings have red paint. But the truth is that the temple walls were originally the same color as the houses'. They should be gray."

To our left as we walked south were rows of old houses. None were as majestic as those we'd seen by the lakes. This had always been a poorer part of town, and it showed in the cramped homes formerly owned by lower-middle-class artisans and shopkeepers.

A few years ago Fang Ke had worked here on a project with some MIT students. The goal was to come up with a feasible plan to renovate the neighborhood, which had been devastated in the 1960s by the destruction of one of Beijing's most famous temples: Huguosi, or the Temple of National Protection. It had been a Buddhist temple but primarily a center of Beijing's largest folk festival on Chinese New Year. The festival had lasted for two weeks, attracting millions of visitors, and had been the focal point of the community for much of the rest of the year. That had made it a target of communist authorities, who pulled it down.

The students had come up with a plan to protect the best-preserved of the homes and build a square in front of the White Dagoba Temple. We walked by the entrance and decided not to go in. The reliquaries had all been destroyed in the Cultural Revolution, and all that was left was the big white dagoba. We wandered around, and Fang Ke took pictures of the neighborhood for his friends at MIT.

Then we walked up the other side of the temple, now heading north. The narrow road met another small street in a slanting X intersection, forming a small square. Restaurants opened out onto the square, many selling spit-roasted chicken. One man stood in front of the glass-enclosed rotisserie, staring at the birds as they slowly rotated, dripping fat.

Farther up the road we saw a giant, ten-story building, gray and in the style of a Stalinist wedding-cake building.

"It was called a 'communism building' by the locals," Fang Ke said. "It was built in the Great Leap Forward when everyone was supposed to live together. It had one kitchen per floor and one group of toilets."

Each of Beijing's four central districts was supposed to have one, the ultimate in communist city planning. Two were built and one torn down. This was the last one standing, and it was unpopular, with people rejecting the lack of facilities and the shoddy construction.

We walked down the street and then cut over toward the dagoba, which loomed over the low buildings. We passed a former lama residence that had Tibetan prayer wheels on the roof. They contained the scriptures and were proof of the lama's devotion, and wealth. The building looked as if it were going to fall over; I wondered how long it would stand.

Fang Ke seemed to be looking for something. He went off to ask for directions and quickly returned.

"It's down one of these streets," he said as we walked by a couple of two-story warehouses that were built next to the temple. We walked through a wholesale meat market selling freshly slaughtered beef and ascended a metal fire escape on the back of one building. Perching on a landing, we stared over the temple and neighborhood.

"There he said," like a connoisseur displaying his favorite painting. "It's so low, we can see everything."

From up above, the old city looked like a charming slum. The eaves still sloped upward, and if one had bad eyesight, it looked beautiful, with the giant white dagoba surrounded by gray one-story homes and shops. But the tiles were falling off most roofs, and repairs consisted of throwing sheet metal over the holes and laying bricks along the edges to weigh it down. In other cases people had tossed what looked like bags of rubbish on the sheet metal. Sometimes people had cemented over the holes. I could see what Fang Ke meant by the need for property rights. If the homes were sold, then owners might invest in their upkeep, as they had for centuries.

"The old tiles are so pleasing to look at. They look like fish scales, shimmering in the sunlight. The old capital . . ." he said, his voice trailing off. "It seems lost, vanished."

That term reminded me of a tome by the historian Susan Naquin, who wrote on Beijing's urban life from 1400 to 1900. Beijing had been a capital for the past six hundred years and during that time had come to symbolize many different Chinas. Especially after the Ming dynasty collapsed in the seventeenth century, writers wrote longingly of the "lost" or "vanished" capital, even though of course Beijing was still standing. What they had usually meant was the loss of one dynasty for another, but their works also had a dreamlike quality, a paean to a bygone era.

It was an exercise repeated in the early twentieth century, when many of the writers were foreign and their laments for the loss of "Old Peking" had a colonial ring. Between the two world wars Beijing was filled with romantic westerners who noted how the new Nationalist government hadn't kept up the temples or monuments. Its decay, they noted, began in the last decades of the old imperial rule, when China's economic and political decline left no money to maintain the temples and palaces that embodied the country's complex religion of ancestor and god worship. Moreover after the emperor abdicated in 1912 many of the temples lost their function. If the emperor was no longer the intermediary between heaven and earth, there was no need for the Temple of Heaven, where he would go to pray for good harvests. The temple stayed (and still exists—it is one of Beijing's best-known tourist sites), but many others fell into decay and were pulled down.

Ms. Naquin was no sentimentalist—indeed her book tries to draw as few implications as possible for the present. But toward the end she allowed herself a few sentences about what had happened to Beijing at the close of the twentieth century. Even though the city lost numerous temples, homes and its great walls in the 1950s and '60s, the destruction during the 1990s, she wrote, was greater than at any other time this century: "My research was not begun as, nor is it now intended to be, an exercise in nostalgia, either for vanished temples or for a lost Peking. . . . Nevertheless, if viewed—just for one moment—against the current destruction of the city, this book reminds even me of a 'record of a dream of a vanished capital.' "

I looked down at the fish scales, their shadows creeping longer as the late-summer sun went down. In the distance the great park of Beihai, where we had met to start our walk, was a giant swath of green. I thought back to Fang Ke's teacher, Professor Wu, and his teacher, Professor Liang. Both had stressed the organic nature of the city, and here it seemed literal. The old city stretched out before us like a broken carapace that the new city was shedding.

•   •   •

Huang Yan was deputy head of urban planning at the Beijing Municipal Institute of City Planning and Design and had been walking around an enormous conference room, crossing over from one gargantuan map of Beijing to another, pointing out historic protection zones. Government officials were reluctant to discuss Beijing's urban planning—probably because it had been so contradictory and such an abject failure. But the city had recently announced a new plan to protect the old town and felt obliged to grant an interview.

"In the fifties to the seventies, about a fifth of the old city was torn down for government buildings," she said. "In the eighties not much happened, and then in the nineties we decided to protect the old city. We issued a document in 1992 identifying twenty-five areas that needed special protection," she said, rapping a ruler on one of twenty-five pink squares in the old town.

"The same twenty-five that were announced in 2000?" I asked.

"Well, yes. For whatever reason that plan in 1992 wasn't fully realized. You see, the only people who care about protecting the old city are intellectuals. Residents only care about raising their living standards," she said with a confident smile.

"What about the class-action lawsuits? Many of those people want to protect their buildings," I said.

"That's for the courts to decide," she said firmly.

I felt like I was in a war room, or a movie set of a war room, because nothing real was going on here. Still, I liked Ms. Huang. She was in many ways similar to Fang Ke. She was a bit older, about thirty-five, and had already studied abroad, something Fang Ke was planning to do shortly. Like him, she was part of a group of Chinese who felt part of the outside world. Her two years at an urban-planning institute in Belgium had influenced her, and she looked distinctly different from most Chinese women. She wore tiny rectangular glasses popular in Europe, a white blouse and a floral-print batik skirt that went down to her ankles. A Chinese person who looked at her would immediately guess that she'd lived abroad.

She had come back to a government job. And like all intellectuals, especially those who have been overseas, her power was limited. The institute wasn't really a key city office. It was a quasi–think tank, where ideas were hatched and sent off to the city's party branch for discussion. Still, she was genuinely concerned about the city but seemed a bit like Fang Ke before his walk with Professor Wu. She didn't live in the old city, and even her institute was located outside of the old town.

"When I visited a *hutong* last year on a bike I realized how hard it was just to ride a bicycle in there," she said. "There are so many cars on them now. The *hutong*s used to be public spaces where children played and old people sat. Now it's too dangerous to do that. The fabric has changed."

"So why not restrict car access," I said. "Like old towns in Europe, you could keep autos on the main thoroughfares and keep them off the *hutong*s."

"The problem, you see, is that the *hutong*s aren't really made for the modern world. It's not just cars, it's other things."

"Like . . ."

"Like gas. The *hutong*s are too narrow for gas pipes. Or sewage. So you see they have to be widened or dealt with in some way."

Maybe Fang Ke had prepped me too well, but I felt I knew her lines better than she did.

"And there's another problem," she said.

"The houses are made of wood?" I said.

"Exactly! You've put your finger right on it."

She'd found an ally.

"Look at European cities. They're made of stone. Not wood. How can you protect wood? You can't. It disintegrates. Old European cities are more modern, even the old parts. They can be wired and there's space for toilets. Beijing is a medieval city. Medieval Paris was destroyed by Napoleon III in the nineteenth century, so when they now modernize old buildings, they only have to modernize structures that are a hundred fifty years old. Ours are five hundred years old."

"So it can't be done," I said.

"Well," she shrugged. "Look at this."

She spread out a big map of the city. It showed the 62.5 square kilometers of the old city, all of which was once inside the city walls and which now was inside the ring road built on the site of the old wall. The old city was shaded in five colors: red, yellow, blue, green and white. Red areas had the strictest protection and included well-known temples and palaces, like the Forbidden City. Yellow was made up of protected streets. Blue was for areas where the "morphology" had to stay the same—street layouts and building heights—but the buildings could be torn down and rebuilt. Green were belts around the protected areas where height restrictions were imposed. In white areas anything was allowed. Most of the map, 62 percent, was white.

Of the remaining 38 percent, about half of it was made up of the Forbidden City and Beihai Park, which formed a giant red and yellow rectangle in the middle of the old town. To the north was another yellow belt of protected areas, which made up much of the area around the Bell and Drum Towers where I'd walked with Fang Ke. These areas were surrounded by a few blue and green belts. A few blotches of yellow or red were dotted on the map, but otherwise it was white.

I looked back on the big map and saw why Old Mr. Zhao's home would be torn down. He lived in a white zone. The plan seemed to be that anything outside these few narrow red and yellow areas would be torn down.

"Look at this," she said, pulling out a large-scale map of one of the yellow belts near the Forbidden City. It was an amazingly beautiful technical work, with almost every courtyard home drawn in and even the ancient trees marked in red. As I studied the map, I noticed that some of the buildings were colored yellow but others weren't.

"On this map, not all the buildings that are in the yellow zone on the big map are yellow on this small-scale map," I said.

"Yes, well even in the yellow zone we can't save all the houses. We'll save about two-thirds. The rest will be torn down."

"So, let me summarize," I said. "Of the 62.5 square kilometers, about 62 percent or two-thirds is open to development. Of the remaining 38 percent, about half is to be protected, so about 19 percent. And of the protected 19 percent, about one-third will be torn down. So the percentage of buildings that will be protected will be about 13 percent of the old town."

"Well, there are the green and blue belts—"

"Which are new buildings with height restrictions."

"Well, we might save a few old buildings in those zones."

After a few pleasantries I left and walked outside. Next door was a bookstore run by the institute and which was devoted to city planning. I asked about Fang Ke's book. It wasn't on sale. Out of stock, perhaps? No, they'd never heard of it.

Old Mr. Zhao finally had his final day in court. It was September 21, 2000, at the Beijing Municipal Second Intermediate Court.

Foreigners were banned, but a Chinese friend went and told me what happened.

The court was located in a tiny room in what seemed to be a regular housing block. At five past nine, the judge and a secretary entered and read the verdict. The reading lasted fifteen minutes, but boiled down it meant this: Old Mr. Zhao had five days to leave his home. If he stayed, the construction company had the right to force him out.

A member of the audience who faced the same problem sighed and said, "This is brutal. We are being robbed."

Lawyer Wu went to talk to the judge. His client, he said, faced a Catch-22: He was appealing a related case but the appeal wouldn't be considered for another month. But according to today's ruling, Old Mr. Zhao's home was going to be torn down in five days. Could the judge extend the five days to thirty so the other appeal could be considered? The judge promised an answer and left.

I went back to Old Mr. Zhao's home a few days later. It was early September and still hot. Dressed in a gray T-shirt and tan cotton trousers, he met me silently at the door and then turned to walk inside. I closed the wooden door behind me, shutting out the busy sounds of the street.

"We're still fighting," he said with a wave of his hand as he shuffled in.

He rattled off a list of prominent Beijing intellectuals who had drawn up a petition in support of him. They included Professor Liang's son, Liang Congjie, and Shu Yi, the son of Lao She, an author who had set many of his short stories and novels in Beijing's *hutong*s. Lao She had been hounded to death during the Cultural Revolution, jumping off a bridge into one of the lakes I had walked by with Fang Ke. His death gave the son an aura of moral authority.

The men had forwarded Old Mr. Zhao's petition to Li Rui-huan, a senior party member who was the official glad-hander of religious groups, intellectuals, ethnic minorities and so on. He was supposed to be a reformer but was about as powerless as the groups he met.

"So," said Old Mr. Zhao. "We've got some people on our side."

"That's good," I said.

"And don't forget what Mayor Jia Qinglin said: 'Respect the opinion of experts.' "

"When did he say that?" I asked.

"In 1999."

It had come in response to a public rebuke delivered by Fang Ke. He'd attended a meeting of experts called to discuss the construction of Peace Boulevard. Because it had involved the destruction of so many historic structures, another petition had circulated and the mayor had called the meeting to assess the situation. A series of mealy-mouthed officials spoke, and at the very end Fang Ke stood up. His book wasn't out yet, but he had penned a few razor-sharp articles for national publications about the boulevard. He had pointed out then what was obvious now: the boulevard would look horrible and few shopkeepers would be attracted to the fake-looking shops that line it.

After pointing out the lack of market research, the flawed assumptions on traffic flows and so on, he concluded with this rather bold statement—bold, at least, for an academic to say to a powerful leader like Mayor Jia: "Reforming old Beijing by constructing Peace Boulevard only shows that the city lacks a clear understanding of the mistakes it has made before and the severe problems that are occurring today that are the results of those mistakes."

It wasn't the most stirring rhetoric, but the essence was painfully blunt: you haven't learned from your mistakes. At the end of the meeting Mayor Jia had made a vague summary, thanked everyone and promised to "respect the opinion of experts."

No one thought that Mayor Jia intended to listen to many experts. Instead, he'd listen to his advisers, who'd tell him to "modernize" the city, advice that not coincidentally would also make a lot of officials rich.

"Well," I said to Old Mr. Zhao, "there's some hope still."

We were sitting down again in his living room. His eyes were hard and clear. He was old and knew the fate that likely awaited him.

"And if . . ." I trailed off.

"I'll never agree with this. When they come to tear it down and bring in the Public Security Bureau and the ambulances— they do this, you know, because people often faint when this happens—I'll go. I'm just a simple citizen. I can't fight the law. but I'll never agree with what they do."

I got a call from Fang Ke in late September.

"I'm going," he said. "MIT has agreed to let me take courses and I got a visa yesterday at the U.S. embassy."

"But the semester has already started," I said.

"It doesn't matter. I'm going to audit some courses and improve my English. Then I'll attend next semester and apply for a fellowship somewhere. I'm going really soon. Tomorrow."

It was one of those unexpected calls one sometimes got from Chinese friends. An opportunity would present itself to leave the country, and suddenly they were going, with almost no notice. I knew he had been planning to go to the United States to study, but I'd thought it would take months. I felt sad. He hadn't saved the old city, I thought, although I knew it was a bit ridiculous to feel that way.

October 26, 2000: Old Mr. Zhao's house was about to be torn down. I got to his house around 9 a.m. The street was partly blocked off and a small crowd had gathered to watch. A few foreign journalists mingled in the crowd, but most of those present seemed to be locals who knew Old Mr. Zhao personally. The local newspapers hadn't been permitted to carry news of his case, so most people didn't know about it.

Old Mr. Zhao had left the night before. A representative from the court had come to tell him that the appeal on his second case wouldn't be heard until after his house was slated to be torn down. The wrecking crew would come the next day, the official told him. Chairman Mao's secret police had stolen his father's library and furniture. Not much was left. He donated his large wooden room dividers to a museum, packed up and that night left his home of fifty years.

Police cleared away onlookers from the front of the house. I breezed past them, pretending to be simply walking down the street on my way somewhere. Old Mr. Zhao's red doors were broken, and I looked in at the little stone wall that is inside every Chinese courtyard house. It is supposed to keep outsiders from looking in and, according to the principles of *fengshui*, evil forces from entering the house. An illegible government proclamation was stuck on it and a dozen peasant workers had climbed onto his roof, just above the stone elephants that were supposed to protect it. The workers ripped up the glazed tiles and then attacked the wooden eaves with crowbars.

As I walked back a second time, a policeman herded me away. He pretended to be friendly and told me that it was "for our safety"—a phrase that in China always means something else. A few other policemen stood nearby. A couple muttered to each other, "What do they want?" and "They should just take off, get out." Two of them strung up police tape that read in Chinese and English "Limit Line."

It was a brilliant, sunny day, a bit cold and hazy but unusually clear. The smog had blown away, and I turned my head upward, soaking in some sun. Nearby was a stall making *jianbing*, a small fried pancake. Another sold newspapers, its rack groaning with a huge array of newspapers that were free to discuss anything, from sex to sports, except for one topic: how people might run their government. A small crowd of people stood and stared, attracted by the police, the foreigners and the peasant workers.

A French artist sat there, sketching the scene in a small notebook. He had just come from the home of Cao Xueqin, the eighteenth-century author whose house was also being leveled. His sketchbook was now open to Old Mr. Zhao's home. The page showed the stone lions and elephants that jutted from the walls. "The doors are superb and the lions really unusual. I've sketched throughout the *hutong*s but haven't seen any like this." A police officer craned over to have a look at what the artist was drawing. He looked bemused and slightly angry.

The street itself was slated to disappear if Beijing won its bid to host the 2008 Olympics. Meishuguan Houjie would be widened and the remaining old buildings leveled. A poster glued to a wall heralded the inevitable change: "Develop Commercial Beijing City—Wangfujing General Commercial Real Estate Development Co." I wasn't sure what the jumble of words meant. Was it an order? A prediction? Next to it was a torn poster: "Beijing City Exhibition on Fighting and Preventing Economic Crimes."

A Chinese photographer took a few photos. She said she had recorded Old Mr. Zhao's home over the past year. "I have pictures from each of the four seasons," she said. Of course, she knew everyone: Fang Ke, Wang Jun and the older generation of preservationists. She was going to exhibit the photos, she said, and invited me to attend its opening.

A group of schoolchildren was trying to walk north on the street, a path that would have led them by Old Mr. Zhao's home. They were stopped by the police line and spilled out into the street. The street started plugging up. A bus stopped. Cars started honking. The police glared at the foreign journalists. "Go home," one yelled. Once we went home, I guessed the "safety" concerns would evaporate and people would be allowed to walk in front of the home, which was now sinking under the workers' pickaxes and crowbars. It would just become another house being leveled in Beijing, a completely normal sight. My presence wouldn't change anything. I turned around and left.

The day after Old Mr. Zhao's home was torn down, I got an e-mail from Fang Ke. It was an essay called "Eternal No. 22"—which was Old Mr. Zhao's house number on Meishuguan Houjie. It was addressed to a group of friends who had been interested in, and in some cases helped fight to preserve, the old courtyard home. He had written it from Paris.

> It's five o'clock in the morning here in Paris,
> and I know that over there in Beijing they are
> tearing down No. 22 Meishuguan Houjie. I
> can't close my eyes; the whole night through I

keep thinking of a way [for the house] to escape. But I know that it's no use. My friends have told me by cell phone that several cars have already been by to carry away belongings, that the street is filled with several hundred police, 20-odd foreign journalists and that earth-moving equipment is waiting by the side.

I can't close my eyes; I feel that from now on I'll never again be able to sleep. Maybe this is just one courtyard home from the late-Ming or early-Qing but why do they want to tear it down? This is something beautiful that our ancestors bequeathed us, another part of our shrinking capital. It's a crime to tear it down!

For two and a half years I don't know how many times I've knocked at that door. Inside was the owner, over 80, of this courtyard home with at least 360 years of history. It had radiantly yellow chrysanthemums and was so peaceful. I don't know how many times over the past two and a half years I sat on the sofa across from Zhao Jingxin, slowly drinking some scalding jasmine tea, enjoying his Ming-era furniture or listening to his news. I knew clearly that this courtyard home was on [the Emperor] Qianlong's map of Beijing, that one of the emperor's doctors had lived here and that Zhao Jingxin's father, Zhao Zichen, had left a few of his belongings here. The father had been a leader of China's Christians and a hero in the anti-Japanese war and found refuge in the house before he was molested [in the Cultural

Revolution]. Once I saw a big white cat that seemed to possess great intelligence comfortably sunning itself in the corridor.

Every time I closed the door behind me and entered the courtyard, it felt like this was the real Beijing. Outside its walls was noise and confusion, but none of it reached the inside. When I talked to Old Mr. Zhao, I had this illusion that nothing was going to happen, as if the world outside didn't exist. This is what a courtyard house is. In the whole world of architecture only a courtyard house could create such an environment and in all of history only a courtyard house could captivate people so. In all the world no other style has been commended or doted on as much as a courtyard house, with so many authors writing about it. How they would tremble today!

I'm really sad. Sad for the loss of an irreplaceable cultural relic, for the violation of Old Mr. and Mrs. Zhao's civil rights. This has been their private property for 50 years, something sacred that they shouldn't be deprived of or violated. After 1982 when land rights were given to the state, citizens still enjoyed the right to protection of property use—how can it suddenly be taken away?

Old Mr. and Mrs. Zhao are so old and for the last two years have had to live in such fear and had such a hard time to protect their home and this national cultural relic. Their spirits are still exhausted and to have such an unexpected outcome! How can glass surreptitiously be smashed, walls pulled down and for the courts to write congratulatory letters like the building can "victoriously be torn down"?

I'm really sad. When I return to Beijing and walk to Meishuguan Houjie, I won't be able to knock on the door and a piece of life's beauty won't exist. Close to 400 years of history will be wiped away cleanly in a few hours by earth-moving machines and spades.

Now that Old Mr. Zhao had lost his suit, I wanted to know how Messrs. Luo and Feng had fared. No news, they said over the telephone, but let's meet anyway. It was early 2001, and they wanted to hear the latest about Fang Ke and Old Mr. Zhao. The second floor of the KFC was as brightly lit as ever, but this time we were able to get Mr. Luo's favorite table in the back corner. I slouched low in the plastic bucket seats and tried to make the call as social as possible.

This time we even ordered some food. As I slurped from my paper cup of Lipton, I made my first blunder.

"Old Mr. Zhao lost his case," I said. "Are you worried about your situation? Maybe it's a bit sensitive?"

Mr. Feng stopped eating. He pushed his tray over to the empty side of the table and opened his briefcase. Out of it he pulled a copy of the constitution. The last sentence in Chapter 1, Article 10, was underlined, and he pointed to it: "The state may, in the public interest, requisition land for its use in accordance with the law." The last five words were underlined twice, the strokes so heavy they almost tore through the paper.

"This is my good-luck charm," he said. "You see how tough

our life is. We have no money and the money we raised has run out. We pay our costs ourselves. We're not against the government, but the government is against us. We've both had to meet with the Public Security Bureau so many times that we know their questions before they ask them. But what we do is in accordance with the law. So I don't think it's sensitive."

"How do you answer when the police ask you?" I asked.

"That we're just using the constitution and our right to sue, that we're apolitical and interested in the law."

I bet that's useful, I thought. Then Mr. Feng smiled and trumped me again.

"What I don't tell them is that I have more legitimacy than a member of the National People's Congress."

I jerked forward. "Huh?"

"We didn't appoint ourselves as head of the lawsuit," Mr. Luo said in his deep baritone. "We were elected. January 2000. A secret ballot. Feng and I got ten thousand free and fair ballots for us. How many people vote for a member of the people's congress? Zero."

Our quiet talk was suddenly very loud. A few heads craned around to take a look.

"Let's go outside," I said.

We finished our teas and walked outside. It was a cold winter day and we clapped our hands to stay warm. Mr. Luo crossed the street and we followed him. We walked behind the Bank of China building and into a maze of *hutong*s.

"This is where I grew up," he said.

We walked silently down one alley, into another and then turned quickly into someone's courtyard home. A small coal oven in the corner gave heat. I sat down on a folding chair next to a card table. The room was neat, but everything was worn to the nub. Even the concrete floor seemed ready to sink down into the earth. The windows were made of wood lattice and glass, but the wood was old and cracked; no one had oiled it for decades and in Beijing's dry climate that meant death. Someone had put in a drop ceiling; I imagined the rafters above it, the elaborate post-and-beam construction waiting for a restorer's hand or the peasant worker's pickax.

The owner of the house was Mr. Luo's previous neighbor. He was a thin man with a two-day growth of beard and a weather-beaten face. The two had grown up together and been fast friends. Mr. Luo's house had been torn down as part of the botched Financial Street development project. The original plan was to extend the street up to the Kentucky Fried Chicken, but the project had run out of money and not even the land where Mr. Luo's house once stood had been built upon. But one day the construction glut would be over and the appetite for more office space return. Mr. Luo's friend knew his house would then fall. Unless, of course, the city had a change of heart.

"We need help," the man said as Messrs. Luo and Feng looked on impassively. "Someone has to change the way the government thinks."

"The lawsuit?" I said, turning to Mr. Feng.

"The last court we could think of has rejected it. We're hoping for help from abroad."

That was usually the sign of a lost cause, and the people who said it knew it. It was like a bankrupt person spending his last dollar on a lottery ticket. But again, I'd misunderstood them.

"What he means," Mr. Luo said loudly, barging into my train of thought, "is that we want you to take this book to Fang Ke. He will help us."

I looked at him in surprise. "What?"

"You are going to go to America, are you not? You will take a copy of our book to him. He will think of something to do."

"Well, I had hoped to see him, but he's just a student at a school. What can he do?" My eyes looked around the room and out into the gray courtyard. An oak tree stood barren in the weak winter light. Would it soon be the lobby of a bank?

"No," Mr. Luo said, shaking his head. "He might not be able to save this courtyard, but he will help people learn about things here. He will come back with new ideas and help us save other streets and other homes."

Fang Ke had joined his wife, Zhang Yan, in Cambridge, Massachusetts. He was due to start soon at a World Bank course down in Washington and had come here for a few months to familiarize himself with the United States and brush up on his shaky English. The course was designed to train young professionals for work in the bank or back in their homelands. It was ideal for him and a chance to put his knowledge of China to practical use, perhaps in the future as someone assigned to fund a bank's urban redevelopment project back in China or another country.

When he came here, he thought of translating his book into English. But as he began to immerse himself in western academia, he set more modest goals for himself. Even though his book was marvelously sourced and footnoted, it was still a polemic tract compared to a western academic study. His book, he was realizing, had been an odd creation. It was supposed to be about architecture, but the outrageous destruction of architecture had led Fang Ke to analyze the cause of this, which he traced to Beijing's corrupt urban planning.

A few months later I got a copy of a paper that Fang Ke presented to a United Nations conference. It had the suitably obtuse title for a western academic paper: "Redevelopment of Historic Neighborhoods of Beijing in a Transitional Economy During

Rapid Urban Development Process." It was also much more detailed in analyzing the economic reasons behind the old city's destruction. Bit by bit, he was reworking his book in a western academic style, making his ideas accessible to people worldwide.

We spent an afternoon walking around Boston, but it wasn't quite the same as in China. Back there he had known the reason for every building's placement, size and shape. Here he was casting an eye at a foreign tradition, figuring out how the lessons learned here could be transferred back home.

"I want to be in China," he said as we rambled through the downtown. "It's not my dream to be here. This is a great place and I'm learning a lot, but it's not my home."

It was a feeling I had never experienced, but I had learned to understand it. It was common throughout China, whose culture and history are so strong that few really break free of its gravity. Like thousands of Chinese students before him, he'd discovered a Chinese grocery store in Boston, bought Chinese ingredients and cooked Chinese food every night. "I think that if you take a person out of their environment, they can't do as much," he said.

Was the same true of his work, I wondered. I couldn't help but draw comparisons between him and his intellectual predecessor, Professor Liang. Both were dedicated to saving the old city and both were supported by remarkable wives who shared their interests. China now was more stable than it was a few decades ago, and I knew that should he return to China, he wouldn't face the persecution that had wasted decades of Professor Liang's life before killing him.

Yet progress wasn't linear. Fang Ke and the home-owners who were suing the government would likely fail in their efforts to save Beijing. Realistically, the government was bent on destroying everything but a few small corners of the old town, turning them into tourist zones where buses could disgorge people for a stroll through the remaining *hutong*s and pick them up a few blocks later to take them to an authentic "old Beijing" restaurant—or maybe a KFC. Beijing was turning into a vanished capital, vanished at least in the sense that it was too late to preserve enough sections of the city so modern-day people could get a feel for China's old political and cultural order.

Now it was night and Fang Ke had to get home to cook dinner. We took the subway back to Cambridge and said good-bye. As he was leaving, I suddenly realized that I hadn't given him Messrs. Feng and Luo's samizdat book.

I handed it over and he cracked one of his trademark grins.

"They're still at it," he said as we shook hands and left.

3 TURNING THE WHEEL

Chen Zixiu traveled alone. It was late Thursday afternoon, and she avoided her neighbors' watchful eyes, slipping out of the house as it grew dark. It was cold, and she was prepared to sleep outside if necessary, bundled up in heavy padded clothes and corduroy shoes with thick cotton soles. She caught the 8 p.m. bus to Beijing and dozed fitfully, wondering what she'd do when she arrived ten hours later.

Her goal was simple: make her way to the city's gargantuan Tiananmen Square and protest the government's crackdown on Falun Gong, the exercise and spiritual movement that she rigorously followed. It had been over four months since the government had banned Falun Gong as an "evil cult," and during that time many people she knew had been detained for refusing to renounce it. Now the government had sentenced senior leaders of the group to years in prison. Ms. Chen decided that her voice had to be heard, so she joined the piecemeal flow of adherents who were making their way to the capital to protest the crackdown.

It was her first trip to Beijing, but she was sure she could find Tiananmen Square. What she needed was advice on how to avoid being caught ahead of time by police, who she'd heard had plugged the side streets leading there. She hit upon the idea of a park. She knew that public practice of Falun Gong was illegal, but in her hometown it was still possible to find Falun Gong practitioners in public parks if one got there very early. Her bus arrived in Beijing just after 4 a.m.—early enough, she figured, to find a few adherents. Picking up a shopping bag that she used to carry her personal belongings, Ms. Chen took a slow, creaky bus to Beijing's biggest park, the Temple of Heaven.

She got off the bus on the park's south side and made her way to the entrance. It was now almost 5 a.m. and the park was open. She paid the equivalent of 25 cents to enter—a lot of money for a retiree living on less than $100 a month. She glanced at a map and decided to head toward the Hall of Prayer for Good Harvests, a beautifully proportioned building that looked like an upside-down top. It was a major tourist attraction, and she figured that visiting it was harmless enough.

She started walking toward the hall, its azure roof peeking above the trees. She looked to her left and right, down rows of locust and scholar trees, where she hoped to see people sitting cross-legged in the initial meditation pose, or maybe starting Falun Gong's slow-motion exercises. But after fifteen minutes she had seen nothing but a few joggers and people practicing Chinese shadowboxing. She trudged forward.

It was bitterly cold, and the sun was a gray smudge on the horizon. She clapped her hands. If she could just find a few adherents, she'd be all right. They'd have a place to stay and could tell her the best way to get past the police checks and into Tiananmen Square.

"Where are you going, grandma?"

She slowly turned around. Two policemen were facing her.

"I'm going to see the temple."

"So early in the morning?" one of the officers said dubiously. He looked at her carefully: a short, stocky woman around sixty years of age, with a square face and roughly cut hair. Her looks, her clothes, her belongings in a shopping bag—all pegged her as a country bumpkin. The officers knew that peasants often came to town to see the sights, but few came alone at 5 a.m.

"Grandma, we have to ask you a question: do you practice Falun Gong?"

Ms. Chen hesitated. Falun Gong was banned, but she wasn't practicing it at that moment. Anyway, Master Li had said that they shouldn't lie; lying was a sin.

"Yes, I do," she said.

"Where are you from, grandma?" one of the policemen said.

"Shandong Province, Weifang City."

"Your ID, please."

She handed it to them. They looked it over for a minute and handed it back.

"Grandma, please follow us. Falun Gong practitioners aren't allowed in the parks."

She started to object, but one of the officers' face hardened. One on each side of her, they escorted her back to the south gate. The two officers accompanied her out of the park and then down a side street. A bus was parked on the right side. An officer opened the door and she climbed up. Inside were half a dozen other people, all from out of town like herself. She had found her fellow practitioners.

Four months earlier, Ms. Chen had been aroused from an almost militant lack of interest in politics. It was July 22, 1999, and a local official from the neighborhood party committee had told her to watch the evening news at seven, saying it would have an important announcement about Falun Gong. Up until then Ms. Chen had avoided the news or reading the newspaper. If the past few decades of China's twisting and turning politics had taught her anything, it was to avoid politics and keep as low a profile as possible. "Focus on your own life and stay out of politics," she used to tell her children. For most of her life that had worked. But this evening she turned on the news, curious to hear what it would say about her precious Falun Gong.

Ms. Chen used to say that Falun Gong was simply an exercise group, but this didn't do justice to the role it played in her life. Shortly after her employer, an auto-parts maker, had given her early retirement in 1997, Ms. Chen had been walking through a park in the early morning on her way to market. A group of a dozen neighbors were doing Falun Gong's calisthenics and invited her to join. She hesitated but on an impulse decided for the first time in her life to indulge herself.

Her life had spanned some of the most tumultuous decades in Chinese history, from civil war in the 1940s through the famines of the '50s, the insane utopianism of the 1960s and now, since the late '70s, economic reforms that had made people more prosperous but also demanded yet another 180-degree change in how Chinese lived and worked. She had raised two children almost alone after her husband died in an accident when she was twenty-five. Now economic reforms had left her with early retirement and little to show for her life but a minuscule pension and a tiny apartment with concrete floors. At fifty-seven, Ms. Chen was already considered old; there was nothing left for her to do except help out with her grandchildren. She needed a hobby, something to do with her life. She tried Falun Gong that morning in 1997 and never looked back.

Ms. Chen had always been active, but the new exercises made her feel younger, suppler, lither. Instead of burning herself out running one errand after the other, she was finally doing something for herself. She also liked the fact that the group advocated a strict moral path based on traditional Buddhist concepts of good works and tolerance. Having grown up during an era when religion was virtually illegal, Ms. Chen found the group's guideposts more relevant than the government's ever-changing ideology, which advocated selfless sacrifice but was widely ignored by corrupt officials and cynical citizens. Exercises that made her feel good and a moral compass for her life—the combination was irresistible.

She had a new routine. She'd get up at 5 a.m. and go to the park for ninety minutes of exercise. It was early, but this way younger practitioners would have time to get home and get ready for work. She spent the rest of the day as before: running errands and helping her children and grandchildren. After dinner she read the moralistic texts of Falun Gong founder Li Hongzhi, who preached ethics—summarized by the three principles of truth, benevolence and tolerance—as well as some idiosyncratic notions, such as the existence of extraterrestrial life. Sometimes members would meet in her living room to discuss texts. Other times she'd watch instructional videos of Mr. Li, whom she respectfully referred to as "Master Li." She owned his two main texts and four of his videos. She went to bed between nine and ten.

But as she sat on her sofa in front of the television, the government was saying that all of this was wrong. The announcer intoned that Falun Gong was an "evil cult" and that the government had decided to ban it.

"We must fully understand the serious consequences 'Falun Gong' will have on the physical and mental health of its practitioners. We must fully understand the utmost importance and urgency of dealing with the issues of 'Falun Gong,' " the announcer said, reading from an editorial that would appear in the next day's edition of *People's Daily,* the Communist Party's mouthpiece.

It didn't make any sense to Ms. Chen, and after the fifteen-minute broadcast she got up and walked to a neighbor's apartment two floors down. Like Ms. Chen, her neighbor had also been a practitioner and had also been at home to watch the broadcast. The seventy-year-old retiree opened the door, her face as distressed as Ms. Chen's. "What does it mean?" Ms. Chen asked. The two sat down and thought for a while. Ms. Chen was deeply depressed.

When Ms. Chen arrived at the park the next morning, most of the group was already there, standing around and discussing the news. Some of her friends said they had suspected that Falun Gong was in trouble because it had been criticized recently in the media for holding a demonstration that spring in Beijing. A couple who had worked in the government before retiring even whispered that some Falun Gong organizers in Beijing had already been detained.

"I can tell you what the newspapers today will say," one of the retired officials said to the group. "They'll repeat last night's announcement word for word. This has become a national issue, a big issue. I'm not coming back here until it blows over."

The group went through its exercises and finished up as usual around 6:30 a.m. Some walked over to a newsstand and picked up the morning papers. The retired official had been right. The papers all had the same article positioned in exactly the same spot on the front page. They all had the same headlines. Ms. Chen studied the article slowly.

> While handling and addressing the "Falun Gong" issue, we must pay attention to ensuring

social stability. Stability is the highest interest
of the country and the people. . . . Without stability, we can accomplish nothing.

For the first time in her life, Ms. Chen began to think hard
about a government policy. She hadn't suffered much during
the Cultural Revolution and during the reform era had concen-
trated on raising her family. But now she began to wonder about
the government. She'd heard rumblings that the group was in
trouble—that Falun Gong had protested in front of the government's offices in Beijing that spring—but how could they ban
Falun Gong without even consulting with practitioners? How
did they know it was so bad? So she took the first step that many
Chinese take when they disagree with the government: she
decided to ignore it.

Her skepticism was born of self-interest, not idealism, but it
grew strongly inside her. About a week after the ban was
announced, Ms. Chen and her friends were stopped by police,
who were waiting for them at the park. Falun Gong was illegal
and they couldn't practice it publicly anymore, they were told.
The group dispersed and went home. But many of them continued to meet, using Ms. Chen's tiny living room as their meeting
point. They didn't plot to overthrow the government or to
oppose its ban. Instead, they simply practiced their exercises and
read Master Li's texts.

Ms. Chen's group was located in about as typical a place in
China as one can imagine. They lived in Xu Family Hamlet in
Weifang, a small city of 600,000 in eastern China. A dusty maze
of poplar-lined dirt roads and bungalows surrounded by crumbling brown brick walls, the hamlet was a typical village being
swallowed up by its urban neighbor.

Weifang, too, was a fairly ordinary Chinese city, one of the seemingly endless number of half-million–population cities in China that are all but unknown to the outside world. Indeed, Weifang might be completely obscure were it not for its claim to be the birthplace of the kite and the location of an annual international kite festival. Otherwise the town was an unremarkable collection of newly built white-tiled buildings, home to several state-run factories and a small private sector. Agriculture still played a big role, and Ms. Chen's hamlet sat right between the cornfields of the North China Plain and Weifang's crowded streets.

By August some people from Weifang had gone a step further than Ms. Chen, traveling to Beijing to protest. They joined others from across China and went to Tiananmen Square in the center of the city to perform their calisthenics publicly, hoping to demonstrate that theirs was an inward-looking group with no interest in politics. Facing the Forbidden City, where Chinese emperors had ruled their vast empire for centuries, they sat cross-legged and raised their arms up over their heads—the starting pose for their exercises. Closer to home in Weifang, practitioners had even organized a sit-down strike in front of the local Communist Party headquarters, likewise conducting exercises in defiance of the ban.

The group's demands might have been simple—an end to the prohibition on Falun Gong—but to a government that brooks no opposition, it was a challenge. Plainclothes and uniformed police quickly descended on the small, scattered protests in Beijing and in provincial cities like Weifang. Batons flew. Thousands were arrested, interrogated and most sent back home with a stern warning.

Ms. Chen had stayed out of the protests, quietly practicing at home with her friends. She couldn't imagine participating in such daring protests, although she was secretly proud that her fellow-practitioners believed in themselves enough to stand up for their rights.

But then, in late autumn, the government ratcheted up the pressure again. First came a Supreme Court decision in early October announcing that existing criminal laws could be used to punish cults. Then came a *People's Daily* article calling Falun Gong a cult. The parliament gave the impending crackdown a legal veneer in late October by passing a "decision" that banned cults. Finally, the Supreme Court ordered lower-level courts not to accept cases filed by Falun Gong adherents.

All this had been preceded by the arrest of all major Falun Gong organizers—people who had served as liaisons between practitioners like Ms. Chen and Master Li, who had emigrated to the United States in 1998. These organizers had distributed Master Li's essays to his followers and did odd jobs like reserve space in the parks for the practitioners. Now the government intended to strike some terror into the Ms. Chens of the world. Like the ban in July that Ms. Chen had seen on television, the government blanketed the country with announcements of the indictments and convictions. Some of the sentences were for up to twelve years in labor camps.

Ms. Chen was stunned. She hadn't known any of the people involved, but the idea that a person would spend a decade or more in a labor camp for practicing Falun Gong angered her. For several months she'd refrained from taking any direct part in the protests, but now she changed her mind, heading off to Beijing to protest, only to be arrested in the Temple of Heaven Park.

Zhang Xueling was at home with her son when the call came from the neighborhood committee. Her mother, Ms. Chen, had been detained in Beijing, the caller on the line said, and Ms.

Zhang was asked to accompany local officials to the capital to bail out her mother. Ms. Zhang immediately agreed to go.

Falun Gong, she thought bitterly. This troublesome organization had been the bane of her family's existence for the past few months. Now, because of it, her mother was in jail and she had to go all the way to Beijing to get her released. It would cost money and none of them had much. Ms. Zhang's husband was a carpenter, and she spent most of her time at home raising her son, working occasionally as a matchmaker.

She sat down to count the money in her purse and collect her thoughts. Falun Gong had started out well enough, Ms. Zhang conceded. Her mother had been, well, cantankerous when she had begun practicing Falun Gong a couple of years earlier. She'd sacrificed much to raise her and her brother and was critical of everyone. It was hard to talk to her without getting into some petty argument.

She remembered how she and her brother had supported her mother's decision to start Falun Gong exercises. Her mother had never been a superstitious or religious person, but the exercises seemed to do her good. And the message of tolerance and doing good works seemed to give her a new outlook.

"She had a bad temper," Ms. Zhang said out loud with a smile. "But then she became a better person."

Still, Ms. Zhang couldn't understand why her mother insisted on continuing with Falun Gong after it had been banned. You could disagree with the government, Ms. Zhang said to herself, but you had to face facts. And the facts were that the government was treating this ban on Falun Gong seriously. Everyone knew that police had searched the homes of people who had led the exercises before the ban. Practicing it was a big risk. She could see that her mother might want to continue practicing alone at home, but inviting friends over seemed to be asking for trouble. And now going to Beijing to protest! What had possessed her mother to do that? An old lady taking a bus to the capital and getting arrested. Maybe this was an evil cult after all, Ms. Zhang thought to herself.

She walked over to the Chengguan Street Committee offices. The street committee is the lowest level in the mighty Communist Party's system of control, one that starts with a few top men in Beijing and spreads down through its 55 million members to every neighborhood. Ms. Zhang had little contact with her street committee—part Communist Party cell, part social services office and part neighborhood watch. All Ms. Zhang could ever remember the committee doing was organizing occasional "hygiene" campaigns to sweep out the streets. Most of their work involved monitoring women of childbearing age to make sure they had only one child. Ms. Zhang was only thirty-two years old but had a six-year-old son, and so she got only occasional visits from the committee.

She walked in and was introduced to three officials from the Weifang City government's Public Security Bureau. They got into a government car, a Volkswagen Santana, and drove to Beijing. After seven hours, they arrived at the Weifang municipal government's Beijing representative office. It was a lobbying-bureau-cum-dormitory of the sort that scores of Chinese cities and provinces set up in Beijing to house local officials visiting the capital. Ms. Chen was being held there, locked in a dormitory room.

Ms. Zhang paid a $60 fine—a month's wages—and her mother was released. The two broke into tears, but Ms. Zhang couldn't resist a mild rebuke.

"Ma," she said. "How could you do this? Coming to Beijing all the way alone? Please come home and don't do this anymore."

Her mother pursed her lips and didn't answer.

The two were escorted back to Weifang in a police car. The whole way back the officials glared at Ms. Chen, occasionally saying how embarrassing the event had been for them.

Responsibility for Ms. Chen was given to the Chengguan Street Committee. It was the head of the local street committee who had told Ms. Chen to watch the evening news in July—a tip that she was doing something dangerous and ought to take care. They felt they'd warned her, but she'd disobeyed and gotten them all into trouble. Now Ms. Chen was under their control.

The women were told that Ms. Chen couldn't be allowed off without further punishment. The attempted protest had hurt Weifang's standing in the capital. Before she could go home, Ms. Chen would have to serve a two-week prison sentence, a form of administrative detention that authorities can mete out at their will. To make sure that everyone in the neighborhood got the message, Ms. Chen would be held in the neighborhood committee office, which was just a few rooms on the ground floor of an apartment building. One of the rooms was converted into a small jail, and Ms. Chen was to be held there for two weeks. She was also barred from practicing Falun Gong or reading Master Li's books. Ms. Zhang had to pay another $45 for her mother's room and board.

On January 3, Ms. Chen celebrated her fifty-eighth birthday in jail. Despite being under day-and-night observation, she was in good spirits. Ms. Zhang went to see her and began to gain renewed respect for her mother.

"She knew she was right," Ms. Zhang said. "All she wanted was the government not to make a criminal out of her because she knew she wasn't a criminal."

In mid-January, Ms. Chen was released but was still watched carefully by the street committee, which paid her regular visits and confiscated her Falun Gong books and videos.

The new year, however, marked an odd confluence of western and eastern millennialism. On the western calendar, the new year was 2000, which many people in China saw as particularly auspicious. The upcoming Lunar New Year, which fell on February 4, was also seen as especially lucky. It marked the start of the year of the dragon, the mightiest animal in the Chinese zodiac. The year 2000, the year of the dragon; this coincidence seemed to herald the dawning of a new age. A mini–baby boom was in the making as couples wanted their child to be born in this doubly lucky year. Politicians talked of the new age being China's. A sense of a new beginning swept the land.

Even China's avowedly atheist rulers got into the act. They staged a quasi-religious ceremony to mark the new millennium, constructing a "Century Altar" in Beijing that featured a giant needle and a gargantuan incense burner that was lit by President Jiang Zemin at midnight, December 31, 1999.

Galvanized by this millennarian Zeitgeist, hundreds of Falun Gong protesters converged on the capital in late January 2000. Arriving in the weeks ahead of the Lunar New Year holiday, they wanted to protest the ban on their group, hoping that the auspicious date would lend luck to their cause. Despite a massive police presence, scores arrived on the square each day to start their exercise routine. Before they got started, police would swoop down on them, truncheons flying, dragging the bloodied people into waiting vans. The scenes were caught on film by foreign journalists and spread around the world. They made their way through the Internet and word of mouth back to people like Ms. Chen.

For Ms. Chen this was another act of barbarism that she couldn't ignore. Like Falun Gong adherents around China, she didn't feel cowed; she felt outraged. Over a meal during the two-week New Year's celebration, she and her daughter talked.

"The government doesn't understand that we are good people, ordinary people," she said. "We aren't against the government. Falun Gong is good for China."

Ms. Zhang sighed.

"Mom," she said. "Be more realistic. People know that you're still following Master Li. You'll only bring trouble on all of us if you keep this up."

But again Ms. Chen went silent, not wanting to get into an argument with her daughter.

Then, on February 16, as the New Year's holiday was ending, Ms. Chen's doorbell rang. It was the local party district chief, a high-ranking official who was responsible for the political behavior of the 50,000 people in his district. With him were half a dozen local officials, including representatives from the Public Security Bureau and the lady from the neighborhood committee who'd warned her before to quit Falun Gong.

Ms. Chen let the cadres in, ushering the chief and his deputies to the most comfortable place to sit, the couch. The others sat on kitchen chairs. Ms. Chen stood awkwardly and offered them tea. They declined. The chief asked her to sit down, and she found a stool under the kitchen table, dragged it out and sat across from him, like a naughty child facing a school discipline board.

"Chen Zixiu," the chief said, using her full name and dispensing with more familiar forms of address. She stiffened. "We've all heard about the protests in Beijing. Our government is very tolerant of such things. Protests are allowed in the constitution, we all know that.

"Look at how you were treated," the secretary continued. "It was embarrassing to us and cost us a good deal of money, but all that happened after you went to Beijing is that you were detained and sent home. Nothing more. You made your point and let's leave it at that, okay? The government does not want any more protests. The National People's Congress [China's parliament, which meets once a year] is going to meet soon and we aren't going to disrupt that meeting with protests. My job is to make sure that people understand that."

Ms. Chen sat quietly and dutifully followed each word in the speech, which the chief had already given to several other adherents. She knew this was important: a personal warning from the party chief. The chief continued. Please, he said to Ms. Chen, don't embarrass your hometown. Be a good citizen. No one likes what's happening, but don't make a scene. You know how things are.

The party chief had stopped talking. The lady from the street committee gave her a big smile and added, "We're all one big family. Let's not upset things."

There was silence again. It was Ms. Chen's turn. Now she was supposed to say something reasonable and agree with them. The party chief would smile, everyone would be relieved and they'd go to the next Falun Gong adherent and make a similar speech. It would have lasted ten minutes and no one would know if she practiced Falun Gong at home.

But Falun Gong teaches something that is common among evangelical religions: that it's wrong not to proclaim one's faith—that it's false to practice in private and deny one's belief in public. Despite the past eight months of government propaganda and her experience in Beijing, Ms. Chen was still a believer. Her answer was simple.

"I won't guarantee to anyone that I won't go somewhere. I have the right to go where I please."

There was an awkward silence. The district chief looked

down, his eyes angry. He'd heard this before from these damned Falun Gong fanatics. He left the next part to his aide, who stood up so he could look down on Ms. Chen.

"So far, the government has treated Falun Gong practitioners like wayward children. But discipline can involve harshness. Think about what your attitude means," he said. The officials quickly got up and filed out of her room.

Ms. Chen sat there and pondered her future. A few hours later she left for her second trip to Beijing.

Falun Gong was part of a remarkable religious rebirth that has swept through China since the late 1970s. While outsiders have often focused on the economic reforms that have transformed China from a communist to a largely capitalist country, the collapse of communism as a religion set forth a profound search for meaning, obvious in the arts, such as the novels of Nobel Prize–winning author Gao Xingjian and on a popular level in the rise of dozens of new religions and the rebirth of older, established ones.

Defining what is a religion, especially in China, can be a tricky business. Unlike western religions, which often try to sharply differentiate themselves from each other, Chinese belief systems happily overlap, drawing on ancestor worship, popular beliefs in spirits, the indigenous religion of Taoism and the ideas of worldwide religions like Buddhism. But after it took power in 1949, the Communist Party imposed a Soviet-style religious bureaucracy over this cacophony of beliefs, legalizing only five narrowly defined religions—Buddhism, Catholicism, Islam, Protestantism and Taoism. The myriad folk religions that over the millennia have risen and fallen like waves of faith across the country were either lumped under Taoism or banned as "feudal superstition." In the most famous case, the government spent years trying to wipe out Yiguandao, or Way of Basic Unity, a syncretic religion that draws heavily from Taoism and also tries to meld in ideas from Islam and Christianity. Thousands of Yiguandao believers were sent to labor camps in the 1950s and forced to confess publicly that the practices were meant to deceive the populace. The group was also charged with treason—complicity with Japanese occupiers during the war—and within a few years was largely destroyed on mainland China.

But about thirty years after taking power, the government all but admitted that Marxism was a useless ideology. It adopted capitalist-style reforms and discouraged leaders from setting up personality cults, such as the one that had centered around the party's totalitarian leader, Chairman Mao Zedong. In effect, it told the Chinese that everything that the totalitarian state had preached—the party leader as god, the primacy of socialism and the goal of communism—was wrong. Predictably, a spiritual crisis ensued. Many turned to the five official religions, which boomed. Temples, mosques and churches were rebuilt, while new monks, nuns, imams and priests were ordained.

But the big religions didn't satisfy everyone's spiritual craving. For years they had been humiliated, their buildings desecrated and their teachings banned. That seemed to break their hold over many in society—who could remain in awe of a god who couldn't protect his own temple from destruction? In addition, the legal places of worship had become unfamiliar. Who knew what went on in a church or a Taoist temple when discussion of them had been taboo for decades and the older generation not allowed to introduce religious practices to the young? Some people also felt that the established religions had discredited themselves by their sometimes toadying association with the authorities. Despite all the humiliations and destruction, their leaders were men who regularly paid their respects to the Communist Party, pretending—or perhaps genuinely believing—that China had religious freedom.

Into the breach stepped a spiritual, slightly mystical branch of Chinese medicine known as "qigong." The term itself is relatively new, dating back only to the 1950s as a catch-all phrase for various exercises whose origin goes back centuries. These exercises try to regulate "qi," a concept in Chinese medicine that is hard to translate but is the equivalent of a life force or energy. Qi travels through the body along channels that, for example, an acupuncturist taps into and regulates by inserting needles into the skin. Qigong—the second part of the word, "gong," means "discipline" or "exercise"—is a way of adjusting one's flow of qi through controlled breathing, meditation and slow-motion calisthenics.

Before the communist takeover in 1949, these exercises had a strong spiritual component. Both Taoism and Buddhism had their own versions of qigong, and they were accepted parts of the religious healing tradition—a bridge to Chinese medicine. Meditation was crucial to the exercises, with the practitioner not just healing his body but his mind as well. But the communists' rise to power put qigong in conflict with the authorities' suspicion of all things spiritual and their decision that the only accepted religions in society were the five authorized ones. That left no room for traditional qigong. What to do? The answer was to make qigong "scientific."

Science may seem an odd champion for something as spiritual as qigong, but it was important because China's revolution, which began in 1911 with the overthrow of the emperor, has had as its goal "science" and "democracy," both of which were seen as the keys to a strong, powerful country. Although the communists didn't give China democracy, they did elevate science to an almost cultlike status—much as in the Soviet Union. The party, for example, practices "scientific Marxism"—its policies are therefore not the whims of a gerontocracy but rooted in eternal, provable truths.

Unscientific things, by contrast, are condemned to eternal damnation. In the communist theology, that means they are labeled "superstition" or "feudal superstition." Religion in general is frowned upon, although the five major religions are accepted as temporary necessities. Other forms of religious expression, however, are "superstitious." Shamanism, for example, has had a long history in China, but it and any sort of ecstatic or mystical practice is now taboo because it is not "scientific."

In an effort to avoid the "unscientific" label, qigong's meditative side was downplayed. Instead, it was heralded as a form of physical therapy supervised by doctors. There was less quiet sitting, and qigong's goals were limited to good health. In addition, scientists conducted experiments that purported to show that its regimen of quiet breathing and meditation helped cure chronic problems, such as respiratory or digestive ailments—conclusions not too different from western studies on the benefit of meditation and relaxation in fighting illness.

Research stopped when the Cultural Revolution was launched in 1966 and qigong went into hibernation. Then, as China emerged from totalitarianism, qigong also revived, this time as a national fad. By the early 1990s, qigong was so popular that people talked of a "qigong craze." Qigong was being practiced in parks and outside apartment buildings. It was so widely accepted that China's communist leaders were said to use it to improve their health.

Many people practiced qigong according to traditional precepts, using it as a quiet, meditative form of exercise that could improve one's energy. But it really caught on when it claimed to promote supernatural powers. Practitioners said they could read words that were hidden—for example, written on paper sealed in an envelope. Other claims included being able to throw needles so fast and so hard that they could penetrate glass, the ability to conduct electricity through one's body or to withstand a blow to the head with a hammer. Military magazines featured reports on qigong, although it's not clear which of these feats the People's Liberation Army figured could help it win a war.

Academics, such as Jian Xu of the University of Iowa, saw in the claims an effort by qigong to win back some of its other-worldly allure. But now, instead of a subtle form of meditation aimed at immortality, qigong had morphed into what he called a "a special, high-powered technology of the self, situated between science and mysticism."

The veneer of scientific respectability—and government control—was given by an organization called the China Qigong Scientific Research Association, which was supposed to register all qigong groups and oversee their "scientific" efforts at improving health through exercise.

That label freed qigong from having to worry about government restrictions on organized religion. Established religions were only allowed to meet in their mosques, temples or churches, and were strictly banned from proselytizing. But qigong was—officially, at least—just an exercise regime. That meant participants could hold meetings in public parks and hand out promotional material to passersby on the street. And, free from the stigma of being a religion, Communist Party members, who are supposed to be atheist, could practice qigong without fear of party censure. Officially, it was simply a branch of medicine that could help cure illness.

◆   ◆   ◆

Millions of Chinese found a deeper meaning in qigong: a rare chance for introspection. One such person was Chen Shouliang, a physicist at Beijing University. In 1984, when he was fifty-three years old, Professor Chen (no relation to Ms. Chen, the Falun Gong practitioner) discovered a cancerous tumor in his neck. Surgery was performed, but Professor Chen was weak and had to give up his promising career as an administrator at the university.

Some years earlier, friends of Professor Chen introduced him to a qigong guru named Zhao Guang, a modest man who lived like a hermit in a tiny, spartan apartment, his only luxury an impressive collection of the Chinese classics. Mr. Zhao had tried to interest Mr. Chen in qigong, but the professor had always been too busy. He had classes to teach and a promising future as a university administrator.

Then, one day in February 1984, they bumped into each other on White Stone Bridge Road. Now the street is a crowded six-lane thoroughfare blanketed with computer shops, but back then it was a narrow, tree-lined road in Beijing's university district. The meeting was an encounter of a mystic, revelatory nature that changed Professor Chen's life and helped solidify qigong's position as an accepted part of Chinese society for the next fifteen years.

Professor Chen was embarrassed when he saw Mr. Zhao. He hadn't taken up Mr. Zhao on his earlier offer and now felt foolish. He badly wanted to learn qigong but didn't want to appear insulting, only interested now that he was ill. But before he could voice his feelings, Mr. Zhao spoke.

"You've got cancer. Now do you have time?"

Professor Chen was surprised. The old master had read his thoughts; he knew that he wanted to learn qigong.

"I do, master. Let me know when it is convenient to come by for a lesson."

"No need," Mr. Zhao said. "I'll teach you here on the street corner, in five minutes."

Mr. Zhao taught him three sentences—mantras, really: Relax your whole body. Breathe calmly and regularly. Keep your thoughts in your belly. The latter was tough. It meant not thinking too much, voiding one's mind. How to do it, Professor Chen asked. Referring to the Buddhist Wheel of Law, which rolls from man to man, place to place, age to age, Mr. Zhao told him: "Think of the Dharma Wheel spinning in your belly. Visualize it turning, overcoming everything else. This will keep your mind off other things."

Mr. Zhao instructed him to do this twenty to thirty minutes twice a day and return a few weeks later for further instruction. Professor Chen did as he was told and went back to Mr. Zhao, who corrected a few errors in his breathing technique. If he kept this up for a hundred days, Mr. Zhao said, Professor Chen would become an adept. One hundred days later he returned to Mr. Zhao, who pronounced him no longer a beginner. He was now an adept, a true practitioner, and over time he started to spread qigong by teaching others.

Professor Chen became more than an enthusiast. As a scientist, he was interested in knowing how qigong worked, so he started conducting studies, hoping to prove that supernatural powers were possible. He surveyed an elementary school class of eight-year-olds, for example, and found that a third could read letters sealed in an envelope. With age, he theorized, we lose our ability to know things intuitively. Qigong, he concluded, helps us regain our youthful innocence. He published his findings in a journal and became a mini-celebrity, often interviewed in the Chinese media. It probably wasn't good science—the study was never accepted for publication at a major international journal and its results have never been duplicated—but it fit perfectly into the 1980s, a period when China was breaking from its totalitarian past and anything seemed possible, even supernatural powers.

His role was important to qigong's reemergence. Some critics in the Communist Party were beginning to voice their disapproval of qigong, saying it was unscientific and, worse, hinting that it was a pseudo-religion. Professor Chen, with his Beijing University pedigree, helped to deflect these criticisms, lending the imprimatur of scientific respectability to the ersatz religion.

I first met Professor Chen in 1994, a time when the "qigong craze" was at its peak. Over several long summer afternoons on the Beijing University campus, Professor Chen gave me his thoughts on qigong's new popularity. Back then, Falun Gong was just getting started and neither of us was aware of it. Instead, it was qigong's claimed supernatural abilities that interested us.

Professor Chen had the air of an amiable conspiracy theorist, the sort of person who refers to articles in obscure journals and magazines in faraway lands as proof of his idea. He was a small man, with short silver hair and a sharp wit, often making jokes at his own expense. But he also had a naïve earnestness about supernatural powers. Once, for example, he asked me if I'd heard of David Copperfield, whom he greatly admired. The CIA was doing research into supernatural powers, he said, as had the KGB before the Soviet Union fell. He mentioned this as something extremely significant, as though the fall of the Soviet Union was somehow a premeditated blow against qigong research. He reminded me of East Bloc scientists who had been cut off from the outside world for so long and whose thinking was so politicized that they could no longer differentiate between hard fact and intuitive conjecture.

His trump card was a dog-eared copy of his study of elementary school students, which he brought out when I mentioned skepticism about his claims.

"Some people just don't want to believe," he said. "But it's all scientifically proven that qigong can give us superhuman abilities."

Not everyone was convinced. A professor from the Chinese Academy of Sciences wrote a book called *Human Supernatural Abilities and Qigong* that tried to debunk some of the more dubious claims of miracles being ascribed to qigong. Indeed, even Professor Chen conceded that he couldn't explain why qigong gave rise to miraculous powers, only that they existed. His only explanation was: "If we can't explain it, it doesn't mean it's nonsense. It's just that science can't explain it."

It was a rationale that helps explain qigong's popularity. Since the nineteenth century, Chinese people have worried that modernization wouldn't allow them to preserve anything from their ancient culture, which they claim goes back five thousand years. The insistence on science—a western invention—as the answer to all questions seemed to threaten the essence of Chinese culture. Did China have anything of value to offer the modern world? Especially in the 1980s and '90s, with China's brand of communism junked in favor of western market economics, many Chinese thinkers worried that China had become nothing more than an outpost of western civilization. Qigong was something that could be of lasting value, something that could even give people superhuman powers, a feat western science couldn't match. To the skeptic who said that qigong's claims weren't provable scientifically, qigong defenders like Professor Chen turned the tables, saying that the West's vaunted science wasn't developed enough to explain qigong.

That nationalistic streak appealed to China's leaders, who

have been eager to wrap themselves in patriotism and national-ism as a way to legitimize their rule. Some leaders were rumored to practice qigong, and qigong organizations received high-level backing.

But qigong was a double-edged sword. Its existence was an admission that Marxism—a western invention, after all—couldn't satisfy China's spiritual needs. The party began to recognize this threat, which was stated explicitly in a popular novel that pitted a qigong master against a party cadre. The author, Ke Yunlu, wrote in 1994 in *The Great Qigong Masters* that just as qigong requires that science books be rewritten, it also requires that political theories be rewritten. His protagonist displays his fan-tastic powers to a local Communist Party leader, but the leader is blind to them and organizes a witch hunt against "reactionary" thinking. The message is clear: the party can't be trusted and will only try to destroy qigong.

The novel was prescient, because the party was indeed dis-trustful of qigong. One reason is that qigong is essentially a pri-vate exercise. Formal religions center on temples, churches and mosques, which the government has been able to control by requiring all places of worship to register with the government and be run by officials loyal to the state. Qigong, however, is focused inwardly—outside the government's control. Yet it is often performed publicly in groups. To a government that is used to controlling all aspects of public life, this is perplexing: qigong practitioners are in public and doing something en masse, so by rights they should be formed in an organization and this organi-zation should in some way be run by the government. But what they are doing together is meditating, an inner discipline that the party can't monitor.

The result was an uneasy standoff through the rest of the 1990s. The government kept trying to organize and control qigong groups, but they kept mutating and expanding, ignoring the government and winning millions of converts.

Falun Gong was the next logical step in qigong's development. While many people continued to practice traditional qigong, using it as a meditation and healing art, more organized groups had been forming since the early 1990s. Led by charismatic leaders, they began distributing texts to adherents. The texts usually contained descriptions of the exercises, but they also contained the moral precepts of the qigong master.

Li Hongzhi formed Falun Gong in 1992 and registered his group the same year with the research association. Master Li's background is unclear, but according to the hagiographic accounts put out by Falun Gong, he was a former government grain clerk, a simple person who achieved enlightenment in an unknown fashion. Like other qigong masters, Master Li wrote down his thoughts, but they were far more sophisticated and complete than earlier efforts at writing texts. While other masters wrote down a few basic moral precepts to go with their exercises, Master Li's two main books, *China Falun Gong* and *Turning the Dharma Wheel*, described a cosmology of heavens and hells, spirits and devils. It was not as complex as the older, better-developed theologies of Buddhism or Taoism, but compared to competing qigong groups, it was a breakthrough: a coherent system of religious thought tailor-made for modern-day Chinese.

While firmly stating that Falun Gong was not a religion, Master Li drew on traditional religions for terminology and symbols. The term "Falun" means Dharma Wheel, or Wheel of Law, the traditional Buddhist symbol of the immutable forces in the world. It was also the same wheel that Professor Chen's guru told him to imagine spinning in his body. It is a well-known symbol of the religion, seen in statues, frescoes or Tibetan prayer wheels—in other words, an established part of Chinese cosmology. Falun Gong's sign is a wheel, a circle made up of a central, counterclockwise-pointing swastika, a traditional Buddhist symbol whose mirror-image was appropriated by the Nazis for their pseudo-religion. The Falun Gong swastika is surrounded by four smaller swastikas and four small yin-yang, or t'ai chi, symbols, a traditional Taoist sign.

At first Falun Gong emphasized its health benefits. Like other qigong groups, Falun Gong claimed that regular practice could maintain good health and even heal serious illnesses. Falun Gong Web sites abroad still carry testimonials of people who were healed by its energy-building exercises. That remains an important claim, with some adherents believing—like Christian Scientists—that medical care is unnecessary.

But over time, the philosophical teachings of Truth, Goodness and Forbearance took on more importance. These three principles require people to live upright lives, to not lie and to follow heterosexual, monogamous lives. Homosexuality is dealt with in only one of Master Li's teachings, but he sharply criticizes it, a stance that critics abroad have used to show Falun Gong's intolerant nature. That isolated reference to homosexuality has now been all but abandoned by the group, which does not feature the speech on its main Web sites. Overall, however, the morality remains traditional, family-oriented—what University of Montreal scholar David Ownby calls "popular fundamentalism," or a return to moral values that many Chinese feel have been lost in the rush to modernization.

Master Li's works also preach exclusivity: either you are with us or you are condemned to hell. To me, this was one of the most unappealing sides to Falun Gong, although I recognized in it the same view found in most major religions. Again, the fundamentalist label seemed appropriate. This was a religion trying to overturn the moneylenders' tables in the temple; it wasn't exactly a feel-good religion.

Interestingly—and here Master Li was in tune with his audience—Falun Gong stresses that it is compatible with science. Indeed, like other qigongs, Falun Gong positions itself as a kind of Über-science, something that is modern but even better than modern. His writings refer to extraterrestrial life and the cosmos, but also of the qigong practitioner's ability to surpass these truths. This was probably one of the reasons why Falun Gong appealed so much to Chinese who grew up in mainland China. The group now has branches in most western countries and throughout the Chinese-speaking world, but its adherents remain overwhelmingly Chinese who grew up in communist China, with its environment of stunted major religions and the elevation of science to a pseudoreligion.

In his writings Master Li emphasized that his teachings simply reveal eternal truths that have been known since time immemorial but which have become corrupted over time. He does not claim to be a messiah or god, only a wise teacher who has seen the light. The group also has no formal religious practice typical of organized religion, such as meeting in a special building, lighting incense or candles or worshiping a figure or book.

It was, however, very well organized. Like a modern corporation, its hierarchy was simple but clearly defined. At the top was Master Li, who gave lectures in China and abroad at conferences. His writings were transmitted via book and Internet, with computer-literate members downloading them from official Falun Gong Web sites and printing them out for those without computers. In China before the 1999 ban each of the country's thirty provinces had an "association" and below them were the thousands of individual exercise groups, each headed by a locally agreed-upon coordinator who arranged the early-morning exercise sessions.

It was this structure that so scared authorities. Falun Gong was banned in 1999 after 10,000 believers protested in front of the government's compound, demanding that the group be recognized as a legitimate organization. Leaders learned that Falun Gong had millions of adherents—one television station referred to 100 million. Although that number was certainly a huge exaggeration, it was clear that the group was as popular as any of the mainstream religions. Shocked, the party banned it and started detaining its leaders and anyone who wouldn't renounce it.

The meeting lasted just five minutes and Brother Li was uncharacteristically nervous. "Here," he said, pulling out a big brown envelope. "Would this be of any use to you?" He looked around and motioned for me to open it.

We were sitting on a park bench in the middle of February, both of us freezing and eager to get going. It was late afternoon and we felt vulnerable, as if the barren birch and scholar trees were watching us. I opened the envelope and pulled out a letter. It was written in pencil on fourteen sheets of tissuelike exercise paper that Chinese students use to write essays. The handwriting was clear and only slightly cursive, the work of an educated woman who had sat down and thought carefully before setting her ideas down in writing.

I skimmed through it, the thin pages snapping in the winter wind. It was a detailed account of a woman's death, with the writer and others apparently present during the woman's interrogation, beating and death.

"May I keep these for a few days?" I asked Brother Li.

He nodded and got up.

"Meet me back here in three days. Make sure you're not being followed," he said in a laconic drawl, barely opening his mouth as he stared into the distance. Then he walked away toward his bicycle.

I'd come to know Li Guoqiang in late 1999 through mutual friends. He was a forty-three-year-old accountant who had worked in a textile mill until losing his job. His transgression was that he had refused to renounce his belief in Falun Gong after it was banned in July 1999. Determined to crush Falun Gong, the government had made belief in it a firing offense. Companies were instructed to purge their ranks of Falun Gong adherents, with state-owned companies ordered to report on employees they suspected had affiliations with the group. He didn't hesitate when asked if he was still a member: he admitted to it and spared his boss the embarrassment of firing him by quitting.

I met him shortly after he lost his job. He was one of the friendliest people I've met, with a ready grin and a slightly shaggy mop of hair that attested to his otherworldly concerns. He had a steady dependability about him that led his friends to give him the nickname of Li Ge, or Brother Li, which could more literally be translated as "Elder Brother Li."

Interested in learning more about Falun Gong, I soon started spending quite a bit of time with Brother Li. Every time we wanted to meet, the drill was the same. I'd go to a pay phone and call him on his beeper. He'd return my call about half an hour later to the pay phone, and we'd make an appointment. It was a time-consuming way to meet, but our home, office and cell phones were bugged, so we had to communicate by public pay phones. The half-hour wait was necessary because he was usually at home when I called and had to go out and find a pay phone. Not unreasonably, he figured that the pay phones near his home were bugged, too, so he would ride his bike to another neighborhood and call me from there.

These security precautions might seem unusual, but they were instantly grasped by ordinary Chinese, such as Falun Gong adherents. Unlike Mr. Ma's peasants, whose efforts to challenge the government were fundamentally legal, Falun Gong had been declared illegal, and there was no question that the government was out to destroy it. In routine life one rarely came across undercover police or agents, yet only a fool didn't know of their existence and would instinctively not trust one's home phone or cell phones.

Initially, such concerns were minimal. In the months after the group was banned in July 1999, the government contented itself with arresting key organizers and leaders, believing that this would suffice to crush the group. It was a reasonable assumption. Most dissident groups, usually made up of intellectuals who wanted democracy and freedom of speech, were easily broken by detaining a few dozen ringleaders.

Falun Gong, however, wasn't like these groups. It was made up of believers in a religious idea—the concept of salvation and immortality—not a mere political idea. Rational theories could be countered with other rational ideas, such as "I like democracy, but I like labor camps less. Therefore, I'll defer my plans for democracy until conditions are riper and meanwhile stay out of prison." Although millions of casual Falun Gong practitioners came to similar conclusions—"I'll practice quietly at home, I won't demand that the ban on my group be repealed"—tens of thousands were like Brother Li: fervent believers who thought that they had a right, even a duty, to stand up for their beliefs. The government had failed to stem this wave of opposition by arresting the group's formal leaders. Now it was arresting grassroots organizers, making our meetings hard to arrange.

I later got to know Brother Li quite well, but our meetings were at first businesslike. I was a reporter who was covering the crackdown on Falun Gong and the resulting demonstrations. He was a Falun Gong activist who had good contacts with the group's underground structure. We'd discuss ways that I could meet activists who were flooding into Beijing for daily protests against the ban. He'd help arrange meetings but would never be present at them.

When I met Brother Li again three days later, I had photocopied the letters and asked him what he intended to do with the originals.

"Mail them to the government," he said matter-of-factly, as if that was a logical thing to do.

Wouldn't the person in the letter get arrested, and wasn't it a bit naïve—that a complaint letter would cause the government to reform itself?

Brother Li shrugged.

"I'm sending a copy to our fellow practitioners in Hong Kong to keep them on file, but what else should we do with the letters? We have to petition the government to change. Do we have another choice?"

We departed and I had more time to read through the letters. I soon decided I had to meet the people described in them. I'd seen accounts detailing police abuse but rarely with enough detail to track down the person and others familiar with the case. But here were names and addresses, all laid out clearly.

My name is Jin Hua. I am 22 years of age. I live in Weicheng District of Weifang City. I am a Falun Gong practitioner. A practitioner was beaten to death this February, and most of the other witnesses under illegal arrest at that time were transferred (elsewhere), or might even be killed, too. In order to prove these things truly happened in the Chengguan Neighborhood Committee training class, including illegal detainment and beating of people, I now set forth what I experienced as a written document, in hopes it can raise the attention of related authorities so that they can punish the evil and the corrupt and stop this from happening again.

I got in touch with relatives and friends of the woman whose death the letter described. Her name was Chen Zixiu, the fifty-eight-year-old grandmother who hadn't heeded the party chief and had returned to Beijing to protest.

Ms. Zhang felt like an unfilial daughter. When her mother had begun to struggle for Falun Gong, she'd been against it, feeling that her old mother was ignorant and backward, wasting her time defending a worthless religion. It's not that she didn't concede that Falun Gong had helped her mother; it had improved her health and temper. But Ms. Zhang was too busy for Falun Gong; she was thirty-two years old, a private entrepreneur and the mother of a rambunctious six-year-old. She had worked in a government-run factory but for the past few years had been a matchmaker, a profession that had been banned by the communists but was now back in favor as a harmless relic of China's past. Plump, with short-cropped hair and a no-nonsense air, she spoke in an equally straightforward manner, only sometimes indulging in imprecisions like "that whaddya-call-it" and "that thingamajig."

Now she regretted having been so harsh to her mother. If she'd been more understanding, she kept telling herself, her mother might be alive. It was a burden that was sometimes crushing, mitigated only by her growing respect for her mother's stubborn insistence on her rights. Slowly, she began to feel that maybe her mother had died for something valuable—a principle.

We met in the seaside city of Qingdao to discuss her mother's death and the letters that Brother Li had let me copy. I later traveled to Ms. Zhang's hometown of Weifang, where she lived a few streets over from her mother's old apartment. I looked at the park where Ms. Chen had first encountered Falun Gong practitioners during her morning walk. I learned how hard Ms. Chen's life had become and how appealing she'd found Falun Gong. I also met the women who had written letters from prison and obtained the letter of another woman who was still in prison. Slowly, I began to reconstruct what had happened to Ms. Chen after the officials had warned her in February 2000 not to go to Beijing.

After delivering their lecture, the officials had gone next to Ms. Zhang, repeating their warning and urging her to control her mother. Ms. Zhang had never been in one room with so many officials. She was petrified and quickly went over to her mother's apartment and pleaded with her to heed the warning.

" 'Stay at home and practice quietly,' I told her. I was having my doubts about the government's ban on Falun Gong, but I could see they meant business."

Ms. Chen didn't listen to her daughter. She left her home that day for the train station, intending to go to Beijing. But she was quickly nabbed by a special squad of informants who roamed the neighborhood looking for Falun Gong participants who dared to leave home. Without knowing it, she had been placed under house arrest; her crime was daring to challenge that by leaving home.

Instead of being sent back home, Ms. Chen was sent back to the Chengguan Street Committee offices. But during the night she managed to escape—exactly how isn't clear, but the prison there was makeshift and the doors might not have had proper locks. She was arrested the next day, February 17, heading again for the train station, where she hoped to go to Beijing to plead her case before the Petitions and Appeals Office, a last resort for people who feel they've been wronged—the same place where Mr. Ma, the peasant leader, as well as several of the urban activists, had taken their cases.

This time the local officials in Weifang wanted to teach Ms. Chen a lesson, so they sent her to an unofficial prison—a "transformation center"—run by the street committee. Its formal name was the Falun Gong Education Study Class. Unlike the room in the street committee's office, the "Study Class" had been properly outfitted to hold people in custody. It was a square two-story building with a yard in the middle. In the corner of the yard was a squat one-story building with two rooms. People who have been there say it was where people who hadn't learned their lesson were disciplined—by torture.

After her mother was transferred to the detention center, officials called Ms. Zhang and said her mother would be released if she'd pay a $241 fine. Ms. Zhang was fed up with the endless "fines." She'd already paid two exorbitant fines to get her mother out of the jail in Beijing. Now the government wanted more, and not a small amount either. It was the equivalent of four months' wages, a staggering amount to come up with on short notice.

But there was more to it than money. She had to admit that she was tired of her mother's insistence on standing up for her rights. If she'd just give in and renounce Falun Gong, the family's troubles would be over. The fines would stop, and her mother could, after a decent interval, still practice the exercises at home. She didn't see the need for all this.

So she told the officials their fines were illegal and that she'd complain to the local procurator's office if they didn't release her mother.

Ms. Chen spent the night in the jail and heard screams from the squat building. That was the usual practice: newcomers spent a night untouched but were able to hear the cries of those who were resisting. That was often quite effective, with many capitulating without having to be beaten. But Ms. Chen didn't renounce Falun Gong. It was now February 18, and before she was led over to the squat building for interrogation, she was allowed another phone call. She called her daughter and asked her to bring the money. Irritated by the troubles brought on by her mother's uncompromising attitude, Ms. Zhang argued with her mother. Give in and come home, she said. Her mother quietly refused. They hung up.

Ms. Chen's ordeal began that night. A practitioner who was in the next-door room later wrote: "We heard her screaming. Our hearts were tortured and our spirits almost collapsed." Thugs hired by the Chengguan Street Committee used plastic truncheons on her calves, feet and lower back, as well as a cattle prod on her head and neck. They shouted at her repeatedly to give up Falun Gong and curse Master Li, according to her cellmates. Each time, Ms. Chen refused.

The next day, February 19, Ms. Zhang got another call. It was a woman on the line, not her mother. Bring the money, a woman told her. Ms. Zhang hesitated. Her mother came on the line. Her voice, usually so strong and confident, was soft and pained. She pleaded with her daughter to bring the money. The woman came back on the phone: Bring the money.

Ms. Zhang got a sick feeling and rushed over with the money and more warm clothes for her mother. But the building was surrounded by agents who wouldn't let her see her mother. Suspicious that her mother wasn't really in the building, she returned home. An hour later a practitioner came to see Ms. Zhang. Falun Gong adherents—including her mother—were being beaten in the center, the practitioner said.

Ms. Zhang raced back with her brother, carrying fruit as a small bribe for the police. She was refused entrance and her money was refused as well. She noticed an old lady in a room and shouted up to her: "Is my mother being beaten?" The old lady waved her hand to signify "no," although later Ms. Zhang said she might have been trying to wave her away from the prison, fearing she, too, would be arrested. Ms. Zhang and her brother went home to a fitful, sleepless night.

That night Ms. Chen was taken back into the room. After again refusing to renounce Falun Gong, she was beaten and jolted with the stun stick. Her cellmates heard her curse the officials—like many adherents, she told them that the central government would punish them once they were exposed. But, in an answer that dozens of Falun Gong adherents across the country say they heard, the Weifang officials told Ms. Chen that they had been told by the central government that "no measures are too excessive" to wipe out Falun Gong. She would recant or the beatings would continue.

Two hours after she went in, Ms. Chen was pushed back into her cell on the second story of the main building. It was an unheated room with only a sheet of steel for a bed. She fell into a delirium and one of her three cellmates remember her moaning "Mommy, mommy."

The next morning, February 20, she was ordered out to jog in the snow. Two days of torture had left her legs bruised and her short black hair matted with pus and blood, said cellmates and other prisoners who witnessed the incident. "I saw from the window that she crawled out with difficulty," wrote a cellmate in a letter smuggled out of prison. Ms. Chen collapsed and was dragged back into the cell.

"I used to be a medical major," wrote another. "When I saw her dying, I suggested moving her into another [heated] room." Instead, local government officials gave her *sanqi*, an herbal remedy for light internal bleeding. "But she couldn't swallow and spat it out." Cellmates implored the officials to send Ms. Chen to a hospital, but the officials—who often criticized Falun Gong practitioners for forgoing medical treatment in favor of their exercises—refused. Instead, a doctor was brought in who pronounced her healthy.

But, wrote the cellmate: "She wasn't conscious and didn't talk, and only spat dark-colored sticky liquid. We guessed it was blood. Only the next morning [the 21st] did they confirm that she was dying. Liu [Guangming, an employee of the local Public Security Bureau who the practitioners say did most of the beating] tried her pulse and his face froze." Ms. Chen was dead.

That evening officials went over to Ms. Zhang's house and said her mother was ill. Ms. Zhang and her brother piled into a car and were driven to a hotel, which was surrounded by police. The local party secretary—the man who had visited Ms. Chen and warned her not to go to Beijing to protest—was present. He told the siblings that their mother had died of a heart attack, but he wouldn't allow them to see her body. After hours of arguing, the officials finally said they could see the body, but only the next day, and insisted they spend the night in the heavily guarded hotel. They refused and finally were allowed to go home.

On February 22, Ms. Zhang and her brother were taken to the local hospital, which was also ringed by police. Their mother was laid out on a table in traditional mourning garb: a simple blue cotton tunic over blue cotton trousers. In a bag tossed in the corner of the room, however, Ms. Zhang spotted her mother's torn and bloodied clothes, the underwear badly soiled. She lifted the new clothes on her mother's body. The calves were black and her back had six-inch-long welts, while her teeth were broken and her ear swollen and blue. Ms. Zhang fainted and her brother, weeping, caught her.

One of the government's most brilliant moves in its persecution of Falun Gong was declaring the group a cult. That put Falun Gong on the defensive, forcing it to prove its innocence, and cloaked the government's crackdown with the legitimacy of the West's anticult movement. The government quickly picked up the vocabulary of the anticult movement, launching Web sites and putting forth overnight experts, who intoned that Master Li was no different from Jim Jones, the head of the Peoples Temple who in 1978 allegedly killed 912 members, or the Church of Scientology, whose members are allegedly brainwashed into giving huge amounts of money.

To prove its point, the government came up with a series of lurid stories about people who had cut open their stomachs looking for the Dharma Wheel that was supposed to spin inside it. Others were presented whose relatives had died after performing Falun Gong exercises instead of taking medicine. The government also tried to cast Master Li as having financially exploited his followers. Snapshots of the group's accounting books were shown on television, purporting to prove that Master Li made huge amounts of money off his books and videos.

The problem was that few of these arguments held up. The government never allowed victims of Falun Gong to be interviewed independently, making it almost impossible to verify their claims. And even if one took all the claims at face value, they made up a very small percentage of Falun Gong's total number of adherents. In any group of several million it is always possible to find several hundred unbalanced people; the government's examples never proved that the number of unbalanced Falun Gong adherents was higher than one would find in a general sample of the populace.

As for getting rich, I had little doubt that Master Li lived a comfortable life in the United States. His books sold briskly there and his conferences were well attended. In China, Master Li's books had sold even better, but in 1996 the group had gotten into a dispute with the qigong research association and its books had been denied a publishing license. Thus during the most dynamic period of the group's existence in China the books and videos were bootleg, so he hadn't received royalties.

More fundamentally, the group didn't meet many common definitions of a cult: its members marry outside the group, have outside friends, hold normal jobs, do not live isolated from society, do not believe that the world's end is imminent and do not give significant amounts of money to the organization. Most importantly, suicide is not accepted, nor is physical violence.

Broader definitions of cults do exist; in the West the anticult movement's chief theorist is the clinical psychologist Margaret Singer, whose 1995 book *Cults in Our Midst*, claimed that "covert, seductive groups are targeting the elderly, the workplace, the family . . . anyone can be a victim." Ms. Singer gives a three-fold definition of a cult, arguing that it has a self-appointed, charismatic leader with exclusive knowledge, a hierarchical structure that is totalistic or all-encompassing and that its members are forced to give a "total commitment" to the group. This definition, however, is extremely broad and could take in many religious groups, such as Christian or Muslim religious orders.

I knew, however, that as a new spiritual movement Falun Gong had attracted some extremely committed—some might even say fanatical—members. During the two years that I interviewed Falun Gong members, I had met members who clearly did see Master Li as a demigod and had centered their life on the group. Between performing the morning exercises and the evening reading of prayers, not much time was left for other activities besides family and work. And some members' insistence on not giving in to the government could be seen as unreasonable. But overall I didn't see an unhealthy rejection of the outside world, at least no more so than I'd seen among many adherents of major religions I'd met over the years. I also thought that many people lost sight of the fact that after Falun Gong had been banned, believers had been fired from their jobs and forced underground. If they lived cut off from society, it was the government's doing, not Falun Gong's teachings.

Again, this is not to say that Falun Gong did not have some troubling beliefs. Its worldview was of unceasing tests that people have to go through to reach a higher plane. Human existence was thus seen as transitory and in some ways worthless—hardly a unique concept but one that could lead some adherents to put their life second to the group's goals. But here I also didn't see much that was all that different from some established religions, which have similar concepts.

The final concern about Falun Gong was on one level irrefutable. Experts on new religions are often concerned that leaders of these groups are still alive. The argument goes that, for example, unlike the Jewish prophets, Christ, Mohammed or Buddha, Master Li was actively preaching. That meant that he could still issue a dangerous statement in the future. With, say, Christ, one can argue over interpretations of his statements but because he is dead (or alive in heaven, depending on one's viewpoint), he is not likely to issue a statement for everyone to take cyanide. With Falun Gong, such a possibility does exist, although

I'd never seen a serious indication that such an order was at all likely. I also wondered if the supposedly safer established religions were that much better; Christ wasn't likely to issue a new statement calling on Christians to commit suicide but arguments over how to interpret his texts had resulted in enough bloodshed to make one skeptical that it was less dangerous than a new religion.

Still, the government's use of the "cult" label was useful. In the West the anticult movement had been losing steam since anxiety over cults peaked in the early-to-mid 1990s. By the turn of the century most anticult activists were confined to adherents of established religions—in other words, people with a vested interest in attacking new groups. In the United States, the most prominent organization, the American Family Foundation, is a Christian-right group, while in Europe the sharpest critics come from the established, state-sponsored churches. In addition, the scientific basis of declaring a group a cult has become suspect. Psychologists are increasingly unconvinced that "brainwashing" can really be performed on people; most people who join cults tend to leave voluntarily after a relatively short time. This is not meant to downplay the damage that small, incestuous religious groups can have on a person or society, but cults are hardly a major challenge facing society.

But China's claim that Falun Gong was a cult gave the western anticult movement a new cause. Many outsiders fixated on the cult label and spent their time debating obscure definitions of Master Li's works, trying to prove that the group was potentially dangerous. One western academic wrote a paper pleading for an understanding of the government's concerns over Falun Gong's teachings, saying it had a legitimate right to fear the group. This even though the government had only interested itself in Falun Gong because of its demonstration in downtown Beijing, not because of its teachings. And most fundamentally, what was often forgotten in the learned discourse was that the government, not Falun Gong, was killing people.

This point was lost on the United Nations, which to its later embarrassment sponsored one of these anticult conferences in Beijing. In an opening address to the "International Symposium on Cults" in November 2000, the director of the United Nations Development Programme in China, Kerstin Leitner, blamed excessive tolerance for the existence of cults. The U.N. tried to distance itself from its role in the conference. Ms. Leitner's speech was not made public, and its existence was at first denied by the U.N.'s Beijing office—even though China's government-controlled media were happily trumpeting the speech as a sign that the outside world approved of its crackdown.

Later, Ms. Leitner told me over lunch that she had indeed given the opening speech and that the UNDP had sponsored the conference. While she said she opposed the crackdown, she said she'd hoped that, by working from within, the U.N. could help moderate the government's excesses.

On one point, however, Ms. Leitner would not back down. And that was that the government had reason to be concerned about groups like Falun Gong. The reason, she said, was obvious to any student of Chinese history: that the country had long suffered from millennial groups like Falun Gong. The government might be overreacting, she said, but it was understandable. It was an argument heard widely: with a history like China's, the argument went, any government would be wary of religious movements—or peasant rebellions or whatever. It was a popular understanding of Chinese history but one that didn't hold up to scrutiny.

Not to say that religious uprisings haven't dotted Chinese history, or popularly been blamed for a dynasty's downfall.

China's first major dynasty, the Han, fell after the country was partially overrun by religious rebels. That uprising gathered steam during the second half of the second century as China was plagued by droughts and floods. Consumed by an internal succession struggle, the Han rulers reacted slowly to the disasters, fueling the rebellion. A family of healers impressed the population with miracle cures, teaching that poor health is due to sin and confession leads to good health—a striking parallel to Falun Gong, which also preaches that its exercises and moral regime can end illness. In A.D. 184 the group, known as the Yellow Turbans, launched an uprising, defeating armies and capturing cities. It was soon defeated but was followed by a wave of similar rebellions, with names such as Black Mountain and White Wave. They, too, were put down, but the Han court eventually lost control of the army and China broke up into warring factions. The country's unity was only reestablished some three hundred years later.

Likewise, the downfall of China's last dynasty, the Qing, was partially blamed on a series of religious rebellions that started in the late eighteenth century and ran through the middle of the nineteenth. The most deadly uprising was the Taiping, or Heavenly Kingdom of Great Peace, a mixture of folk religion and Christianity. Its founder was convinced that he was the younger brother of Jesus Christ and preached a rigorous moral code, as well as fiery opposition to the Qing. His armies overran much of south and central China, and after ensconcing himself in Nanjing he ruled a huge swath of China for eleven years. The Taipings were finally destroyed by the Qing's foreign-backed armies, but millions died in sieges, countersieges and scorched-earth offensives. The Qing collapsed a few decades later, in 1911.

In traditional historiography, such groups are usually given a disproportionate role in a dynasty's downfall. They are seen as wild, uncontrollable forces whipped up by demagogues, much like peasants. This, some analysts have argued, is how we should see Falun Gong. Indeed, the existence of groups like the Taipings are seen as explaining or justifying how the communists have dealt with Falun Gong.

This sort of argumentation strikes me as deeply flawed. Most obviously, Falun Gong differs from these other groups in an important way: it does not advocate violence and is at heart an apolitical, inward-oriented discipline, one aimed at cleansing oneself spiritually and improving one's health.

But more fundamentally, the existence of uprisings like the Yellow Turbans, Taipings or even Falun Gong must be seen as a sign of, not the cause of, a dynasty's troubles. Just as the Taipings' rise was due to the Qing's increasing incompetence, corruption and inability to deal with China's contact with the West, so, too, is Falun Gong a reaction to problems in modern Chinese society. A competent regime can deal with floods and droughts; an incompetent one is riven by factions and unable to succor the poor, leading them to find comfort in religious movements and even to rebel. Popular governments have a moral authority that lays claim to its subjects' allegiance—people believe that the rulers should be in power because they are moral and rule well. Corrupt, ossified regimes, regardless of the era, rarely win much loyalty.

Punctually at 8 p.m., Sima Nan strode onto the stage and sat behind a desk. A lamp shone on his face while he talked into a microphone, shock-jock style. "You call yourself Communist Party cadres?" he bellowed. "When you joined the grand party of Marx, Lenin and Mao you swore to atheism, but some of you are cadres by day and proselytizers by night."

His audience of 1,500 sat riveted. They worked for the Wuhan Iron & Steel Works, a venerable communist factory that had more than 10,000 employees. It was August 1999, and the local Communist Party cell was worried that many of them were still Falun Gong adherents even though the government had banned the group a month earlier. Unsure how to cleanse their ranks of Falun Gong, they'd invited Sima Nan, a government-sponsored cult-buster to the grimy metropolis of 7.4 million to give a stern lecture to senior cadres and workers it suspected of still following Falun Gong.

Sima Nan was perfect for the part, a thick, powerfully built former qigong fanatic. Like Professor Chen, he had once believed that qigong could give one supernatural powers. But unlike the amiable academic, who clung to this belief and defended it with questionable science, the forty-four-year-old former journalist had long discovered that most "special powers" granted by qigong were indeed David Copperfield routines that a clever person could learn. Since the early 1990s he'd labored with the conviction of a born-again atheist to expose qigong frauds, developing a performance that had been honed to spellbinding perfection. His message was not always easy for the party to swallow, but at heart he fundamentally supported it and remained a member.

Now he launched into a surprisingly frank criticism of how the Communist Party has failed to fill China's spiritual vacuum. Ever since China's traditional religious world collapsed along with the imperial system in 1911, he said, Chinese have searched for a new spirituality. When the communists took over in 1949, Chairman Mao usurped the role of God.

"But since Chairman Mao's death in 1976," Sima Nan said, leaning across the table to the microphone, "China has been spiritually adrift. We are looking for something to believe in.

Capitalism isn't a religion, so some people are looking for something else."

Especially pitiable, he said, are old party members trying to regain their youth.

"They used to get the best girls," Mr. Sima said as the auditorium roared with laughter and the local party secretary, sitting in the first row, squirmed.

"Now they're just old guys in apartments looking to be strong again."

He then grabbed the microphone and strode across the stage, his powerful arms bulging through his blue banker's suit. Stripping off his jacket, he piled eight bricks on the head of a volunteer from the audience, climbed on a chair and swung a sledgehammer down onto the bricks. Five shattered, but the young man remained standing, somewhat surprised that his head was in one piece.

"Physics," Sima Nan shouted at the audience. "I only smashed five bricks. The bottom three cushioned his head. Magic had nothing to do with it."

Next, he picked up a glass tumbler and another brick. Mimicking a qigong master, he pretended to breathe his qi on the glass to turn it into "iron glass." He then picked up a brick in one hand and the glass in the other and hit the glass against the brick, careful to make sure the thick base of the glass struck the brick first. The brick broke. People whispered in amazement that the glass must truly have been transformed into "iron glass." Looking disgusted at the audience, Sima Nan explained how the thick base of the tumbler is actually stronger than many bricks. To show that thin glass isn't stronger, he smashed the rim of the glass against the brick, shattering the glass into pieces. He topped off the sequence by eating the thin shards, washing them down with water. He later explained that he'd simply practiced carefully grinding glass with his molars; as long as he drinks water the glass powder goes down fine.

After four hours his assistant dragged him offstage and into a waiting car for a late-night flight home to Beijing. Eager to toe the government line and rid their factories of Falun Gong adherents, many other factory managers had hired Sima Nan, who was now a hot commodity. He'd even won a recent "Hero of Atheism" award.

On the flight back we discussed what a shock Falun Gong was to the government. The iron and steel works was a Communist bastion, built during China's first five-year plan in the 1950s. But local party officials had estimated that hundreds of the plant's Communist cadres were still refusing to give up their belief in Falun Gong, preferring to follow Master Li instead of Chairman Mao.

"Remember how I joked to the steelworkers about the old party cadres who believed in qigong's supernatural powers?" he said. "For years the party flirted with qigong and even embraced it. But they don't really understand it. Sure, the tricks are appealing, but what really attracts people is the spirituality."

The man who really understood Falun Gong lived in the Temple of Universal Succor. No one talked to him and his advice was shunned. He was by now a virtual recluse, a hermit embittered that the world had ignored him. His name was Chen Xingqiao, a lay Buddhist who'd been fascinated and repulsed by Falun Gong for half a dozen years.

It was early evening when I got to the temple, already getting dark as I made my way in. The entrance had been hard to find on the busy commercial street outside, but inside I found a spacious series of courtyards arranged one after another deep into Beijing's alleys. I walked back from one courtyard to another, past shrines that were empty but for giant wooden statues and the occasional monk reading by candlelight. Most monks were hurrying to supper back in their living quarters, and the incense sticks before the statues were slowly burning down. I stopped and listened to the faint echoes of the city, savoring the quiet.

Despite the tranquil scene of devotion, the temple was primarily a bureaucratic center. It housed the China Buddhist Association, the organization charged with administering the country's 13,000 temples and its 200,000 monks and nuns. Mr. Chen worked for the association's monthly magazine, the *Voice of Dharma*, where he was an editor. Many of the monks I'd just seen worked for the association, and although they were saying their evening prayers, they spent most of their time as little more than employees of the tourist industry, collecting tickets and selling books or souvenirs.

I slowly worked my way back through half a dozen courtyards to Mr. Chen's tiny office. I lost my way and only found him with the help of a friendly cleaning lady. At forty-three, Mr. Chen cut a detached, slightly hostile figure. He was tall and thin, with a carefully combed head of hair and small eyes that carefully watched the world. As he told me his story, I could see that his caution had served him well, allowing him to move up the bureaucratic ladder from a remote province to the association's head office in the capital. But I was also aware from talking to others that Mr. Chen was more complicated than that. He was also a practicing Buddhist, someone who believed in its teachings and studied them carefully. He typified China's religious associations: a legitimate believer who realized he was making compromises but felt he had no choice.

Mr. Chen first came across Falun Gong in 1994, when he still lived in Harbin, a northern city that lies about a day's drive from the Russian border. I had been in Harbin around the time that Mr. Chen lived there and remember it vividly. Many of China's painful economic reforms—especially the closing of state enterprises, which later led to high unemployment across the country—had begun in Harbin due to its history. The city and the rest of China's northeast had been colonized by Japan, which built heavy industry. Later came the big steel mills and gargantuan machine tool factories built by China's communist economic planners. By now, these factories were out of date and crumbling under the onslaught of free-market competition. This disproportionate concentration of rust-belt industries meant that layoffs started here earlier, giving the city a rotten feel even in the early 1990s. Later a common sight across China, Harbin early on had legions of unemployed camped out on its sidewalks, selling trinkets and leftover products from their bankrupt enterprises. Brazen prostitutes and seedy karaoke lounges were ubiquitous. The appeal of a doctrine promising salvation was obvious.

But something deeper made this region receptive to Falun Gong only two years after Master Li had founded it. In centuries past it was home to non-Chinese tribes like the Manchus—hence the name Manchuria that Japan used and which remained in popular western usage until recently. The Manchus conquered China in the seventeenth century and ran it for nearly three hundred years. During this time they limited the number of ethnic Chinese—the "Han"—allowed to settle in the Manchus' ancestral homeland, hoping to preserve the region's mixed agricultural and hunting economy. The Manchu empire eventually collapsed and the region became overwhelmingly Chinese, but it still retains some of the flavor of a frontier. Unlike China's cultural heartland, where Mr. Ma led his peasant rebellion, this was on the fringes of China's cultural influence. Instead of denuded hills and tiny temples, here were thick forests and a tradition of shamanism—much closer culturally to Siberia and Mongolia. A religion drawing on this mysticism would find a sympathetic hearing.

A friend took Mr. Chen to hear Master Li speak at the Harbin Ice Hockey Rink, which Falun Gong had rented for the week. It was a revival-style meeting, part of the group's expansion beyond its base in nearby Liaoning Province. "A friend said that Li was a 'great Buddha' and knew I was interested in Buddhism. I thought I might as well go along and listen. It couldn't hurt."

Inside the rink, a stage had been set up, and Master Li addressed the people sitting in the stands. Sometimes adherents would recount their tales, sharing experiences and trying to show how useful Falun Gong had been in ridding believers of illness and pain. During breaks people milled around in the hallways, looking at information posters describing Falun Gong's tenets and how to meditate.

But Mr. Chen didn't like what he heard. Part of Master Li's speech, he said, denigrated Buddhism, which Falun Gong sometimes portrays as a slightly degenerate, worn-out religion that has run its course. Mr. Chen's temple in Beijing, for example, with its mixture of politics and religion, wouldn't meet with approval from many Falun Gong adherents.

As a committed Buddhist, Mr. Chen was slightly insulted.

"I wasn't too impressed. He seemed to be teaching a basic-level qigong and his own personal theory on life. But a lot of people there were really impressed. They're not too familiar with religion and other teachings, and they don't understand much. Many hadn't heard of any religion through the media or at school, so for these people this was really something fantastic. He talked about 'Buddha law' and spent half the time criticizing other qigong masters."

Mr. Chen said that government allegations that Master Li enriched himself through Falun Gong were probably exaggerated, but he said that in the early 1990s, at least, Falun Gong was a profitable business. He estimates that about 4,000 or 5,000 people attended the revival and that each paid 53 yuan to listen to the ten lectures. That's only about 5 yuan, or 60 cents, a lecture, but all told, the Harbin conference still grossed about 200,000 yuan, or about $25,000. After costs, it still probably earned half that—a very tidy sum for the China of that time.

"I went back for the last lecture," Mr. Chen said. "I left thinking it was strange but nothing important. Just a typical northeastern thing. Northeasterners like things big and exaggerated and simple," he said with a laugh, consciously repeating stereotypes of northeastern Chinese. "There were dozens of these qigong guys all around the northeast then, and such boastful teachings were common. I thought he was a crook."

But during the next two years Mr. Chen found it increasingly hard to ignore Falun Gong. Thanks to fervent proselytizing, the group became the most popular of the new religions. Almost every park in Harbin featured a Falun Gong exercise spot. Corner bookstands were lined with the group's books and videotapes. Many Buddhists were even returning their statues and Buddhist sutras, or holy texts, to temples, saying they weren't as powerful as Mr. Li's main work, *Turning the Dharma Wheel*.

At the time, Mr. Chen was only a part-time volunteer at the local chapter of the Buddhist association and earned his living as an administrator at the Harbin Measuring & Cutting Tool Works, a giant state enterprise that then had about 8,000 employees. Falun Gong believers practiced for an hour every morning in the front yard of the plant and met for discussion groups in the evening. They urged Mr. Chen to join them.

He still had a bad impression of the group from the revival

he attended in 1994 but was curious. He picked up a copy of Mr. Li's book and spent several months studying it. His conclusion: Falun Gong was a heretical offshoot of Buddhism that tried to legitimize itself by misappropriating traditional religious terms such as Dharma Wheel.

Basically, Master Li's works call for a reevaluation of Buddhism. The Law of the Buddha, he says, has not been properly conveyed to mankind. Buddhist scholars, for example, quibble over words and categories, paying too much attention to scriptures. Instead, the true "Buddha Law" encompasses the entire universe, and at its core are three principles: Truth, Benevolence and Tolerance. While science has made massive strides forward, it is limited to explaining material existence.

"What can be understood with modern human knowledge is extremely shallow and tiny," Master Li wrote in the introduction to *Turning the Dharma Wheel.* "Only through the Buddha Law can the mysteries of the universe, time-space and the human body be completely unveiled. It is able to truly distinguish what is righteous from evil, good from bad, and eliminate misconceptions while providing what is correct."

People can only improve themselves, Master Li wrote, by cultivating themselves—by meditating and behaving according to the three principles of being truthful, benevolent and tolerant. As people improve, they reach higher and higher levels of cultivation. Eventually, they escape mortal concerns, like illness, and become immortal.

After learning what Falun Gong stood for, Mr. Chen wrote a 20,000-word essay called "Revealing the Original Face of Falun Gong—a New Kind of Folk Religion" and gave it to the local office of the China Buddhist Association.

But Mr. Chen's analysis was too penetrating and his remedy too radical for China's rigid officialdom. The country's religious bureaucracy recognizes only five religions and limits their growth by banning proselytizing. But Mr. Chen noted that qigong groups like Falun Gong had registered themselves as simple exercise groups and thus labored under no such restrictions.

Mr. Chen's solution: unshackle established religions so they could compete on equal terms. If Falun Gong could hold meetings in sports stadiums and recruit passersby in the park, why not allow Buddhists to do the same? The response from officials, though, was predictable: they ignored his proposals. "They were just interested in keeping everything quiet," Mr. Chen said.

Open discussion of Falun Gong would also expose the central paradox in official policy. Acknowledging Falun Gong as a religion would mean officials would either have to allow a new religion to register, or ban it. Registering a new religion is impossible in China—it hasn't happened in five decades of Communist rule—while banning it would be an admission that the government had allowed a religion to flourish for years in the guise of an exercise group.

Mr. Chen's frustrations came to a head later in 1996, when the Harbin city government convened a meeting called "Socialism and Buddhism." As a senior lay member of the city's Buddhist community, Mr. Chen attended and brought up Falun Gong for discussion.

The issue died after just a few minutes' debate. Representatives from the police said they could act only when a disturbance occurred, while officials from the religion bureau said they are allowed to oversee activities only inside established places of worship, according to people present at the meeting. "It fell through the cracks, so the government simply ignored it and hoped it would go away," said an official at the Harbin Public Security Bureau who attended the 1996 meeting. Adds Mr. Chen:

"It was a new religion, but no one knew what to do about it because new religions are illegal. Therefore it didn't exist."

Mr. Chen decided that if the bureaucracy wouldn't act, he would prod it by publishing his essay, which the local Buddhist association had forwarded to its national headquarters. He appealed for help to its head, Zhao Puchu, a rare figure who managed to remain respected in religious circles while maintaining the trust of party officials.

Mr. Zhao liked the essay and sent it to China's leading party newspaper, *People's Daily*. The paper initially wanted to publish a condensed version in its elite "Internal Reference" edition, which is read by the country's top leaders. But after the newspaper asked Mr. Chen for permission to run such a version, a senior editor killed it. "Several things prevented us from running it," said an editor at the newspaper. "Foremost was that he talked too frankly about religion. We just can't do that."

Mr. Zhao then ordered that the tract be published in early 1997 in *Religious Trends*, an internal publication of the Buddhist association. After a further year of effort, he got the essay printed by a publishing house run by the party's religious affairs office.

These were victories, but small ones. Reflecting government suspicion of religion, *Religious Trends* was allowed to be distributed only to members of the Buddhist association, so its impact was negligible. He also managed to get the manuscript published, but by a tiny publishing house. The book was deemed too sensitive to distribute to bookstores, so interested readers had to contact the publisher in Beijing and pick it up in person.

Mr. Chen said that during the next year, 1998, he was contacted by members of the China Atheist Association, including cult-buster Sima Nan. They also opposed Falun Gong and wanted a copy of his book. He sent one over, but as a Buddhist, Mr. Chen didn't like what they stood for. "I criticized Falun Gong, but I also talked about the need for religion," Mr. Chen said.

We had been speaking for more than an hour and it had grown pitch black outside and Mr. Chen's office was chilly. His spirits sank as he thought of how the atheists had hijacked the debate over Falun Gong. "Their criticisms are so crude. Their arguments are like objecting to a fake bottle of liquor because it has alcohol in it—not because it's fake and dangerous. So by this logic, all liquor, real or fake, is bad. That's how they treat Falun Gong. They say Li Hongzhi is wrong because he claims to be a god and gods are bad. But what they're doing is criticizing all religions."

Crude or not, it was the atheists who brought down Falun Gong.

Leading the atheists' attack was one of China's most famous scientists, He Zuoxiu. I had heard of Professor He before. He was a semipublic figure, the sort of person who, like Mr. Chen, is more complicated than he first seems. People in Falun Gong portray him as a government pit bull, the stooge who adds a veneer of scientific respectability to the government's attacks on the group, much like Professor Chen had lent credibility to qigong in years past. But Professor He is also a man who speaks his mind and had written letters to the government protesting a planned theater in downtown Beijing. The egg-shaped glass-and-steel theater was President Jiang Zemin's pet project, but that hadn't stopped Professor He from criticizing it as too modern for a building across the street from the Forbidden City.

When I called, he was wary, until I said I didn't want to talk about the theater. He'd received a lot of flak for opposing it, he said, and wanted to let that issue cool down. His work on Falun

Gong, however, had recently been met with government approval, so he quickly invited me over to his spacious but simple concrete-block apartment. Before opening the steel security door he peeked at me through a watch hole. He laughed apologetically. "I've been a target of these Falun Gong types and can't be too sure," he said, tramping into his living room with a motion for me to follow.

He was a rumpled seventy-three-year-old, energetic and quick-witted, if slightly grubby and unkempt. His fingernails were dirty and his unwashed hair stuck straight up. He wore a track suit and plastic sandals. He gave the impression of being either a devil-may-care intellectual or a lunatic.

No sooner had he sat down than he jumped up again and walked to a bookcase, pulling out a plastic envelope, the sort used to store evidence. He unzipped it and carefully pulled out a copy of *Turning the Dharma Wheel*. "I saw it displayed on a roadside stand and was curious what nonsense people were reading," he said, "so I bought it."

As I gingerly opened Exhibit A, Professor He reached over and pulled a receipt out from the back flap. It was dated November 4, 1996. "I thought the book had to do with Buddhism, but I was intrigued because the publisher was the China Broadcast & Television Publishing House. I thought it was strange that a publisher that's supposed to be propagating government information would be spreading Buddhism."

Professor He figured he'd report on the publishing house. After all, such texts are usually only published by obscure companies, such as the one that put out Mr. Chen's treatise on Falun Gong that same year. But then Professor He read the book and became even more fascinated. Here wasn't a simple book on Buddhism but an original religious text, one that outlined a new theology designed to replace major religions. China already had five legal religions, which as an atheist he thought was bad enough. Now here was another. Worse, it was brazen enough to publish its tract with a publishing house run by the Ministry of Propaganda.

Then Professor He became involved in a research project at his institute, the Chinese Academy of Sciences' Institute of Theoretical Physics. He put the book on his shelf, intending to come back to it later. Like Mr. Chen, he forgot about it for two years.

By this time, 1998, Falun Gong had exploded in popularity, spreading from Mr. Chen's home in the far north to China's big cities in the south. It had in effect become China's unofficial sixth religion, boasting millions of adherents.

It spread widely on university campuses, even to Professor He's institute. In March 1998, he said, one of his students started to practice Falun Gong compulsively. He refused to eat, lost weight and was sent to the hospital. The next month he was sent to a mental hospital where he stayed for one year. Falun Gong adherents say that such behavior is simply that of a psychologically unbalanced person, but Professor He attributed the young man's behavior to his new passion.

In June 1998, Beijing Television came by his institute to film a report. As usual for China's state-controlled media, it was planned as a puff piece. But Professor He asked if he might air some criticism of his research institute. Coming from Professor He, a respected party member, the criticism couldn't be that controversial, so the producer agreed. "I said we have good things at our institute, but bad things, too. We have people who believe in Falun Gong so much that they've become schizophrenic," he said, recounting his words with a grin.

The day after the show aired on May 11, 1998, Professor He realized he was in for a fight. That morning half a dozen Falun Gong adherents showed up at his house and sat in his living room for three hours, arguing with him. "I showed them that I'd read their book, and all the parts that I thought were nonsense," he said. "It was a bit unpleasant having all these people coming to your home, but in the end we just agreed that we didn't agree and they left."

Professor He promptly called the television station and found out that a few hundred Falun Gong adherents were outside the station with pickets. Fresh from his experience with the argumentative students, Professor He urged Beijing Television not to buckle. "The idea that they could protest outside a major organization of the party was unimaginable," he said.

But, as Mr. Chen the Buddhist administrator had learned two years earlier, Professor He soon discovered that officials were bent on the path of least resistance. The number of protesters outside Beijing Television quickly grew to 2,000—all peaceful and orderly but shocking to authorities in Beijing, which hadn't seen a significant demonstration since the student protests in Tiananmen Square in 1989. With the ninth anniversary of those demonstrations rapidly approaching—the anniversary always being a sensitive time on China's political calendar—leaders ordered the television station to end the Falun Gong protests at any cost.

The station quickly complied. To show goodwill, it handed out two thousand boxed lunches—one for each protester—and promised to air a sympathetic portrayal of the group. The next day the show ran as promised, the protests dispersed and quiet returned to the Chinese capital.

Professor He was incensed at the weak-kneed television managers. He did more research and got a copy of Mr. Chen's book. Through contacts in the party, he learned that it had regularly yielded to Falun Gong protesters. Over the past few years several media outlets—estimates range as high as fourteen—had been besieged by Falun Gong adherents angry at reports casting doubt on its claim to foster good health through exercise. In almost every case, the media had backed down, printing or airing apologies to Falun Gong.

Most, Professor He learned, were simply taking their cue from the State Press and Publication Administration, which controls content in China's media. The office had a "three nots" policy on qigong, including Falun Gong: media should not be for it, should not be against it and should not label it good or bad—part of the agency's general policy of avoiding anything controversial.

Newspapers had been following this rule since 1996, when a leading party paper gave in to Falun Gong's first protest. On June 17, 1996, a writer using the pseudonym Xin Ping, wrote in the *Enlightenment Daily* a book review critical of Master Li's work:

> Recently, booksellers in every side street and alley have been selling *Turning the Dharma Wheel,* which is a book propagating feudal superstition and false science. Of all the books I've read, *Turning the Dharma Wheel* is the most wildly arrogant and outrageously boastful.

That incensed Falun Gong adherents, who protested outside the newspaper's office. The newspaper issued a retraction apologizing for the piece. Alarmed at the whiff of controversy, officials in the China Qigong Scientific Research Association expelled Falun Gong, while the State Press and Publication Administration banned Master Li's works, such as *Turning the Dharma Wheel*. [Falun Gong says it voluntarily left the association because Master Li felt it was corrupt.] But the government took no action against Falun Gong for its protest, and the retraction stood. That set a precedent for the other media outlets, which also issued apologies or retractions whenever they criticized Falun Gong.

To the stability-minded mandarins who run the country, this seemed like sound policy, one that the Beijing Television protests bore out. Opening up a messy debate about Falun Gong would have sparked more protests and allowed people such as Mr. Chen to call for religious freedom. Banning it, on the other hand, seemed pointless because the group was otherwise harmless. Few considered the lesson that Falun Gong was learning: that demonstrations were acceptable and achieved results

Professor He decided to force the party to change its policy—and unlike Mr. Chen, he had more ways to make society take notice of Falun Gong. As a famous academic researcher and government loyalist, he was a member of a top-level consultative committee that advises the Communist Party on policy. Although largely powerless, the committee provided Professor He with some cover to step up his criticism of Falun Gong.

He started by sending a letter to President Jiang Zemin, warning him that a new religion with tens of millions of followers was spreading across China. The letter, which he titled "Reckless Falun Gong," was written by Professor He and five fellow members of the committee. There was no reply.

Refusing to be discouraged, Professor He began writing articles for any publication that would accept his work. Most followed the party's three-nots campaign, but a few regional journals, unaware of the central government's policy, were happy to run articles by the famous scientist. "The bigger papers . . . were afraid they'd have to apologize," Professor He said. "So I had to publish in these small newspapers and magazines."

While Professor He plugged away, Falun Gong enjoyed a banner year in 1998. Though its founder, Master Li, had emigrated to the United States, he returned occasionally to coordinate activities and stayed in close contact with practitioners through a tightly knit organization. Critics such as Professor He continued their pinprick attacks, but the party's do-nothing policies coupled with Falun Gong's assertiveness had marginalized them.

"The government was mostly supportive of us," said Zhang Erping, a Falun Gong spokesman who lives in New York told me in a telephone interview. "Many top leaders seemed to support us."

This impression was understandable but wrong. Most of China's leaders didn't accept or agree with Falun Gong; their crude governing apparatus had simply kept them in the dark, capable only of stifling public debate on the new religion. That was about to change, not because leaders had become wiser, but because Falun Gong was to make a tactical mistake.

As 1998 wound down, Professor He decided to write a short commentary for a small student magazine called *Science and Technology Knowledge for Youth*. The article, "Why Young People Shouldn't Practice Qigong," was one of his typical blasts at all forms of qigong, which he said was more suitable to older, less-active people. Young people, he said, shouldn't sit around meditating; they should be out exercising, running, jumping and in general being as vigorous as he still was. Halfway through the article, Professor He mentioned Falun Gong and then, in a key phrase that angered the group, referred to Master Li in a mildly derisive term as its *toutou,* or "boss."

The response came quickly. The day after the magazine was printed, protesters arrived at its offices on the campus of Tianjin Normal University, located in the port city of Tianjin, about a hundred miles east of Beijing. From April 20 to 23, as many as 6,000 occupied the university, demanding a retraction.

The group's response seemed excessive—after all, the magazine is not widely read and few would have noticed if Falun Gong had let the issue rest. Part of its insistence on apologies and retractions is certainly the self-righteousness found in many religions—the idea that any criticism is an insult against an eternal truth. But there was more to it than that. Falun Gong activists also knew that in communist China small critiques in the media are often a thin wedge. Indeed, the infamous Cultural Revolution began with the critique of a play that might have allegorically criticized Chairman Mao. The group may have been overzealous, but in many ways it understood perfectly how the communists ran society.

This time, however, there would be no retractions. "The publishers called me," Professor He said. "And asked me what was going on. I told them that as a science publication, they had better not print a retraction. They had a duty to the truth." The editors held the line.

With no apology forthcoming, angry Falun Gong members then made their fateful decision to seek help from the very top echelons of the party in Beijing. It was a turn of events that even Professor He couldn't have foreseen. He had hoped his magazine articles would attract leaders' attention; instead, his articles provoked Falun Gong into delivering his message for him.

The protest was like a mirage. It materialized during the morning of April 25, 1999, as Falun Gong adherents converged on the Communist Party's headquarters in central Beijing. Then, after about six hours of quiet sitting outside the compound's perimeter, it slowly vanished as the protesters went home at dark. There were no placards, no shouting, no disturbances. Only about 10,000 people quietly challenging the government to legalize their group.

The leadership compound is called Zhongnanhai, which means Central and South Lakes, in reference to the two lakes around which the group of imperial palaces and modern buildings is grouped. The protesters had gathered to the north, south and west of the compound—the east side abuts the Forbidden City. It was the heart of communist power, just as it had been the heart of imperial China for six centuries.

The quietness only made it odder, even unnerving. Police cars had blocked off the main roads leading to the protest, and central Beijing was turned into a giant pedestrian zone. As I walked by the wall of people, I could only wonder what it was like inside for the government. They could hear nothing, but they knew that under their noses, without any warning from the country's vaunted Public Security Bureau, a group had formed, one whose exceptional organizational power could pull off this well-disciplined demonstration. I heard later that some frantic officials remembered Professor He and called him up, demanding material on Falun Gong. He couriered over a packet, including Mr. Chen's book.

Some of the protesters sat on the ground practicing their exercises, while others stood around, waiting for something to happen. Most were suspicious of outsiders, unwilling to talk or to criticize the government.

"We don't want to say anything," an old man said. "You cannot solve our problem, only the government can do this. Therefore, we want to talk only to the government."

Although Falun Gong would later say that the protest was spontaneous, a fair degree of planning had clearly gone into it. The protesters seemed to have unofficial marshals, who made sure that the protest stayed quiet and that no one said anything. Most seemed to be from Beijing, but from the accents, I and other reporters there knew that some protesters were from Falun

Gong's homeland in northeastern China. Perhaps they had been in Tianjin for the first protest against Professor He's article and made the short trip to Beijing for this protest.

The police presence was light, a reflection of the shock that had engulfed the government. The party maintained, and had largely convinced outside observers, that it had a firm grip on China. Stability ruled in China, unlike those other ex-communist countries that were beset by turmoil. And while China certainly did not have any wars going on and by many measures was stable, here was something that didn't fit: 10,000 people who had somehow been organized without the government's knowledge. In my experience, whenever two or more democratic activists got together they'd be busted. How had 10,000 members of a new religion been organized to travel to Beijing? I wondered if the government's control over society could be as strong as we imagined, or if it wasn't hollowing out.

As I walked on, I saw a policeman ask a group of three elderly women what they were practicing. He shook his head in bewilderment when they said Falun Gong.

Nearby, a young man from the Beijing Post and Telecommunication University said he had come to demonstrate because he'd heard that Falun Gong had been libeled in a student newspaper somewhere. He was clearly referring to the Tianjin article but didn't know the details. It seemed that someone had told him to come down to protest and he'd obeyed.

After walking along the north end of the compound, I wanted to turn left and head south along the side of the compound. The road was blocked, but some marshals tried to keep order.

"Pedestrians, please walk on the right side and do not stand on the road," a middle-aged woman told people entering the street.

I spoke to another old man, who said he was from Hebei Province, which is located next to Beijing.

"Falun Gong is great," he said, dressed in a white shirt, windbreaker and baggy cotton trousers. "If you practice it, you won't get sick. The government could save a lot of money on health care if it allowed Falun Gong. That's why we're here: to make the government understand this."

"Why does the government need to understand this?" I asked.

"It's been criticized in some newspaper. We think it's going to be banned."

"Which paper?"

"I don't know, some youth newspaper. It doesn't matter. We just want to be a legally recognized form of qigong. That's it."

"How long have you been here?"

"Since seven-thirty a.m. I came here after my morning exercises."

Then a young lady came up and stopped him from speaking.

"We don't allow interviews," she said. "Sorry."

The old man kept quiet and I moved on.

Many Beijingers stopped and asked questions, but likewise were met with silence.

"What do you want?" a young man said after stopping his bicycle in front of a group.

No one answered.

He shrugged.

"I've never heard of a demonstration where no one says anything," he said and then biked on.

Other locals were less blasé.

"You're just causing trouble," one said to an old man. "Don't rock the boat," another said a bit later. "Look at the disturbance you're causing," a woman said to a third group. "This is only going to cause trouble for you and all of us. Don't be so selfish."

The comments reminded me of the remarks that family members might make about a troublesome relative: Don't speak about that because it'll only set him off. It was the way a lot of citizens around the world are forced to deal with their governments—as an unpredictable force that is better left alone.

The ordinary citizens' instincts were accurate. The decision to protest in Beijing was a colossal miscalculation by Falun Gong. A crackdown was inevitable and anyone not completely naïve or blinded by belief could see that.

I walked along farther and saw a group of people reading a letter. It was from the Beijing Public Security Bureau and the city's Petitions and Appeals Office. "The government has no intention of banning Falun Gong," the letter read. "Appeals should be made through the usual channels."

That promise turned out to be false, but at the time it seemed reasonable. A group of demonstrators reportedly went inside the leadership compound and met with Premier Zhu Rongji, who also made conciliatory remarks. By nightfall the protesters had dispersed.

But the government soon made its true feelings known. President Jiang Zemin issued an open letter to all senior leaders, calling Falun Gong a threat to the party's authority. In the letter—which was also read aloud in party cell meetings, so everyone got the message—Mr. Jiang chastised the government's security apparatus for allowing the protest to take place.

"We called for 'stability above all,' but our stability has fallen through," Mr. Jiang wrote. "Our leaders must wake up."

Soon, the creaky government bureaucracy that had ignored and unwittingly encouraged Falun Gong for years started to formulate a response to the group. But there was to be no public discussion on religious freedom, as Mr. Chen wanted, nor the sort of robust, no-gloves debate favored by Professor He.

Instead, the party took the only action it knew. It set up a bureau called Office 610—named for the date, June 10, when it was formed. Its job was to mobilize the country's pliant social organizations. Under orders from the Public Security Bureau, churches, temples, mosques, newspapers, media, courts and police all quickly lined up behind the government's simple plan: to crush Falun Gong, no measures too excessive. Within days a wave of arrests swept China. By the end of 1999, Falun Gong adherents were dying in custody. In February 2000 it was Ms. Chen's turn.

The day after seeing her mother's corpse laid out for cremation in February 2000, Ms. Zhang decided she'd find out who killed her mother. "I felt that something wasn't right, and that they were hiding something," she said. "None of it made any sense."

She hit upon a simple task to start her quest: to obtain her mother's death certificate. Police or hospitals are supposed to issue to family members who request it a person's death certificate, a single piece of paper that confirms that the person is dead and states the cause of death. Ms. Zhang wanted the certificate so she could launch a complaint about how her mother died. Without the certificate, she couldn't request an official investigation—the courts needed proof that her mother had died violently. So she set out to prove that her mother had been killed.

She met with her brother, a twenty-eight-year-old mechanic, and he agreed they should act. But he was not sure what to do. The death certificate seemed like a good idea, but he had no idea how to obtain it. How about asking at the police? he suggested. Ms. Zhang went to her husband and he also agreed that something should be done, but he also was of little help, other than advising caution: "I didn't think it'd lead to much but, if she had to do it, it's okay," he told me later. "It was a matter of family honor."

What I liked about Ms. Zhang was her bluntness and stubbornness. It was obvious that she had no experience with politics and, at least at first, had little idea how China's political system worked. That was unsurprising because like most Chinese, Ms. Zhang had avoided politics, a messy subject that was only trouble.

In fact, she was once the sort of person who floated easily through reform-era China, taking advantage of the party's cautious economic reforms and relatively relaxed grip on society. She'd worked first as a clerk at a department store, later improving herself by taking accounting classes in her spare time. She married, had a son and went to work as a bookkeeper. Later, after neighbors praised her skill in arranging a few marriages, she worked as a freelance matchmaker—not arranging marriages as traditionally was done, but introducing potential brides and grooms to each other.

Her appearance added to the impression that she was a very ordinary person. She wasn't dressed like many of the Falun Gong bumpkins from the countryside—unlike her mother, for example, she didn't wear old-fashioned padded jackets and cloth shoes. Instead, she wore dark polyester slacks and bright printed blouses, unchic by the standards of China's big cosmopolitan cities but the uniform of a slowly modernizing, slowly prospering hinterland of a billion people. Her hair was cut short, which was practical, but in a concession to fashion was sometimes permed. Her eyes, dark and clear, were remote when she spoke, as though she was trying to visualize what she was saying.

Now she was trying to see justice done for her mother. It was hard to imagine such an abstract idea, but she pursued it with a matter-of-fact air that I often saw in China's lower classes. There was no hopelessness, only a shoulder-to-the-wheel attitude of people used to struggling and not getting very far. She cried in front of me only once, when describing how she'd refused to pay her mother's fine the day before she was beaten to death. Mostly, though, she was coolly analytical and indefatigable, wanting only to get on with it and obtain that piece of paper.

She turned first to the hospital. They told her that they had just issued a paper ordering the crematorium to burn her mother's body. It wasn't the death certificate, but it confirmed that her mother was dead and stated the cause. She decided to get a copy of that document and went back to the hospital. A receptionist sent her to an official in the records department who handed her a piece of paper on hospital letterhead. It was addressed to the local street committee and read:

Citizen Chen Zixiu from your district suffered from heart attack and died suddenly at 9:30 a.m. on Feb. 21, 2000, in this hospital after unsuccessful rescue attempts. The corpse has been kept in mortuary for more than 30 hours, and spots have appeared (on the skin). As it has started to rot and the hospital can't maintain it longer, please inform relatives of the dead to transfer the corpse to funeral parlor as soon as possible.

WEIFANG MUNICIPAL HOSPITAL

FEBRUARY 22, 2000

Stamped at the bottom was the hospital's seal. Ms. Zhang studied it for a few minutes. This couldn't be true. She spoke to the official: "A heart attack? What about the bruises? The broken teeth? The blood? I want a copy of the death certificate." The official looked at her like she was mad. She asked to see the corpse again. The official went out, came back five minutes later and said it was impossible. It was in storage and couldn't be brought out without proper authorization. Would she please make arrangements to have the body cremated?

Ms. Zhang left in a daze. It was slowly dawning on her how difficult her battle would be. She went home and conferred with her brother. They'd read about China's legal system, which was in the news all the time, with reports of people suing each other for this or that. It wasn't quite like the lawsuit-happy United States, but China was developing into a litigious society, and the party was trumpeting this in the media as a sign that the country was maturing and that a credible legal system had been created. Ms. Zhang decided to sue the government, demanding that it issue the death certificate.

But unlike the peasant champion or the dispossessed home-owners—who at least could give the appearance that they were simply suing in the name of lower taxes and cultural preservation—Ms. Zhang was challenging the government's stated top priority: crushing Falun Gong. Here one couldn't argue that this was a simple administrative lawsuit; this was as political as it got. She learned this when she called lawyers for help. None would even allow her in the front door for a consultation, let alone file a suit on her behalf. She spent the next three weeks going from one lawyer to another, until finally one told her that they'd been instructed by the government not to handle cases regarding Falun Gong.

On March 17, Ms. Zhang got a letter from the hospital saying her mother's body would be cremated that same day. She called the hospital and said she was launching an inquiry into her mother's death. Don't cremate the body, she said. The official on the phone told her to write a letter. She did but figured the exercise was hopeless and that her mother would be cremated.

Next, she sent letters to the State Council, the highest body of civilian power in China, and to local media, demanding that the state send her a copy of her mother's death certificate. They ignored her. The police, however, didn't; for the next six weeks she was interrogated repeatedly for what she calculates was a total of 107 hours. Finally, in late April, she was sentenced to fifteen days in prison for "distorting facts and disturbing social order."

The detention was a turning point. "I was thrown in with common criminals and could finally see the injustice that my mother had suffered," Ms. Zhang told me after she got out of prison. "I decided to learn everything I could and challenge the authorities using their own language."

Upon her release, she stopped working as a matchmaker to devote herself full-time to pressing her mother's case. She bought handbooks on the law and learned how to make official requests for documents and how to appeal refusals. Her husband remained passively supportive, accepting the family's reduced income but never actively helping her.

She reminded me of Mr. Ma, the peasant lawyer. Like him, she'd taught herself about the law and developed a sophisticated knowledge of appeals and procedures. But Mr. Ma had organized what amounted to a political movement against the government—a band of peasants who traveled hill and valley to spread the word of fair taxes. Others, like Mr. Fang the architect, showed how a person could mobilize thousands by force of intellect, cleverly negotiating his ideas through the barriers and reefs of censors and bureaucrats. Ms. Zhang, though, was more typical. Like most Chinese, she had few allies and little sophistication. She was one person fighting a small battle, the consequences hers to bear.

She was aided in many practical matters by Falun Gong adherents who had withstood the government's onslaught. Brother Li, for example, had given me some of the original documents and had later smuggled them out of China. He and others helped Ms. Zhang find accommodations and locate the petitions and appeals offices. Knowing their location was important because—in another sign of schizophrenia—their location was kept a secret. It was like a test: if you can find us, you can complain to us. "Only they [the Falun Gong adherents] could really understand the frustrations I had and the hurdles I had to face every day," she said to me during a trip to Beijing.

Adherents like Brother Li had managed to survive the government's crackdown by putting together an ad hoc group of volunteers, interchangeable activists who could step in when any were jailed. Before the crackdown, Falun Gong was carefully organized like the government, with a structure that paralleled the government's hierarchy. That was quickly smashed by the Public Security Bureau, which threw thousands in jail. Now it was the Brother Lis of China who were holding the movement together and helping people like Ms. Zhang along the way.

In early July, I set out with Brother Li on a bike ride through the city. Throughout the summer we took several of these trips, avoiding tails and meeting up at a sports stadium in eastern Beijing to tour through the city and chat about life.

We discussed almost anything imaginable, but we always returned to his beliefs. I think he saw in me a possible convert. Like an evangelical Christian, who believes that everyone should be saved and genuinely wants to share the Word with the unbelievers, Brother Li wanted me to understand the good news of Falun Gong. This was a system of beliefs that had made his life meaningful, setting out a strict moral code that stood in contrast with what he saw as the amorality of daily life in China. It was a complete cosmology, with a creation story, and a promise of salvation and heaven—and of hell to those who did not believe and follow. Of course, he'd want me to know about such a gift, and I accepted his solicitousness as it was meant: as a token of friendship and genuine concern.

Not that I could really get my head around much of the teachings. I had a hard time with the main text, *Turning the Dharma Wheel*, because to me it lacked the beauty of, say, the Buddhist sutras or other religious classics. I could see why the text might be appealing to many mainland Chinese, with its simple language, appeal to science and emphasis on personal health. Perhaps I just lacked this personal history, but in my mind Master Li's writings lacked the genius that had touched some of the writers of the sutras, the Taoist canon, the Bible or the Koran. But I was always eager to talk to Brother Li about how he felt about the texts, and how he interpreted Master Li's message.

One hazy morning we set off on our simple steel-framed bikes toward Tiananmen Square. It was two weeks before the first anniversary of the government's July 22, 1999, ban on the Falun Gong movement, the startling announcement that Ms. Chen had heard on her television. Brother Li knew that scores of out-of-town adherents who had been undeterred by the death of Ms. Chen and others would soon descend on Beijing to appeal against the crackdown. His plan was to help prepare for their arrival. Today was a scouting day, and he intended to provide information on the likely police presence around the square to any adherent who called him for information.

He could expect many calls in the coming weeks. His beeper number was well known among the informal network of protesters, and our two-hour ride was punctuated several times by pager messages from Falun Gong members requesting help. "Everyone decides for themselves how to be of most use," he said to me as we set off west toward the square. "This is something I can do."

Like our bicycle ride, that year, 2000, was interspersed with the unexpected. The government had an overwhelming advantage over Falun Gong and looked like it would crush the group. But for a year now, small people like Brother Li had resisted, succeeding in staging regular protests in the Chinese capital. They'd be arrested, beaten and some, like Ms. Chen, killed, but their faith kept them coming back. It was at times sickening to watch, like a boxer whose fight should be called before he is permanently injured. But it was also uplifting. A decade earlier a sustained series of protests in the face of a government crackdown would have been inconceivable. Now they were so common that the foreign media soon tired of them and at times only the duty-bound foreign wire services sent reporters.

As Tiananmen Square came into sight, Brother Li's beeper went off. It was a message to call a pay phone in Beijing. Brother Li angled his one-speed black bike over to the curb and stopped in front of a bank of pay phones. A wave of cyclists rushed past, and as he dismounted, he noticed that all the phones were occupied.

Experience quelled the temptation to turn on his cell phone. Not only can conversations be monitored, but the phones are dangerous even when they are only switched on. That's because security agents can figure out which transmitter the phone is getting its signal from. In a city like Beijing, where a high density of mobile phones means transmitters are located every few blocks, police could trace Brother Li from one signal tower to the next, triangulating his position and following him through town.

A few weeks earlier one of Brother Li's associates was almost nabbed when he used a mobile phone to set up a meeting. A novice to the group's security measures, he arrived at the rendezvous point to find the area crawling with suspicious-looking people. Although he jumped into a cab and left, the two followers he was supposed to meet were detained. Caution was paramount.

Finally, a public phone came free and Brother Li called. From the receiver came an excited voice—that of a Falun Gong practitioner from northeast China who was in the capital to find someone to help her send an e-mail to the outside world. She told Brother Li that a teenage Falun Gong believer had died trying to escape from police custody by leaping from a train. Like many Falun Gong newcomers to the city, the woman had heard of Brother Li through a friend of a friend. Brother Li had no idea who she was, but after talking to her for a while, he figured she wasn't a police plant. He agreed to meet her later in the day.

"You can usually tell if the people are genuine," he said, hopping on his bike and heading back down the road in the stifling heat. "They make references to things that the police wouldn't know about and have this earnest air about them."

The woman, who had spent the previous night outside in a park, was desperate for accommodation. Practitioners used to stay with Brother Li, but his three-room apartment in Beijing's eastern district was now watched by security agents. Like most people who had continued to practice Falun Gong during the year since the crackdown, the woman had been fired from her job and had little money. She could survive only through the generosity of fellow practitioners.

Helping her was easier because the government's grip over society was continuing to relax. Not too long ago—until the mid-to-late 1990s, depending on the part of the country—state-run factories paid for all manner of social benefits, including insurance, pension and even local schools. Paramount was housing, which was handed out by employers, be they factories or ministries. Truly private companies were few, and even they had to offer some sort of housing. That meant that neighbors knew each other—they were, after all, colleagues. And the blocks where they lived were guarded by retirees who certainly would know if an outsider was living there.

But as reforms took hold, profits took precedence over control. Companies realized they couldn't be competitive in a market economy if they had to run apartment blocks and provide other social services. So apartments were sold off and began to change hands. Residents couldn't always assume that their neighbors were from their company. They got used to having strangers living next to them. So, too, the watchmen, who no longer could be sure of who was living where.

Brother Li and his colleagues used these changes to their advantage. A fellow Falun Gong adherent who worked for a textile company had an extra apartment, and Brother Li could let the woman stay there without anyone noticing. Over the phone he promised the adherent a place to stay and gave her his friend's beeper number. Another little task accomplished.

As we pedaled across the north end of Tiananmen Square, we didn't attract much attention. Beijing is full of foreigners, and one biking with a Chinese person hadn't been a novelty in years. For his part, Brother Li looked like any of the thousands of other cyclists who at that moment were riding past the cavernous square. Wearing a striped short-sleeve shirt and black polyester pants, he cut a trim figure, his face often breaking out into a broad, easy smile as we chatted. But then his eyes, usually languid and distant, suddenly lit up.

"There and there," he said, making quick mental notes. "The police are all along the entrances to the pedestrian underpasses"— useful information that he would later share with adherents arriving in Beijing.

We met again the next day and cycled past Workers' Stadium

in Beijing, talking about his beliefs. For weeks now he had been agonizing over whether to go to Tiananmen Square himself and protest. He brought up Ms. Chen's death and said he was sure he could resist the torture. After all, he said, it was his duty to let the government know his feelings toward the ban. But he also knew that he was of more use out of jail, where he could continue to coordinate protests.

It was a debate that consumed many Falun Gong adherents. Back in the United States, Master Li had recently started publishing new essays on his Internet site. Computer-literate adherents printed them out and distributed them widely. One, "Toward Consummation," was distributed in August 2000 and was widely reprinted. In it Master Li argues against worldly attachments. In Falun Gong's sometimes turgid jargon, he also urged adherents to protest—to "step forward" and show their belief in the Fa, or immutable law of the universe: "What's unfolding at present was arranged long ago in history. Those disciples who have stepped forward to validate the Fa in the face of the pressure are courageous and admirable."

He wasn't directly ordering people to protest, but the message was clear. It was similar to the Christian idea that one has to "stand up for Jesus." Given the current crackdown, however, I was frightened at the thought of people being encouraged, even if only indirectly, to protest. I kept my thoughts to myself, silently hoping that Brother Li wouldn't go to the square.

His beeper went off again and he pulled over to make a call. It was an adherent from Guangdong Province in the south who had been in Beijing helping people from her region survive in the distant capital, with its incomprehensible dialect and tight security.

A few months earlier the woman had debated going to

Tiananmen Square to protest—an act that always winds up with arrest and detention without charge. At a meeting with Brother Li before heading back, the woman, a thirty-two-year-old unemployed English teacher with a pale face and a tiny voice, decided not to protest. Instead, she said she'd return to Guangdong to tell about the situation in Beijing. "Many followers need to be reminded that others are protesting. This will give them courage."

Now she was calling to say she had made it back safely and to ask for any news. Most of the contact between regions was to exchange basic intelligence—where police are active and who is out of jail and how they can be reached. Members also share stories of police abuse and protests to bolster their spirits. Brother Li told her that demonstrations have been going on daily, even if on some days only a few made it to Tiananmen Square.

We were at a pay phone in a kiosk, and with the vendor listening to our end of the conversation, Brother Li didn't speak too explicitly.

"We've still got a lot of friends visiting town. We're still very active," Brother Li said, referring to the protests. "Let everyone know we're fine in Beijing."

He hung up and we continued to ride. We passed through the capital's bar district, a narrow street lined with pubs called Durty Nellie's and Nashville and, at night, with prostitutes and revelers. In his mind the risks he took were worthwhile because his faith stood in direct contrast to this moral decay. After decades of communist attacks on people's beliefs, morality had been damaged. Brother Li felt he was helping to restore standards.

Not too long ago Mr. Li had given little thought to such spiritual matters, striving for the promotions and business trips abroad that define success in modern China. He had worked as an accountant at a textile mill, got married and had a son. A year ago, just before the ban was announced, he heard about Falun Gong, and began to practice, at first out of curiosity but then with increasing fervor.

About six months later Brother Li was suddenly forced to decide how much Falun Gong meant to him. Worried about pressure from their government masters, managers at his state-owned mill told him that he should stop practicing. The decision, he said, was easy: he quit his job and since then has occupied his time with odd jobs and with helping the movement survive.

He was living on a monthly $40 stipend from the local welfare office, an amount so small that he liked to say he reminded himself of the famous Chinese aphorism "The great hermit lives in the city"—which means that anyone can be a hermit in a remote mountain cave; resisting the temptations of the material world while among people was a greater feat. Accordingly, he had stripped his life down to the simplest of clothes and only one luxury: a pair of black plastic wraparound sunglasses against the blinding summer sun. Pagers were cheap here, and so were phone calls. He had bought his cell phone, which he rarely used now, when he had a job. With his wife's salary as a clerk in a factory, the Li family just made ends meet.

"We live in a bad world, one that needs good people who believe in doing good deeds," Brother Li said quietly, embarrassed at having to explain his beliefs. "Life is a test to see if you can be a good person."

He was interrupted again by his pager. We coasted to a stop next to a telephone by the side of the road. It was another follower from Guangdong Province who needed a fellow believer picked up at the airport. Brother Li quickly called a Falun Gong member who drove an unregistered cab—one of the thousands of private taxis that had sprung up in recent years. The cabby agreed to take the passenger without charging; another problem solved.

Arrest was always on Brother Li's mind. To minimize risk he followed a few basic rules. Meetings with adherents lasted just a few minutes. Calls were clipped and ambiguous. Sensitive information was exchanged only in person. Pagers changed as often as he could afford—he had gone through three in the past four months. With adherents regularly arrested, he knew that phone lists, some of which must have his beeper number on them, would fall into police hands. Once police knew his account, they could tell the pager companies to hand over the lists of people who'd left messages for him, a disaster the movement couldn't afford.

We rode around for another hour. Brother Li noted a few pay phones for future use and headed home. The temperature was over 100 degrees, and even Brother Li, usually so cool and calm, started sweating.

He was continuing to agonize over whether he should go to Tiananmen Square to protest. In some ways, a key weapon that Falun Gong practitioners had in their battle against the Public Security Bureau was the randomness of their actions. While protests increased in intensity around certain anniversaries, protesters went to the square almost daily, driven by the dictates of their conscience. Now Brother Li's conscience told him to go to the square. "I feel it is my duty to let the government know it's wrong," he said. "But if I stay out of prison, I might be of more use."

As he weighed his options, the one thing he didn't consider was his timing—but his turned out to be impeccable. Two days later he and his wife went to Tiananmen, sat cross-legged in the Falun Gong meditating position and were quickly thrown in jail. It was early enough in the month so the judges weren't yet hand-ing down the heavy sentences that some later got for protesting directly on the July 22 anniversary. In fact, as a first-time offender, he was held only fifteen days. But it was long enough for his stay to overlap with the wave of arrests that flooded the prison around the anniversary and the accompanying police brutality. He saw a fellow prisoner beaten unconscious. His wife went on a hunger strike to protest the cramped conditions of ten women to a cell. Suddenly, in late July, he was released.

But as we dismounted to catch our breath, it was still early July, and all he knew was that it was his turn to test his faith. It was late afternoon and the cicadas drowned out everything but Brother Li's voice.

"You know my decision," he said. "I'll call you when I get out."

Unlike Brother Li, Ms. Zhang was also helped by her fame. The United Nations, for example, had cited her mother's case in its triennial review of China's compliance with the U.N. Treaty Against Torture. The U.S. Department of State also drew attention toward it.

That seemed to prevent police from touching Ms. Zhang. After she was briefly detained in April, police left her alone. One friend of hers said she seemed to have a shield around her—while other government opponents were sentenced to long jail terms, she remained free, largely because of the international attention. To some degree I knew that I was like a scientist who changes the thing he is observing simply by observing it. I never told her what to do or gave her any encouragement at all. Indeed, weeks went by without our speaking to each other, and she never called me. But I am sure that my articles in the *Wall Street Journal* allowed her to stay free when others might have been jailed. To that degree, I abetted her quest; without the coverage, she might have vanished into the prison system.

Ms. Zhang's efforts continued to center on her mother's death certificate. After the police and the crematorium refused her requests for the certificate, she decided to go through more formal channels, filing written requests for the certificate.

After being released from detention in late April, she spent most of May shuttling between offices of the Public Security Bureau in her hometown. Officials at the district office told her that they couldn't release the death certificate and that she should appeal to the higher-level bureau that controls the municipality. That bureau referred her back to the district office, arguing that the lower-level office had to furnish a copy of records before the higher-level office could act. Back at the district office, officials said nonsense: the highers-up didn't need the certificate. Go away.

Frustrated, Ms. Zhang decided in early June to bypass the squabbling officials in Weifang by appealing to officials in the provincial capital, Jinan. Her goal now was to push the provincial procurator's office, which acts like a prosecutor's office in the United States, to file criminal charges against the local Public Security Bureau for failing to release the death certificate.

But the procurator's office, which works closely with security forces, told her to file a civil lawsuit. When she approached lawyers, however, they told her the Ministry of Justice had issued a directive to all lawyers in the country ordering them not to accept cases related to Falun Gong. Stymied again, she headed for Beijing and the central government's Petitions and Appeals Office, where Mr. Ma the peasant champion had been beaten up a year earlier.

I caught up with her in June, a few weeks before my bike ride with Brother Li. Her six-year-old son in tow, she trudged through the heavy heat toward the Petitions and Appeals Office of the State Council, which is the highest executive body in the central government. Each city, county, province and many ministries have their own petitions office—the Shaanxi farmers, for example, had tried to file a grievance with their local district government's appeals office. But Ms. Zhang was now at the pinnacle of all appeals offices. It was a Mecca for lost causes, the central magnet for the legions of Chinese who felt they'd suffered injustice.

The Petitions Office was located in the south of the city, near a filthy canal. The street had a few scrawny trees that were withering in the dry Beijing air. As we walked down the street, I felt I was back in Shaanxi on the Loess Plateau, the white tile and concrete of Beijing as monochromatic as the barren yellow soil of China's cultural heartland.

As Ms. Zhang hurried from the subway toward the Petitions and Appeals Office, she passed groups of people who, like her, were availing themselves of their right to petition. It was a tradition that went back centuries, and which the party has maintained as a safety valve. We stopped for a moment to look at one bedraggled peasant crouching over a sheaf of papers, moving his pen in the air, trying to remember how to write the word "expropriate." His clan had been trying for fourteen years to recover land that they say had been taken illegally by officials.

The building's entrance is in an alley and is watched carefully by plainclothes police. I drifted back, letting Ms. Zhang walk ahead toward the office. A dozen agents with shifty stares and mobile phones watched her. Security agents at the entrance to the alley stopped her and asked if she was a Falun Gong adherent. Those who answer affirmatively are turned back or even arrested. Ms. Zhang, though, could truthfully say that she didn't practice Falun Gong and that her problem was a simple case of police abuse. She walked in. I peeled back and waited for her down the street.

Two hours later she came out, shaking her head. "They said it was a criminal case and should be handled by the Public Security Bureau's appeals office," she said, walking back along the garbage-filled canal. "That's my next stop," she said, and disappeared into a subway station.

Ms. Zhang hesitated before going to the Public Security Bureau's appeals office. It wasn't the fear of stepping inside the bureau's offices, a move that would brand her forever as a troublemaker. Instead, it was worry for her son that made her think twice. He had been crying at the sight of uniformed men ever since police had started harassing the family. She didn't want to upset him anymore and wondered whether she was going too far. Perhaps she should just go home. But she knew she had to go through with this. We met later that morning at another subway station and headed to the office.

We were in one of my favorite parts of Beijing—the old city that the urban activists like Mr. Fang were trying to save. The bureau was located in an old courtyard house that used to belong to a prince in the royal family, which was deposed in the 1911 revolution. Like most palaces, it is discreetly located behind a gray-washed wall, the only clue to its noble ancestry being the broad red doors with stone lions out front. I thought back to other former palaces I'd visited, trying to imagine the odd mixture of modern state power and feudal elegance that this office incorporated. I imagined the four wings of a traditional Chinese building set on each side of a small square courtyard. In the middle: a shady plane tree planted several hundred years ago, its impenetrable foliage rising over the slate roofing tiles and upturned eaves. It was a fitting place for Ms. Zhang to take her appeal, as she followed in the wake of Chinese down the centuries who asked the emperor for help, each sure that if only his majesty knew the truth, the problem would be solved.

It was nearly noon when she arrived and visiting hours were already over for the morning. Another defeat. The adrenaline that had kept her going the past few days ebbed. Her son scampered away, hoping his mother would follow.

Ms. Zhang took a deep breath and decided to visit one more place before giving up. Beijing is dotted with several lesser petitions offices that belong to various minor ministries. Maybe just one of them, she said, could help. Nearby was the petition office of the All-China Women's Federation, a government-run organization that is supposed to look after the interests of China's 650 million women. She grabbed her son by the hand and headed over.

We lost our way in the maze of alleys that make up Beijing's slowly shrinking old city, but finally found the unmarked office. I waited outside, then followed in behind her. The woman behind the reception desk looked up, and Ms. Zhang quickly stated her case. I stood back, holding a map and pretending to have a question about directions. The woman listened carefully to Ms. Zhang, nodded and sighed. Then she pushed her glasses up on the bridge of her nose and spoke carefully: "Rule of law is still rudimentary right now. This case will be hard to solve, but you have to go back to the Public Security Bureau."

The answer was blunt, but was the first civil reply Ms. Zhang had received from the dozens of bureaucrats she had approached. Her courage grew. She gathered up her son and headed out into the heat, vowing to return to the Public Security Bureau in the afternoon.

At 2 p.m. she walked up once again to the unmarked door. Her son had fallen asleep. Ms. Zhang carried him slung over her shoulder and pushed open the red door.

An hour later she emerged, her face beaming. She carefully held a letter sealed by the Public Security Bureau that she suspected contained orders for the local security bureaus to give her the death certificate. She shook her head in amazement. "I don't know," she said, letting her son down gently to the ground as he woke up. "Maybe I can finally get an answer."

Back in Weifang two days later she went straight to the local office of the Public Security Bureau. When an official there opened the letter, she caught a glimpse of the brief order: "Handle this case in writing"—in other words, give a written response. Ms. Zhang was ecstatic. If police had to give a written answer, they couldn't deny her the certificate, she reasoned. A written denial could be appealed, so they'd have to finally give in and hand over the document she'd sought for months.

But then days passed without reply. She returned again and again to the local bureau until finally someone in the office told her that the local police had decided to ignore the order from Beijing—after all, who was going to call them to account?

As the stifling summer slowly came to an end, Ms. Zhang began to realize that she wouldn't get her mother's death certificate. The experience, though, had transformed her. She was still the woman from Weifang who spoke Mandarin Chinese with an accent, lapsing into folksy expressions. She still dressed simply and occasionally permed her hair. Yet she had insights into China that a normal person would never have. Local people, like the peasants in Shaanxi, might know about a local injustice. But like Mr. Ma the peasant champion and Mr. Fang the architect, Ms.

Zhang had been forced to examine her life and her country in ways that most people do not. She did not have a sophisticated political vocabulary, yet I found it easier to talk about China with her than with almost anyone else I'd encountered in China. One didn't have to ignore topics such as repression or pretend that huge segments of one's life were off limits. She knew that. Yet she loved China in ways that I could understand—we both enjoyed green tea, the country's simple northern food, and the dusty beauty of the North China Plain.

The experience also taught her to write essays, something she hadn't done since high school. The constant flow of petitions and appeals that she had to produce focused her mind and forced her to express her frustrations with pen and paper. In September we met for a coffee in Beijing and she handed me an essay she'd written by hand. It was titled "I Am Willing to Trust the Government, But Can the Government Convince Me?"—a description of her travails and the lessons she'd learned.

The process of petitioning, she wrote, "enabled me to meet people being treated unfairly and to listen to the ridiculous things that happened to them. Apart from Falun Gong practitioners, who are taken away by the public security, less than 10 percent of those [other] petitioners expect to have their problems settled. Most petitioners only get a chance to exchange their complaints with each other and end up with empty pockets. Among the dozens of officials who received my petition, nobody talked to me for longer than fifteen minutes and most of them were impatient."

It was a telling comment on the archaic process of petitions and appeals. The petitions system bankrupts already poor people, sometimes leaving them stranded in Beijing, unable to afford the train ticket home. I thought back to peasants I'd seen outside the Petitions and Appeals Office. I'd gone there numerous times during my seven years in China and met people who'd been in Beijing for years on end, hoping for an audience with the elusive powers that run the country.

As I read on, I realized that Ms. Zhang had become convinced of the need for basic freedoms in a way that the elite of China, most of them corrupted by money or proximity to power, still have not grasped.

"I didn't quite understand Mother's act [of protesting]," she wrote. "On last April 25, I objected to the gathering [of Falun Gong demonstrators]. But after a long march to Beijing this time, I realized that a single person can do nothing to settle any problem. A big crowd of petitioners like in the April 25 affair would cause enough attention. These people petitioned in a peaceful and polite way for the benefit of the group. Seeing the anger and the sadness of other petitioners, I am calm. I'm lucky because I know the reason why we can't make it."

In other words, people have a right to protest, but individual efforts, like her own, are doomed to failure. That is why, she has learned, "we can't make it." It is a sad realization to come to after months of frustration and anger. Similar conclusions had led people like Mr. Ma to organize larger-scale protests and people like Mr. Fang to effect change slowly, by force of his ideas. She has come to realize what all people who want to change China eventually learn: the current system is at a dead end, but its death is not in sight.

After reading Ms. Zhang's essay I tried to call her but could only reach a neighbor of hers in Weifang. The Falun Gong community in the small city is suffocating, the woman said. I asked her what she meant, and she said that more practitioners have died in the months since Ms. Zhang's mother's death. I had been vaguely aware that the suppression was continuing, but with the protests in Beijing slowing down, I hadn't paid as much attention to the movement. Then she told me that up to another dozen had died in police custody just in this one small city.

I stood at the side of a dark road that ran between a highway and an industrial park. It was cold and dry, but the stars couldn't penetrate the blanket of smog that was choking north China. The industrial park was dark and I could barely see the ground below me. The woman next to me pulled a green army coat up around her neck.

"Be patient," she said. "He's waiting out there somewhere. He saw us get out of the taxi and walk down this road. If we're not being followed, he'll come down and pick us up."

"And if he doesn't come?" I said.

"Then we're being followed and will be arrested," she said, suddenly breaking out of her Falun Gong seriousness and into a schoolgirl's laugh. "We'll go to labor camp together."

"No," I said, playing along with the joke. "You'll go to the labor camp. I'll just be expelled from China."

"Yes," she said, breaking into a fit of giggles and laughs. "You'll be expelled from China, but you'll write me letters in the labor camp."

We suddenly felt depressed and stopped our banter. I'd met this woman a year earlier during the first, almost euphoric wave of protests against the government. We had become e-mail pen pals over the intervening months. At times, she simply talked about her life and interests, but it was like talking to a fundamentalist in any religion—friendship is possible but the lack of shared belief is hard to overcome. I didn't believe in Falun Gong and this was something she couldn't understand. Some months later, before I left China, she sent me a handwritten letter in English that tried to bridge the gulf:

> in many respects you differ greatly from me. but I still tell you: look at "zhuan fa lun [*Turning the Dharma Wheel*]." I know you have one. a good deal of the importance of the book lies in its later influence. you must have a book. I hope you'll always be in touch with me from now on. I want to know if you're fine. write a letter to me. ok?

After a few minutes of waiting I looked up and watched a car crawl along the highway, slow almost to a stop and turn down our road.

"Our friend or the Public Security?" I said.

"Our friend," she said. "Look at the make."

I understood why the car was so slow. It was an old gray Moscow, straight out of the 1950s Soviet Union. It was clearly not the cops, who wouldn't be caught dead in such an old rattle-trap. The design was given to China by the Soviets as a kind of development aid. Although China's auto industry had since moved forward by leaps and bounds, the car was still built and given to army officers as a kind of cheap perk, almost an insulting sign that the army is poor. Cops were different. They were more corrupt than army officers and drove around in confiscated luxury cars or at least in products of foreign-Chinese joint ventures like the Volkswagen Santana.

The car bumped and shook, a dark outline against the glow of the city. Dirt blew across our boots as the first winds of winter blew down from the Mongolian Plateau.

My friend got in the front seat and I got in the back. The

driver wore an appropriately conservative Mao suit, with a collarless woolen jacket buttoned up to the top. Once worn by almost all Chinese, it is now a sign of the wearer's age. The man was a poor Communist Party cadre in his sixties with a brush cut and a clipped, matter-of-fact way of speaking. The suit fit him. So did the car, however he had come by it.

He carefully pushed the gearshift forward, finessing the clutch so the gears wouldn't grind, made a three-point turn and drove back to the highway. In a few minutes the dark suburbs gave way to dimly lit streets. The woman in the front seat reached back and pushed my head down so I wouldn't be visible from the outside. I was back in Weifang, where so many Falun Gong practitioners had been killed.

Weifang hardly seemed like the sort of place that would become the focal point of tragedy. I'd thought that if one were trying to find an Anytown in China, Weifang might be it. It has a famous past as a commercial center and is the hometown of flowing, silk-covered Chinese kites. Today, it is a small industrial center in one of China's wealthiest provinces and boasts a per capita income just above the national average.

Like most Chinese cities, Weifang felt more rural than its population would indicate. Officially, the greater metropolitan area had 8 million residents, but this included a huge swath of densely populated countryside. The urban center had just 620,000 people, and its streets were filled with farmers driving their tractors to markets.

This would be my last trip here and the preparations had been far more elaborate than those for my other trips. Earlier, I'd simply contacted acquaintances on public phones and hopped on a plane. Now the government's campaign against Falun Gong had gained traction. Like all things the government undertakes, it had started slowly, with a few hundred arrests and a few dozen people sent for long stays in labor camps. But now, nearly eighteen months after it had begun its campaign, the government had mobilized itself fully against the spiritual group. I'd often thought of China's government as akin to a medieval siege engine. It wasn't elegant and was hard to maneuver, but could be deadly when finally set up. Now it was in place and had found its distance. Falun Gong, as an organization in China, was being pulverized, and here in Weifang I could see the rubble.

Although my friend Brother Li was not in jail, many others like him around the country had been imprisoned. In the past the government let him and others like him out of jail after a few weeks. Now if they had any involvement in organizing opposition, they received three years, the theoretical maximum the government could detain someone without charge. In practice, a three-year sentence can be renewed indefinitely. The ability of the group to organize protests was knee-capped. Protests were dwindling in size, while the jails bulged with prisoners. Anecdotal information suggested that criminals were being released to make room for Falun Gong adherents, while *laogai*—reform-through-labor camps—which are not supposed to be used to house people detained without charge, were serving exactly this function.

Falun Gong activists had countered by adopting the most sophisticated underground organizing methods they could think of. For this trip to Weifang, for example, I'd been in e-mail contact with someone who went by the alias of "Mike." He was a graduate of Tsinghua University, China's top technical and scientific university. Midway through 2000 he had contacted me, advising me that in the future all e-mail communication with Falun Gong adherents must be done by encrypted e-mail. I wrote back saying that I was only in e-mail contact with those living in the United States, so such secrecy didn't seem warranted and might attract government attention. He wrote back and told me that the government could read my e-mail going to the United States even though I used a Hong Kong–based server. In addition, he said obliquely, by using encrypted e-mail I could contact other Falun Gong members—the few, presumably, who were computer-literate and not in jail.

Encrypted e-mail, relatively little used in the West, soon became a standard way of communicating with people in even fairly backward cities like Weifang. After you got the hang of it, encryption was easy to use. It involved downloading free software off the Internet (www.pgp.com) and creating a "key." You used the key to "lock," or encrypt, e-mails that you sent to others, as well as to "unlock" and read encrypted messages sent to you. Only the creator of the key has the password, so only I, for example, could read encrypted e-mails sent to me. It's a bit like having a locker that is closed with a lock that only two people can open—the sender and receiver of the e-mail.

With this software in place, I had sent Mike a note telling him I wanted to go to Weifang and asking for suggestions. Ms. Zhang was now so heavily watched that the police surely had her beeper number and had tapped her phone. That also was true for others I'd previously contacted—all were under heavy police watch. Even meeting people like Ms. Zhang would be tricky because she was often followed. So we arranged for me to contact other people. A few encrypted e-mails later, we'd worked out the details. Several days later I was on my way to Weifang.

According to human rights groups and my own research, by December of 2000 at least 77 Falun Gong adherents had died in police detention. That meant that Ms. Chen hadn't been an anomaly—a significant number of adherents were dying in custody. Not only that, but a huge number were dying in Ms. Chen's hometown. Weifang, with less than 1 percent of the national population, accounted for 15 percent of those deaths. Clearly, Ms. Zhang's mother hadn't been an isolated case. Something was wrong in China's treatment of prisoners, but something was especially wrong here in Weifang.

As we drove through the empty streets, I asked the driver what he did. It turned out he worked for the city government and had been a devoted Falun Gong adherent for five years. It had caught on early here and across Shandong Province, a densely populated coastal region that has developed rapidly in the past decade. I tried to find out why it was so strong here. The northeast made sense. Chinese culture's hold on it was more tenuous and Master Li came from that province. But Shandong was as Chinese as it got. Confucius was born here and this was a stronghold of China's indigenous religion, Taoism, one of whose holiest mountains lies not far from Weifang.

Some people I'd talked to thought that the group's Shandong organizers were especially gifted; others noted that Master Li paid a successful visit to the province several years ago. I could never really find a satisfactory answer, but what was clear was that by the time of the crackdown, Weifang had one of heaviest concentrations of believers in the province, with an estimated 60,000 adherents, according to an unpublished government report.

After a while the woman told me to get down on the floor of the back seat. She tossed a blanket over me and said not to move. We stopped, turned into a housing compound and drove passed the guardhouse where the doorman kept track of people's comings and goings. No one was on duty this late at night and our biggest threat passed. A few moments later we stopped, I pulled a large, floppy hood up over my blond head and adjusted my scarf so it covered everything but my eyes. Then I put on my gloves, got out of the car and fixed my eyes on the pavement. I followed the two into an empty apartment building, up two flights of dusty concrete stairs and into our haven. The apartment had five small rooms: a living room, two bedrooms, a kitchen and a toilet. The heating wasn't working, and there was hot water thanks only to a gas burner. The electricity worked, but the apartment was almost barren except for the odd chair, a tatami in one room and a few pieces of calligraphy. The newly whitewashed walls gave the feeling that I was in the workshop of a supercool artist, a minimalist who had hung a few pieces of his work on the walls.

Instead, I was in an abandoned apartment that my companion was using as a safehouse for a few weeks. She'd painted the walls and hung a couple of pieces of calligraphy and pictures that a fellow practitioner had painted for her. One of the pieces of calligraphy was of the three core beliefs of Falun Gong—the characters for Truth, Benevolence and Tolerance. It was done in thick, precise strokes, the work of a self-confident amateur. Another picture showed bamboo bending with the wind, a traditional motif that symbolized the virtuous person's ability to bend but not break. It was an interesting choice of symbols because the group was taking the opposite course of action—it was standing upright and the wind was threatening to break it.

The driver dropped off a roll of bedding for me and a McDonald's bag that had a fish filet in it and a cup of hot chocolate. "We wanted you to have something to eat that you would like," he said with an embarrassed smile. He left to fetch some Falun Gong adherents who wanted to meet me. Over the course of the next days I also went out, mostly at night, and met some contacts I'd made through friends. By the third day I had a fair picture of how the government had operated here and what had gone wrong. Finally, nearly a year after Ms. Chen had been beaten to death, I understood why.

* ✦ ✦

Officials in Beijing had set up the framework that led to the killings in late 1999. Impatient with the continued flow of protesters from around China into the capital, they decided that drastic measures were needed. So they reached for a tried-and-true method of enforcing central edicts, one honed over centuries of imperial rule.

Based on the twenty-two-hundred-year-old *bao jia* method of controlling society, the system pushes responsibility for following central orders onto neighborhoods, with the local boss responsible for the actions of everyone in his territory. In ancient times, that meant the headman of a family or clan was personally responsible for paying taxes, raising troops and apprehending criminals.

This method of rule was carried on by the Communist Party, especially after it launched economic reforms in the late 1970s. In the spirit of the times, it put an economic spin on the system, signing "contracts" with peasants and factory chiefs, who had to deliver a certain amount of grain or industrial output but were given latitude over the methods used. By the late 1980s provincial governors were also signing similar contracts, being held personally responsible for maintaining grain output in their province or holding down births to a certain level. This led to well-known abuses, such as forced abortions and sterilizations, because the end, not the means, was all important.

This showed that, instead of creating a modern system to rule China, the government still relied on an ad hoc patchwork of edicts, orders and personal connections. It was a classic pattern of a system under pressure: instead of universal principles and laws, the system reduces itself to the most fundamental of human relationships: favors. Rule of law was the goal, but here, as with the peasant champion or the urban activists, laws were secondary to rule by friendship, alliances and obligations.

Now, the problem was Falun Gong. Weifang officials (none of whom were Falun Gong adherents) I talked to, including some in the party's key "organization department," said central authorities told them that they would be held personally responsible if they didn't stem the flow of protesters to Beijing. As in years past, no questions would be asked about how this was achieved—success was all that mattered.

Weifang officials knew the policy meant trouble for them. China has other concentrations of Falun Gong believers, such as in the northeast. But those areas are remote from the capital. Weifang is located just three hundred miles southeast of Beijing, making it easy for protesters to travel to the capital even after the city had taken the initial precaution of sending security agents to train and bus stations to head them off before they left town. The authorities' worries were justified; I remember one forty-eight-year-old practitioner confirming this: "After a while the police were waiting for us at the train station, so we started to bike and walk to Beijing. It takes four days to bike to Beijing, twelve days to walk. I did it both ways."

As the flow of protesters continued into the new year, central authorities didn't have far to look to find a scapegoat. The man held responsible was the province's boss, Wu Guanzheng, Shandong's sixty-two-year-old party secretary. Party Secretary Wu was a member of the Communist Party's twenty-one-member Politburo, making him one of the most powerful men in China. But Party Secretary Wu was in a precarious position. Most Politburo members are central government officials. Only two governors sit on the Politburo: Party Secretary Wu and the party secretary of Guangdong Province, which doesn't have many protesters. That meant Party Secretary Wu was a focal point of Politburo meetings called to discuss the protests.

One Weifang official put it like this: "The central government told Party Secretary Wu that he was personally responsible. He risked losing his job if he didn't do something. Everyone knew the pressure he was under."

While the official told me his story, I thought back to one of the first letters I'd read from Weifang. A young woman had written the letter to "Uncle Wu." At the time I wondered who that was—some powerful relative who could save her, or perhaps the head of the neighborhood committee? Now I realized it was Party Secretary Wu, the man behind the terror in Shandong.

> Uncle Wu, How do you do!
>
> I'm one of your common people, an originally happy kid, a treasured child of my parents, and a widely known Falun Gong practitioner. Like all other Falun Gong friends, I learned to be a good person through Falun Gong, to have good health and to please my parents.
>
> But, Uncle Wu, I am more and more scared these days. I come across things I never dared to think about.

The letter writer went on to explain about how she had been thrown out of university for practicing Falun Gong and later detained for practicing Falun Gong and for trying to deliver a letter to Party Secretary Wu.

> Why should I be put into jail for practicing Falun Gong and following the doctrine of Truth, Benevolence and Tolerance? Why can't I go to school? I can't get an

answer. Those jailers always made fun of me and beat me with bamboo sticks. They cut my hand, it was very painful and scars still exist now. I lost weight inside and Mum was sick outside for my sake. She couldn't fall asleep at night because of missing me, she kept crying and in this very short period of life she turned very old. Uncle Wu, if your relatives, your kids, were beaten this way, you must feel pain too.

We youth are the hope of the future, but we're scared of society. Uncle Wu, our hope is relying on your effort, please help us!

The letter was dated February 2000 and signed by a practitioner from Weifang. It was followed by a postscript:

Uncle Wu: Before I sent the mail, I heard another piece of news. . . . A practitioner was forced to jump out of the third floor [of the detention center where the practitioner had been held] and was sent to hospital. Another one was forced to commit suicide by hitting himself against a wall. When will this hell on earth end?

Party Secretary Wu almost certainly never saw this letter. Instead, he was busy transferring the pressure he was receiving from the Politburo. First, Weifang city officials say, he ensured that every official in the city knew what was at stake by calling a meeting of police and government officials to a "study session." There, the central government's directive was read out loud. "The government instructed us to limit the number of protesters or be responsible," a government official told me.

Such methods quickly led to abuses. Several Falun Gong adherents imprisoned by local police early this year said their captors told them that their continued protests threatened to derail officials' careers. "One policeman beat me with a truncheon," said a forty-three-year-old factory worker imprisoned in December 1999. "He said we were responsible for his boss's political problems."

That detainee was beaten after being arrested in Beijing and transferred back to Weifang. City officials said such arrests reflected badly on Party Secretary Wu and the rest of the province because people arrested in Beijing are booked by central security agents and their hometown noted. Statistics were then compiled and provinces with a high number of protesters—like Shandong—criticized. Beating people in Weifang prisons might eventually deter protesters, but this would take time. Authorities wanted results immediately.

So, early in 2000, local officials devised a plan to skirt Beijing's monitoring of their performance. Like many other cities, Weifang maintains a permanent representative bureau in the capital, the place where Ms. Chen had been taken immediately after being arrested in Beijing. I'd been by the bureau several times. It was a two-story building with chrome-plated pillars and looked like a bordello or a karaoke lounge. Located near Rear Lake in the old part of Beijing, the office was surrounded by police cars with Shandong license plates. The office usually had twenty staff members, but by early 2000 the number was doubled, and supplemented by a dozen police officers.

According to an employee in the office and Falun Gong adherents who were arrested, Beijing police had a mutually beneficial agreement with Weifang police. Weifang residents detained in Beijing would simply be handed over directly to the small city's police on duty in the capital. They'd be jailed in the representative office until transportation could be arranged back to Weifang. This suited Beijing police, who were able to shift some of their work burden. And it helped Weifang's image, because the detainees wouldn't be booked in Beijing prisons and show up on the central government's tally of laggard provinces.

Few detainees say they were beaten in the Beijing representative office. Instead, they were sent directly to one of seven "transformation centers"—like the one where Ms. Chen had ended up. It was at these unofficial prisons that the killings occurred.

I walked by several of these centers in Weifang. One morning I left the apartment early and walked down a street where efforts at building a sidewalk had been abandoned and paving stones lay haphazardly over the cold dusty ground. Trees were bare and a few enterprising shopkeepers stared as I walked past the stores they were unshuttering.

I stopped before a gate that had a vertical white sign out front with printed black letters that read WEICHENG DISTRICT TEXTILE FACTORY STORAGE DEPOT. The entry was barred by a rusty metal gate. I looked in and saw several four-story buildings made of yellow brick that rose seamlessly out of the yellow soil. This was a "transformation center," according to prisoners. It looked empty. I pushed the fence and it wobbled.

A man suddenly hopped out of a small hut inside the gate.

"Whaddya want?" he said, suddenly stopping in his tracks at my foreign face.

"Kites. Kite museum," I said in the worst Chinese possible.

He waved his arm for me to go away. "There are no kites here. This is a government office. Take a taxi to the center of town," he said.

I nodded in agreement, thanked him and walked away.

Along with use of these "centers" came the final ingredient needed for the killings to take place: fear of financial ruin.

Instead of just threatening to ruin local officials' careers,

Party Secretary Wu's colleagues in the provincial government started to fine them as well. The new twist was simple: The provincial government fined mayors and heads of counties for each Falun Gong practitioner from their district who went to Beijing. The mayors and county heads in turn fined the heads of their Political and Legal Commissions, holding them responsible. They in turn fined village chiefs, who in turn fined the police officers—who administered the punishment. The fines varied from district to district, but in one Weifang district the head of the Political and Legal Commission was fined 200 yuan per person protesting in Tiananmen Square, or about $25—a potentially ruinous amount given that his monthly salary is only about $200, according to one of the official's colleagues.

The fines were illegal; no law or regulation has ever been issued in writing that lists them. Officials say the policy was announced orally at government meetings. "There was never to be anything in writing because they didn't want it made public," a member of the city's Political and Legal Commission told me.

Thus a chief feature in torture victims' testimony is that they were constantly being asked for money to compensate for the fines. That's why Ms. Zhang was told to pay a $241 fine in exchange for her mother's release. When she balked, her mother was held another night and beaten to death. I was lucky to have introductions to the officials I talked to. Normally, it would have been impossible to see officials; and all previous efforts at seeking official interviews had been fruitless. But by going through friends, in this case a foreign friend who had relatives living in Weifang, the officials were sure I was trustworthy and wouldn't betray them.

Privately, they told me that they worried that the crackdown had been a terrible mistake. "I wonder why we spend so much time doing this," said the official from the party's organization department. "We need to undertake economic construction, not beat people."

He and others said that none of the police directly involved in the deaths have been reprimanded. "Reprimanded, for beating a Falun Gong disciple? Don't be ridiculous. You know the motto: 'No measure too excessive,' " an official told me with a sarcastic laugh. In fact, the three officers who oversaw Ms. Chen's interrogation have since been promoted, they say, true to the tradition of giving local authorities a free hand, no questions asked.

The cumulative effect is that at least 11 Falun Gong practitioners died from abuse they suffered in Weifang prisons, according to family members and officials I talked to. An independent human-rights monitoring group in Hong Kong, the Information Centre for Human Rights and Democracy, verified one more death in Weifang. According to the center, the rest of Shandong accounts for another 12 victims, for a total of 24. The next-highest number of deaths is 14 for Heilongjiang Province, the place where Mr. Chen saw Master Li speak at the hockey arena in 1994.

Besides the deaths, which the Information Centre estimated at over 100, the policy seemed to split China in ways that were hard to quantify. Society was polarized and many people turned against the government. A friend of mine liked to argue against this, saying the crackdown showed that Chinese actually didn't care much about each other or the discrepancy in what they saw and what the government said. There was no solidarity with the persecuted, unless they were family members or personal friends. It was like the traffic accidents that one sees in big Chinese cities—crowds only gather to stare; almost no one stops to help. No wonder the government could hold on to power so easily, he said. It doesn't have to divide and conquer its enemies; they are divided of their own accord. I had to agree with him, because I rarely encountered a person who got really angry about the way the government treated Falun Gong adherents. While some far-thinking people saw the campaign as unjustified and cruel, most simply shrugged and wondered why people bothered to stand up for something they believed in. Concerned with their daily struggles, they couldn't understand why Falun Gong believers insisted on exercising publicly. "Why not just exercise in the living room?" was the most common response I got when I asked about the repression of Falun Gong.

But longer term, society was suffering from the government's one hundred battles a day against Falun Gong and its innumerable other opponents, real and imagined. The sheer number of those jailed—I would conservatively estimate that 30,000 passed through jails during the first two years of the crackdown—meant that many hundreds of thousands more were touched in some way by the campaign.

The woman who met me on the outskirts of Weifang, for example, came from a good family of government officials who all believed in Falun Gong. The last I heard of them the family was split, with the young woman moving from one safe house to another. The parents, meanwhile, had been released from jail and promptly fled to live with relatives in the countryside. If they returned home, the local street committee would come by and demand they denounce Master Li, something they couldn't do.

I wondered at the scores of neighbors who knew that the family's apartment was vacant because of government terror, who knew of their flight to the countryside and the young girl's resistance. The way housing is distributed to government officials, all the people in the apartment building would have been colleagues of the parents. Their children, too, would have gone to university and have been classmates with the young woman. What would these hundreds of people think of the government? How much trust would they have in the ability of the Communist

Party to lead the way forward? And all these hundreds of doubts stem from just one family's suffering. Multiply it by the tens of thousands of Falun Gong adherents who went to labor camps, the peasants who sued and lost, the residents whose homes were demolished.

Eventually, I made it to Weifang's impressive kite museum. I was ready to leave town. My taxi was outside waiting. I walked up to an employee.

"Have you ever practiced Falun Gong?"

His eyes widened and he laughed nervously. "No, why?"

"I was visiting friends here, and one family told me that their grandmother was beaten to death in a transformation center, the one up in Weicheng District, the Chengguan Street Committee. I guess it's pretty dangerous to practice."

He was unpacking boxes of kites, carrying huge stacks of the featherweight boxes into a storage room from a trolley. Then he stopped. It was one of those moments of quiet civic courage that one encountered increasingly in China: "No one can talk about these things," he said. Then without stopping, he added brusquely, "But a lot of people know."

I met Ms. Zhang during my last trip to Weifang but only briefly; the police were outside her house almost all the time, and she had only been able to get away by feigning to go to the market and instead hopping in a cab and traveling across town to meet me. She said she should have been jailed long ago but credited the international publicity and pressure that had accompanied her mother's case with keeping her free.

Slowly, though, that pressure on China was easing. As the international community lost interest, authorities felt they had nothing to lose by detaining Ms. Zhang. In April 2001 she was picked up by police and taken before an administrative hearing officer. Denied access to a lawyer, she was tried in secret and given three years' "administrative detention," a form of punishment sanctioned by the law. Essentially, the law gives security services the right to jail anyone they want for up to three years— a term that can be extended indefinitely. It was the sort of extra-judicial punishment that, in a more extreme form, had claimed her mother. Three years later, Mrs. Zhang was released from jail and sent home, where she lives quietly with her family. Her jailing was brutal on several levels. Her efforts had been aimed at figuring out the law and getting it to work for her. Now she was being told that this was illegal. And she'd essentially given up her efforts at redressing her mother's death. "Now is a time for waiting," she told me during our last meeting in Weifang. "China isn't ready for change."

It was a change from her earlier determination to push change at all costs. She explained it to me during an earlier trip to Beijing, in August, shortly after she'd written her essay. We had gone for a walk along Beijing's main drag, Chang'an Boulevard, a broad Stalinist-style avenue that in the early 1990s had been almost devoid of traffic. Now it was choked with private cars, buses and taxis, which had squeezed the once-generous bike lanes into narrow, crowded corridors along the side of the road. It was hot and we took a seat on a bench. The sidewalks were filled with people, and no one took notice of us as she talked.

"While I was in jail earlier in the year, the only people who were good to me were Falun Gong prisoners," she said slowly, looking down at her feet. The guards had been horrible and the common prisoners were bribed to make her life miserable. When she returned to her cell after an interrogation, the prisoners would also berate her, telling her to give up her struggle for justice. Sometimes they'd take her food away—always, she was sure, at the guards' instruction, and in exchange the prisoners obtained some small benefit, like bigger rations or early release. She began to doubt human goodness until she started to read the Falun Gong texts that had so captivated her mother.

"I used to be a materialist and believed that everything in life could be gained from hard work," she said. "But Falun Gong makes more sense. At its root are three principles: Truthfulness, Compassion and Tolerance. If we adhere to these, isn't that a deeper meaning to life?"

She said she had started to attend gatherings of practitioners who still meet in secret. They are people of different social status, of different incomes and different backgrounds. But, she says, they treat each other as equals and are nice to each other. "I never knew that a group of people could get along so well," she said, shaking her head and smiling.

Increasingly, she said, she was turning her attention to her son, a reminder of the grandmother who was so fond of him. He was due to start school in September and Ms. Zhang was worried about the government textbooks that he would be reading, with their heavy emphasis on patriotism and nationalism. So she decided to start teaching him the principles of Falun Gong, as a counterweight to the materialism of daily life.

"I teach him that when someone hits him, it's the person who hit him who is wrong," she said as we looked at the people jostling each other on the street and crowding onto the buses. "His grandmother had this belief. I have it now, and so will he."

I asked her if she'd lost faith in the government and in China. She hoisted her duffel bag off the ground and put it between us on the bench. Out of it she pulled a creased, marked-up copy of her essay, opened it to the last page and folded it in half. She pointed to the last line and read it out loud: "China is still trustworthy, we're still waiting."

Notes

A book written in a narrative form is ill suited to footnotes, which break the flow and rhythm of the tales. Readers, though, have a right to know where the information came from. To reconcile these two desires I've included endnotes. Unlike footnotes, these are not numbered and so don't break up the flow of the stories. But they do allow curious readers to learn where I obtained information. For those who see in this exercise nothing but pure pedantry, you are probably right; please feel free to ignore the next few pages.

I have not included notes explaining every fact in the book. Some facts, such as China's population or the location of Weifang, are obvious and don't need sourcing.

Likewise, I have not explained in the notes the source of every quotation. This is a work of journalism, and all quotes are from interviews with the people who said them or from court documents. When accounts differed, I gave precedence to scenes that I witnessed directly or to direct interviews. I tried in all cases to obtain as many sides of the story as possible in order to verify accounts, but was sometimes denied access to participants. In these cases I have relied on the standard journalistic principle of obtaining two witnesses who did not consult with each other before talking to me, and then taking the most conservative version of events. In the case of Chen Zixiu, for example, her words are taken from people who heard her speak them. Many of these quotes first appeared in the *Wall Street Journal*, and the citations are noted below. I have used people's real names except when this could imperil their safety; these cases have also been noted below.

PROLOGUE

10   "Rulers and ruled wage one hundred battles a day": The Han Feizi quote is often translated as "Superior and inferior wage one hundred battles a day," referring to the ruler as the superior and his ministers or subordinates as his inferiors. Like all philosophical works, however, the quote has been interpreted and translated in many different fashions. Kung-Chuan Hsiao points out this translation and the broader significance of the quote in his book *Rural China: Imperial Control in the Nineteenth Century.*

PART I: THE PEASANT CHAMPION

15   One commonly hears: Here I am referring to the endless magazine and newspaper articles and books touting China's economic future. Almost all focus on big, prosperous coastal cities like Shanghai or Shenzhen.

16   "disturbing social order": The charge "disturbing social order" is one of the most criticized in the Chinese penal code because of its broad scope. It is commonly used to round up undesirables of all shades, from dissidents and labor activists to those who get in the way of China's Olympics redevelopment plan. See reports by Amnesty International, China Labour Bulletin, Human Rights Watch, or Human Rights in China.

18   This was a moment I'd rehearsed several times: This next section on how Chinese hotel rolls are handled is drawn from personal experience, as well as conversations with dozens of journalists and hotel managers who have told me about the regulation of registering at hotels. The rules seem to vary from province to province and even district to district, which

accounts for the differing experiences journalists have faced when traveling without official permission.

19 Their solution had been to hire a lawyer and charge the government: The Peijiawan case is described in detail in Ian Johnson, "Mass Leverage," *Wall Street Journal,* March 26, 1999, A1, or Minxin Pei, "Citizens v. Mandarins: Administrative Litigation in China," *China Quarterly,* December 1997, pp. 832–62.

24 But the changes did have: The most common method of measuring a government's tax revenues is the ratio of revenues to gross domestic product. From 31 percent in 1979, the year reforms begin in earnest, the ratio declined to 10.7 percent in 1995. By contrast, most developed countries have ratios of 30 to 50 percent. Since then the ratio has edged up but remains low.

25 This was reinforced by advice: The China 2020 reports (available online from World Bank publications), for example, discussed the need for a tax system but didn't explore the need for popular support.

26 User fees suddenly began appearing: Limiting users fees was a theme throughout the premiership of Zhu Rongji. See "Farmers Praise China's Anti-Poverty Goals" by William Foreman, Associated Press, March 9, 2003.

28 Messrs. Zhao and Shao walked gingerly: I have changed these men's names to protect their identities from the authorities.

38 Recently, a national newspaper had published a letter: The essay "The True Feelings of a Township Party Secretary" by Li Changping appeared in *Southern Weekend.* I am indebted to David Cowhig, formerly with the U.S. Embassy in Beijing's Environmental, Science and Technology staff for pointing out this essay on the embassy's extremely informative Web site, which he maintained. The translation is also his.

41 A more typical product of his time was Wu Hanjing: I am indebted to Zhang Lijia for pointing out to me the existence of the Mao temples.

57   This is a key distinction: See, for example, Lubman, pp 299–19.

59   The exact number of farmers: In China, plaintiffs are allowed
      to join a suit after it has been filed. Most initial reports spoke
      of 5,000 coplaintiffs. Human Rights in China estimates
      20,000 eventually filed. In 2001, locals spoke of 68,000 having
      joined the initial suit, but this is impossible to verify.

86   I found a fax waiting: The fax was from the Information Cen-
      tre for Human Rights and Democracy. See BBC Monitoring
      Service, August 16, 2000.

PART 2: DREAM OF A VANISHED CAPITAL

105   Today, despite some impressive efforts at restoration: Esti-
      mate drawn from author's survey of maps, Chinese guide-
      books and interviews. This number will likely increase in the
      coming years as temples are restored and new ones in the sub-
      urbs built. Still, the overall picture of a dramatic decline in
      religious life is valid.

112   Throughout the 1990s: See, for example, Susan Naquin, espe-
      cially the epilogue, pp. 706–8.

115   To put it in context: This calculation is based on a 2000 gross
      domestic product of 217.4 billion yuan. If inflation-adjusted
      figures are used for the city's output in the 1990s, the rough
      comparison holds.

157   The pieces are on display: Thanks to Pete Hessler for point-
      ing this out.

163   It was an exercise repeated: See, for example, Arlington or
      Bodde.

PART 3: TURNING THE WHEEL

187   Anyway, Master Li had said: I use the title "Master Li"
      because this is how his adherents refer to him.

193   But then, in late autumn: The chronology for measures taken
      against Falun Gong is reliably reported in Human Rights
      Watch, *Dangerous Meditation*.

202   Into the breach stepped: For an excellent history of how the term qigong was created in the 1950s, see Miura.

204   Academics, such as Jian Xu: The citation is from Xu Jian, p. 985.

210   Li Hongzhi formed Falun Gong: History according to Falun Gong informants and books. A complete history of the group has yet to be written, but the government uses many of these dates.

211   Master Li's works also preach exclusivity: Falun Gong adherents dispute this interpretation, yet it is a subtext found in many writings.

217–23 Quotes from Ian Johnson, "A Deadly Exercise," *Wall Street Journal*, April 2, 2000, p. A1.

224   Broader definitions of cults: See Singer, pp. 3–9.

226   One Western academic wrote a paper: See Patsy Rahn's "The Falun Gong: Beyond the Headlines," presented at the American Family Foundation's Annual Conference, April 28, 2000.

232–47 Quotes from Ian Johnson, "A Blind Eye," *Wall Street Journal*, December 13, 2000, p. A1.

257–66 Quotes from Ian Johnson, "Brother Li Love," *Wall Street Journal*, August 26, 2000, p. A1.

Selected Bibliography

Arlington, L. C., and William Lewisohn. *In Search of Old Peking.* Hong Kong: Oxford University Press, 1987 (orig. 1935).

Bei, Dao. "13 Happiness Street." In *Seeds of Fire, Chinese Voices of Conscience.* Edited by Geremie Barme and John Minford. Hong Kong: *Far Eastern Economic Review,* 1986, p. 2.

Bodde, Derk, and M. L. C. Bogan. *Annual Customs and Festivals in Peking.* Taipei: SMC Publishers, 1994 (orig. 1936).

Bredon, Juliet. *Peking.* London: T. Werner Laurie, 1922.

Fairbank, Wilma. *Adventures in Retrieval.* Cambridge: Harvard University Press, 1972.

———. *Liang and Lin: Partners in Exploring China's Architectural Past.* Philadelphia: University of Pennsylvania Press, 1994.

Fang, Ke. *Contemporary Redevelopment in the Inner City of Beijing* (in Chinese). Beijing: Zhongguo Jianzhu Gongye Chubanshe, 2000.

Han, Feizi. *Han Feizi Jijie.* Taipei: Shijie Shuju, 1990.

Hsiao, Kung-Chuan. *Rural China: Imperial Control in the Nineteenth Century.* Seattle: University of Washington Press, 1960.

Human Rights Watch. *Dangerous Meditation: China's Campaign Against Falungong.* New York: Human Rights Watch, 2002.

Liang, Sicheng. *Zhongguo Jianzhu Shi.* Tianjin: Baihua Wenyi Chubanshe, 1998.

Liang, Ssu-ch'eng (Sicheng). *A Pictorial History of Chinese Architec-*

ture. Edited by Wilma Fairbank. Cambridge: MIT Press, 1984.

Lubman, Stanley. *Bird in a Cage: Legal Reform in China After Mao.* Stanford, Calif.: Stanford University Press, 1999.

Miura, Kunio. "The Revival of *Qi*: Qigong in Contemporary China." In Livia Kohn, ed. *Taoist Meditation and Longevity Techniques.* Ann Arbor: University of Michigan Press, 1989, pp. 1–40.

Naquin, Susan. *Peking: Temples and City Life, 1400–1900.* Berkeley: University of California Press, 2000.

Singer, Margaret Thaler. *Cults in Our Midst.* San Francisco: Jossey-Bass, 1995.

Turner, Karen G., James V. Feinerman and R. Kent Guy, eds. *The Limits of the Rule of Law in China.* Seattle: University of Washington Press, 2000.

Watson, Burton, trans. *Han Fei Tzu Basic Writings.* New York: Columbia University Press, 1964.

Wu, Liangyong. *Rehabilitating the Old City of Beijing.* Vancouver, B.C.: University of British Columbia Press, 1999.

Xu, Jian. "Body, Discourse, and the Cultural Politics of Contemporary Chinese Qigong," *Journal of Asian Studies,* vol. 58, no. 4 (1999), pp. 961–99.

Acknowledgments

Readers will have to indulge me for three paragraphs while I thank a host of friends, colleagues and mentors. Although for most people their names will mean little, their sheer number show that behind every book, especially one on such a complicated topic as China, are dozens of people whose moral and intellectual support were crucial.

First, many journalists have nothing but criticism of the Chinese government for hindering their work. That is sometimes justified, but I'd like to thank the more liberal members of the Ministry of Foreign Affairs in Beijing for allowing me to serve as a journalist in China for seven years. If the ministry's rules and regulations were followed to the letter, every one of the roughly four hundred foreign journalists in China should be expelled. I thank the ministry's officials for interpreting the rules liberally, thus allowing me and others to take advantage of China's blooming civil society and penetrate the country in ways that our predecessors couldn't have imagined possible.

Also thanks to: Mr. Harold Givens and Dr. and Mrs. Jean Battle, who over the years have been generous in their moral support and faith; my adviser at the Freie Universität Berlin, Erling von Mende, whose wide-ranging intellectual interests allowed me to broaden my understanding of China in a very congenial setting; Stephen Feldman of Asian Rare Books, who provided many stimulating and hard-to-find volumes over the years; the former foreign editor of Baltimore's *The Sun*, Jeff Price, who took a chance on sending me to China in

1994; the participants of the chinapol listserv, which was founded by Rick Baum of UCLA and has provided a wealth of stimulating ideas; Brock Silvers of the Taoist Restoration Society (www.taorestore.org) for insightful conversations on Chinese religion; the *Wall Street Journal*'s page-one editing staff for its work on the original Falun Gong series; the *Journal*'s foreign editor, John Bussey, whose unwavering faith in the Falun Gong story was crucial during a very trying period; my former bureau chief at the *Journal*, Marcus Brauchli, who taught me how to write features and helped edit this book; Toronto-based freelance writer Lorne Blumer for his editing work; Jane Kramer of *The New Yorker* for helping to find a beginning to the book; Chris Calhoun at Sterling Lord Literistic for his support and advice; Dan Frank at Pantheon for his superb editing; Calum Macleod, Leslie Chang, Reginald Chua, Charles Hutzler, Mark Leong and Dali Yang, for conversations and suggestions that helped enormously over the years; and to many Chinese friends and associates who helped out with introductions and, most importantly, unstinting friendship—for obvious reasons most must go unnamed, but I'd like to mention Eldridge Lee and Zhang Lijia for companionship on trips to the Loess Plateau and the rest of China.

Special thanks to: Pete Hessler of *The New Yorker*, for his extraordinary help in editing this book; my wife, Elke; and finally to my parents, to whom this book is dedicated, for never—well, rarely—criticizing their unfilial son even as he spent years abroad.

Index

Peijiawan case, 19–21, 295*n*
  amount won in, 69
  backlash after, 60
  illegal taxes and, 19–21, 38
  Ma peasant lawsuit compared
      with, 21, 30, 38, 56, 57,
      59, 60, 62, 64, 66, 75
Pennsylvania, University of,
      123, 127
People's Daily, 190, 193, 239
People's Republic of China
  fiftieth anniversary of, 132
  millennialism in, 197, 227
  "social peace" campaign in,
      132
  social polarization in, 288–9
  spiritual crisis in, 201–2,
      230–1
  see also China; *specific topics*
Peoples Temple, 223
Petition and Appeals Office,
      Beijing, 76, 219, 251,
      267–9, 272–3
petitions, petitioning, 52, 133–4
  of Falun Gong, 216
  as imperial era relic, 66–7
  of lawyers, 85–6
  of peasants, 29, 31, 32, 33, 64,
      84
  of Zhang Xueling, 267–73
  for Zhao Jingxin, 133–4, 136,
      169, 170
photographs, 13, 54–6, 127, 174
  color, 97, 98
  in Fang Ke's book, 115, 118
Pictorial History of Chinese

Architecture (Liang
      Sicheng), 122–4, 127–8
Pingyao, 134
police, *see* Public Security
      Bureau
Politburo, 282–5
Political and Legal Committee,
      Weifang, 287
political reforms, 7, 8, 24, 81
politics, Chinese view of, 147,
      187–8
population density, 113, 119,
      160–1
Post and Telecommunications
      Ministry, Chinese, 51
poverty, the poor, 15, 24, 55, 130
Press and Publication Bureau, 94
Propaganda Ministry, Chinese,
      242
Property Management Office,
      Chinese, 108
property rights, 148, 163, 176
Protestantism, 200, 203
protests, 5–6
  anniversaries of, 5
  Falun Gong, 70, 185, 190–3,
      195, 197–200, 213, 216,
      226, 243–51, 258–9, 262,
      263, 265–6, 273, 274,
      277, 282
  by peasants, 16, 25, 27–8, 40,
      62–5, 67–8, 70, 81, 273
  Zhang Xueling's views on, 273
public opinion, destruction of
      Beijing's old city and,
      91, 95